LIBRARY OF NEW TESTAMENT STUDIES
676

Formerly the Journal for the Study of the New Testament Supplement series

Editor
Chris Keith

Editorial Board
Dale C. Allison, Lynn H. Cohick, R. Alan Culpepper, Craig A. Evans, Jennifer Eyl, Robert Fowler, Simon J. Gathercole, Juan Hernández Jr., John S. Kloppenborg, Michael Labahn, Matthew V. Novenson, Love L. Sechrest, Robert Wall, Catrin H. Williams, Brittany E. Wilson

Women in John's Gospel

Susan Miller

LONDON • NEW YORK • OXFORD • NEW DELHI • SYDNEY

T&T CLARK
Bloomsbury Publishing Plc
50 Bedford Square, London, WC1B 3DP, UK
1385 Broadway, New York, NY 10018, USA
29 Earlsfort Terrace, Dublin 2, Ireland

BLOOMSBURY, T&T CLARK and the T&T Clark logo are trademarks of
Bloomsbury Publishing Plc

First published in Great Britain 2023
Paperback edition published 2024

Copyright © Susan Miller, 2023

Susan Miller has asserted her right under the Copyright, Designs and
Patents Act, 1988, to be identified as Author of this work.

For legal purposes the Acknowledgements on p. x constitute an
extension of this copyright page.

All rights reserved. No part of this publication may be reproduced or transmitted in
any form or by any means, electronic or mechanical, including photocopying,
recording, or any information storage or retrieval system, without prior
permission in writing from the publishers.

Bloomsbury Publishing Plc does not have any control over, or responsibility for, any
third-party websites referred to or in this book. All internet addresses given in this
book were correct at the time of going to press. The author and publisher regret any
inconvenience caused if addresses have changed or sites have ceased to exist, but can
accept no responsibility for any such changes.

A catalogue record for this book is available from the British Library.

Library of Congress Control Number: 2022023541

ISBN: HB: 978-0-5677-0822-9
PB: 978-0-5677-0823-6
ePDF: 978-0-5677-0824-3
eBook: 978-0-5677-0825-0

Series: Library of New Testament Studies, volume 676
ISSN 2513-8790

Typeset by Newgen KnowledgeWorks Pvt. Ltd., Chennai, India

To find out more about our authors and books visit www.bloomsbury.com
and sign up for our newsletters.

To Joel Marcus with love

Contents

	Acknowledgements	x
	List of Abbreviations	xi
1	Introduction	1
	Recent research on women in John's Gospel	1
	The approach of this study	6
	A feminist interpretation of John's Gospel	7
	A literary reading of John's Gospel	11
	John's Gospel and the synoptic gospels	12
	The Johannine community	15
2	The mother of Jesus (2.1-11)	19
	Introduction	19
	The portrayal of the mother of Jesus	21
	The conversation between Jesus and his mother	22
	The revelation of the hidden Messiah	26
	Discipleship and the mother of Jesus	29
	The mother of Jesus and the new creation	30
	The mother of Jesus and the Johannine community	33
	Conclusion	35
3	The Samaritan woman (4.1-42)	37
	Introduction	37
	The portrayal of the Samaritan woman	39
	The conversation between the Samaritan woman and Jesus	42
	The revelation of the hidden Messiah	45
	Discipleship and the Samaritan woman	48
	The Samaritan woman and the new creation	52
	The Samaritan woman and the Johannine community	55
	Conclusion	57

4 Martha and Mary of Bethany (11.1-44) — 59

Introduction — 59
The portrayal of Martha and Mary — 61
The conversation between Martha and Jesus — 63
The conversation between Mary and Jesus — 68
Martha's confession of faith — 71
Discipleship and Martha and Mary of Bethany — 73
Martha and Mary and the new creation — 75
Martha and Mary of Bethany and the Johannine community — 78
Conclusion — 81

5 Mary of Bethany (12.1-8) — 83

Introduction — 83
The anointing of Jesus in the four gospels — 84
The portrayal of Mary of Bethany — 87
Discipleship and Mary of Bethany — 91
Mary of Bethany and the new creation — 94
Martha and Mary of Bethany and the Johannine community — 98
Conclusion — 100

6 The women at the cross (19.25-27) — 101

Introduction — 101
The portrayal of the women at the cross — 102
Discipleship and the women at the cross — 106
The mother of Jesus and the Beloved Disciple — 108
The mother of Jesus and the new creation — 112
The mother of Jesus and the Johannine community — 115
Conclusion — 118

7 Mary Magdalene (20.1-18) — 121

Introduction — 121
The portrayal of Mary Magdalene — 122
The conversation between Mary Magdalene and Jesus — 125
Discipleship and Mary Magdalene — 130
Mary Magdalene and the new creation — 132
Mary Magdalene and the Johannine community — 134
Conclusion — 137

8	Conclusion	139
	The portrayal of women	139
	The discipleship of women	142
	Women and the new creation	144
	Women and the Johannine community	147
	Conclusion	150

Bibliography	153
Index of References	163
Index of Authors	177

Acknowledgements

This book has developed over a number of years and I am grateful for the help of many people. I would particularly like to thank Professor Helen Bond, Professor Louise Lawrence and Professor Sean Adams for their support. I am thankful for opportunities to teach courses on Women and Gender in the New Testament at the University of Edinburgh and the University of Glasgow, and I am now looking forward to teaching a course on this subject at the University of Aberdeen.

I am also grateful for opportunities to present papers on my research at the Annual Meeting of the Society of Biblical Literature and at the British New Testament Conference. I would like to thank Dr David Lamb, Professor Andrew Lincoln, Dr Wendy Sproston North, Dr Pete Phillips, Dr Janet Unsworth and Professor Catrin Williams for friendly and inspiring conversations.

My parents have given me encouragement and support throughout the time I have been writing this book and I wish they could see the published version. In the final stages of this book, I've spent happy times with Joel Marcus and his daughter Rachel in North Carolina. I would like to thank Joel Marcus for his love and faith in me. I dedicate this book to him.

Abbreviations

AB	Anchor Bible
ABRL	Anchor Bible Reference Library
BA	*Biblical Archaeologist*
BETL	Bibliotheca ephemeridum theologicarum lovaniensium
Bib	*Biblica*
BibInt	*Biblical Interpretation: A Journal of Contemporary Approaches*
BJS	Brown Judaic Studies
BTB	*Biblical Theology Bulletin*
CBQ	*Catholic Biblical Quarterly*
IEJ	*Israel Exploration Journal*
Int	*Interpretation*
JBL	*Journal of Biblical Literature*
JEH	*Journal of Ecclesiastical History*
JJS	*Journal of Jewish Studies*
JSNT	*Journal for the Study of the New Testament*
JSNTsup	*Journal for the Study of the New Testament, Supplement Series*
JSOT	*Journal for the Study of the Old Testament*
JTS	*Journal of Theological Studies*
NCB	New Century Bible
NICNT	New International Commentary on the New Testament
NovT	*Novum Testamentum*
NTOA	Novum Testamentum et orbis antiquus
NTS	*New Testament Studies*
RB	*Revue biblique*
SBL	Society of Biblical Literature
SBLDS	SBL Dissertation Series
SBLMS	SBL Monograph Series
SBLSP	SBL Seminar Papers
SJT	*Scottish Journal of Theology*
WBC	Word Biblical Commentary
WUNT	Wissenschaftliche Untersuchungen zum Neuen Testament
ZNW	Zeitschrift für die neutestamentliche Wissenschaft

1

Introduction

Recent research on women in John's Gospel

John's Gospel contains a number of distinctive accounts of women that do not appear in the other gospels. The mother of Jesus draws attention to the lack of wine at the wedding at Cana, and she prompts Jesus to carry out his first sign (2.1-11). The Samaritan woman engages in a conversation with Jesus at a well in Sychar, and she responds positively to his gift of living water (4.1-42). Martha and Mary of Bethany send word for Jesus's help when their brother, Lazarus, falls ill. Martha confesses her faith in Jesus, and Mary anoints Jesus's feet with expensive perfume (11.1–12.8). The mother of Jesus, her sister, Mary of Clopas and Mary Magdalene are witnesses to the crucifixion (19.25-27). Jesus announces to his mother that the Beloved Disciple is now her son, and he tells the Beloved Disciple that Mary is his mother. At the end of the gospel Mary Magdalene goes alone to Jesus's tomb. She is the first person to see the risen Jesus, and she passes on the news of the resurrection (20.1-18).

John's presentation of the women in these narratives differs in several ways from the portrayal of women in the synoptic gospels. The synoptic gospels contain short accounts of the meetings between women and Jesus such as the account of the gentile woman who seeks healing for her daughter (Mt. 21.21-28; Mk 7.24-30) and the account of the visit of Jesus to Martha and Mary (Lk. 10.38-42). In the synoptic gospels women are often silent as in the account of the healing of a woman with a haemorrhage who is praised by Jesus for her faith (Mt. 9.18-26; Mk 5.21-43; Lk. 8.40-56) and in the account of the healing of the son of the widow at Nain (Lk. 7.11-17). John, however, develops extended conversations between women and Jesus in which women grow in their understanding of Jesus's identity. The Samaritan woman recognizes Jesus as a prophet, and she wonders if he could be the Messiah (4.29). She leads the people of her town to Jesus, and they recognize him as 'the Saviour of the World' (4.42). Martha confesses her faith in Jesus as 'the Messiah, the Son of God, the one coming into the world' (11.25). Initially, Mary Magdalene believes that the risen Jesus is the gardener but in the course of her conversation with Jesus, she recognizes him as her teacher and Lord (20.18). John's distinctive portrayal of women raises questions about his development of traditions that feature women. Why has John highlighted the presence of women such as the mother of Jesus, the Samaritan woman, Martha and Mary of Bethany and

Mary Magdalene in his gospel? What factors have influenced John's presentation of women characters?

The prominence of women in John's Gospel has encouraged several scholars to examine the roles of women in the gospel. Raymond Brown notes that the Samaritan woman is depicted as a missionary, since she leads the people of her town to Jesus, and Mary Magdalene is portrayed as an apostle because Jesus first appears to her and then asks her to tell the disciples about the resurrection.[1] Brown proposes that John presents women as disciples since Martha and Mary are described as those whom Jesus loved, and Mary Magdalene is identified as one of Jesus's 'own' because she recognizes Jesus when he calls her by her name. Sandra Schneiders, moreover, observes that women are not portrayed as one-dimensional characters but as rounded individuals who often act in unconventional ways such as the Samaritan woman who takes the public role of bearing witness to Jesus, Mary of Bethany who anoints Jesus's feet with expensive perfume, and Mary Magdalene who visits Jesus's tomb alone at night and engages in a conversation with a man whom she believes to be a stranger.[2] As John Rena argues, women take part in the main events of the gospel: the Samaritan woman acts as a missionary, Martha confesses her faith in Jesus, Mary anoints Jesus, the mother of Jesus is a witness to the crucifixion and Mary Magdalene is the first person to see Jesus after his resurrection from the dead.[3]

Several monographs have been written which explore the portrayal of women in John's Gospel. Martin Scott proposes that John's use of wisdom traditions as a source for his Christology has influenced his presentation of women, and he suggests that women are portrayed as the disciples or 'handmaidens' of Jesus Sophia (cf. Prov. 9.3).[4] Scott argues that the Samaritan woman is depicted as 'Sophia's maidservant' since she calls others to meet Jesus, and he proposes that Jesus's love for Mary, Martha and Lazarus may be compared to the love of wisdom for her followers. Scott's work highlights the discipleship roles of women characters, but his book is mainly concerned with the relationship between wisdom traditions and John's Christology. Additional research is needed to account for John's distinctive portrayal of women characters. Other scholars such as Robert Maccini have explored the relationship of women to a specific theme in John's Gospel.[5] Maccini examines the ways in which individual women are portrayed as witnesses to Jesus, and he argues that there is no difference between the presentation of female and male witnesses. Not all commentators, however, give a positive interpretation of women in John's Gospel. Adeline Fehribach develops a feminist interpretation of John's portrayal of women.[6] She proposes that John restricts

---

[1] R. E. Brown, *The Community of the Beloved Disciple: The Life, Loves, and Hates of an Individual Church in New Testament Times* (New York: Paulist Press, 1979), 183–98.

[2] S. M. Schneiders, 'Women in the Fourth Gospel and the Role of Women in the Contemporary Church', *BTB* 12 (1982): 35–45.

[3] J. Rena, 'Women in the Gospel of John', *Église et Théologie* 17 (1986): 131–47.

[4] M. Scott, *Sophia and the Johannine Jesus*, JSNTSup 71 (Sheffield: Sheffield Academic Press, 1992), 241–52.

[5] R. G. Maccini, *'Her Testimony Is True': Women as Witnesses according to John*, JSNTSup 125 (Sheffield: Sheffield Academic Press, 1996), 240–7.

[6] A. Fehribach, *The Women in the Life of the Bridegroom: A Feminist Historical-Literary Analysis of the Gospel of John* (Collegeville, PA: Liturgical Press, 1998).

the discipleship roles of women because she interprets the primary purpose of the women characters as one of supporting the role of Jesus as 'the Messianic bridegroom'.

Initial research on the portrayal of women in John's Gospel focuses on the relationship between women and discipleship. The development of literary approaches to the New Testament has led other scholars to compare the characterization of women with men in John's Gospel.[7] Colleen Conway compares the role of female characters with that of male characters including Nicodemus and the Samaritan woman, Martha and Peter, Mary of Bethany and Judas, and Mary Magdalene and the two disciples at the tomb.[8] She points out that the female characters are all portrayed positively, whereas the blind man and the Beloved Disciple are presented more favourably than the other male characters. Conway rightly notes that characters including women who are not part of the structures of power and authority are seen in a more positive light than other characters in John's Gospel. Margaret Beirne also compares John's portrayal of female and male characters but she selects different 'gender pairs' from those of Conway, and her work centres on the mother of Jesus and the royal official, Nicodemus and the Samaritan woman, the man born blind and Martha, Mary of Bethany and Judas, the mother of Jesus and the Beloved Disciple, and Mary Magdalene and Thomas.[9] Beirne argues that women are portrayed as disciples of 'equal standing' with men, since women and men both respond to Jesus with faith and at times struggle to understand him.

John's portrayal of women as examples of discipleship has prompted some scholars to explore the ways in which the female characters illustrate the historical situation of women in the Johannine community. Sandra Schneiders notes that John's presentation of the meetings between women and Jesus suggests that he has knowledge of women who take part in theological debates and who have the roles of missionaries in the early church.[10] Mary Rose D'Angelo proposes that John's portrayal of women as prophetic figures reflects the charismatic nature of the Johannine community which did not have clearly defined leadership roles and fixed structures.[11] In addition, Adele Reinhartz argues that the portrayal of female characters in the roles of teachers, prophets and apostles indicates that they may have held similar positions in the Johannine community.[12] Reinhartz, however, believes that the portrayal of women is ambiguous because John does not clearly identify women as 'disciples'. She argues that Mary Magdalene's meeting with the risen Jesus is superseded by accounts of resurrection

---

[7] For an analysis of the literary features of John's Gospel, see R. A. Culpepper, *Anatomy of the Fourth Gospel: A Study in Literary Design* (Philadelphia, PA: Fortress, 1983).

[8] C. M. Conway, *Men and Women in the Fourth Gospel: Gender and Johannine Characterization*, SBLDS 167 (Atlanta, GA: Society of Biblical Literature, 1999).

[9] M. M. Beirne, *Women and Men in the Fourth Gospel: A Genuine Discipleship of Equals*, JSNTSup 242 (Sheffield: Sheffield Academic Press, 2003), 219–23.

[10] Schneiders, 'Women', 38–9.

[11] M. R. D'Angelo, '(Re)Presentations of Women in the Gospels: John and Mark', in *Women and Christian Origins*, edited by R. S. Kraemer and M. R. D'Angelo (Oxford: Oxford University Press, 1999), 137.

[12] A. Reinhartz, 'Women in the Johannine Community: An Exercise in Historical Imagination', in *A Feminist Companion to John*, edited by A.-J. Levine with M. Blickenstaff, vol. 2 (London: Sheffield Academic Press, 2003), 26–33.

appearances to the male disciples. Reinhartz suggests that John may wish to support the leadership roles of women but she believes that he has been constrained by the tradition that Jesus is mainly accompanied by a small group of male disciples and by the views of his community that women are not disciples.

Our review of recent research on women in John's Gospel indicates that scholars give different interpretations of John's portrayal of women and their roles as disciples. Their research raises questions about the factors which have influenced John's portrayal of women and the role of women in the Johannine community. In this study we will assess John's portrayal of women in the context of his apocalyptic world view. John portrays Jesus as the Messiah and the Son of God who has come to bring humanity eternal life and to inaugurate the new creation. John's Gospel includes a number of accounts that feature conversations between Jesus and women. Women are among those who recognize the identity of Jesus and confess their faith in him as the Messiah and Son of God, and they are associated with the development of the Christology of John's Gospel. We will explore John's portrayal of women in relation to his definition of discipleship and his understanding of the new creation.

Recent scholars note the influence of Jewish apocalyptic traditions on the development of John's theology.[13] John Ashton proposes that the main theme of the gospel is the revelation of God in Jesus and the human response to this revelation.[14] As Ashton observes, the association of apocalyptic literature with expectations of an imminent end of the world has led to the view that John's Gospel does not reflect apocalyptic thought. This perspective, however, does not take into account the Johannine emphasis on the revelation of heavenly mysteries to human beings (cf. 1.51). The revelation of the heavenly mysteries is a characteristic feature of apocalyptic writings and John's Gospel.[15] Nevertheless, John's Gospel also contains some allusions to the end-time. Although John emphasizes the gift of eternal life in the present, he includes some references to future eschatology (5.25-29; 6.39, 40, 44, 54; 11.24; 12.48).[16] In apocalyptic texts the world is ruled by Satan, and God intervenes to bring about a new age of peace and well-being. Judith Kovacs rightly argues that apocalyptic

---

[13] J. Ashton, *Understanding the Fourth Gospel*, 2nd edn (Oxford: Oxford University Press, 2007). Recent work which highlights the influence of apocalyptic thought on John's Gospel incudes B. E. Reynolds, *The Apocalyptic Son of Man in the Gospel of John*, WUNT 249 (Tübingen: Mohr Siebeck, 2008); C. H. Williams and C. Rowland (eds), *John's Gospel and Intimations of Apocalyptic* (London: T&T Clark, 2013) and B. E. Reynolds and G. Boccaccini (eds), *Reading the Gospel of John's Christology as Jewish Messianism: Royal, Prophetic, and Divine Messiahs*, Ancient Judaism and Early Christianity 106 (Leiden: Brill, 2018).

[14] Ashton, *Understanding*, 6–7, 307–29.

[15] For an analysis of the role of the revelation of mysteries in apocalyptic writings, see C. Rowland, *The Open Heaven: A Study of Apocalyptic in Judaism and Early Christianity* (New York: Crossroad, 1982), 9–48 and J. J. Collins, *The Apocalyptic Imagination: An Introduction to the Jewish Matrix of Christianity* (New York: Crossroad, 1984), 1–32. Rowland emphasizes the importance of visionary experiences in his study of apocalyptic literature. On the other hand Collins stresses the significance of apocalyptic eschatology in which revelation is concerned with the imminent intervention of God who will bring the present age to an end.

[16] For a study of John's eschatology, see J. Frey, *Die Johanneische Eschatologie: Band II: Das Johanneische Zeitverständnis*, WUNT 110 (Tübingen: Mohr Siebeck, 1998).

traditions of cosmic combat have influenced John's presentation of the death of Jesus.[17] As she points out, Jesus's death is depicted as a victory over Satan, the 'ruler of the world' (12.31-32). John's Gospel, however, differs from Jewish apocalyptic texts since Jesus has overcome the 'ruler of the world' through his death on the cross but his disciples still experience persecution in the world while they await his return (15.18–16.4).

In this study we will explore John's portrayal of women in relation to the apocalyptic theme of new creation. In John's Gospel Jesus overcomes the power of evil, and he inaugurates the new creation. The Johannine prologue alludes to the creation account in Genesis and introduces the theme of new creation. The opening of the prologue (ἐν ἀρχῇ, 1.1) echoes the first verse of Genesis (ἐν ἀρχῇ, 1.1 LXX). Jesus is identified with the word which is present with God before creation comes into being. John's identification of Jesus with the word recalls God's act of creation through his word in Genesis (cf. Ps. 33.6; Wis. 9.1). His use of creation imagery is a common feature of Jewish apocalyptic writings. As D. S. Russell notes, the prophecies of Isaiah associate the end-time with the creation of new heavens and a new earth (Isa. 65.17; 66.22) and apocalyptic writings depict the end-time in terms of a new creation (cf. *1 En.* 91.16; *4 Ezra* 7.30-36; *2 Bar.* 3.7).[18] In the New Testament Paul also describes the end-time as a new creation (καινὴ κτίσις, 2 Cor. 5.17; Gal. 6.15). Jeannine Brown analyses the Johannine theme of the renewal of creation, and she argues that Jesus is the Messiah who has the role of bringing God's creative work to completion.[19] Brown proposes that John's identification of Jesus with light and life evokes the creation account in Genesis (1.4, 5, 9). This association is continued in the course of the gospel since Jesus is portrayed as 'the light of the world' (8.12), 'the bread of life' (6.35) and 'the way, the truth and the life' (14.6). Carlos Raúl Sosa Siliezar notes that John places creation imagery at strategic places within the gospel including the prologue and Jesus's Farewell Discourse in which he refers to the 'foundation of the world' (17.5, 24).[20] At the end of the gospel Jesus's act of breathing the Spirit into his disciples (ἐνεφύσησεν, 20.22) is reminiscent of God's act of breathing life into Adam (ἐνεφύσησεν, Gen. 2.7). Siliezar argues that John employs creation imagery in order to associate the creative activity of Jesus with God's work of creation in Genesis. As Siliezar points out, John presents Jesus as the agent of creation and of salvation.

---

[17] J. L. Kovacs, '"Now Shall the Ruler of This World Be Driven Out": Jesus' Death as Cosmic Battle in John 12:20-36', *JBL* 114 (1995): 227–47.
[18] D. S. Russell, *The Method and Message of Jewish Apocalyptic 200 B.C.-A.D. 100* (London: SCM Press, 1964), 280–4.
[19] J. K. Brown, 'Creation's Renewal in the Gospel of John', *CBQ* 72 (2010): 275–90. Other scholars who have examined the Johannine theme of new creation include P. S. Minear, *Christians and the New Creation: Genesis Motifs in the New Testament* (Louisville, KY: Westminster John Knox, 1994), 82–102. Minear assesses the theme of new creation in relation to John's presentation of human beings as those who must be born from above. See also J. A. Du Rand, 'The Creation Motif in the Fourth Gospel: Perspectives on Its Narratological Function within a Judaistic Background', in *Theology and Christology in the Fourth Gospel: Essays by the Members of the SNTS Johannine Writings Seminar*, edited by G. Van Belle, J. G. Van der Watt and P. Maritz, BETL. 184 (Leuven: Leuven University Press, 2005), 21–46.
[20] C. R. S. Siliezar, *Creation Imagery in the Gospel of John*, LNTS 546 (London: Bloomsbury, 2015), 191–203.

In John's apocalyptic world view women and men are caught up in the struggle between the powers of light and darkness. In the prologue Jesus is described as the true light coming into the world which enlightens every human being (1.9). John, moreover, depicts a cosmic struggle between light and darkness in which darkness fails to overcome the light (κατέλαβεν, 1.5). This verse alludes to Jesus's victory over evil at the crucifixion when he casts out 'the ruler of the world' (12.31; 14.30). The verb καταλαμβάνω, however, may also be translated as 'comprehend' which suggests that the darkness did not comprehend the light.[21] The Johannine prologue introduces the paradoxical thought which lies at the heart of the gospel. The world was created through Jesus but the world did not recognize him. He came to his own but his own did not accept him (1.10-11). As Adele Reinhartz points out, the cosmological story of the word made flesh forms a framework for the historical story of Jesus's conflict with his human opponents.[22] This conflict focuses on the identity of Jesus as the Messiah and Son of God. Jesus's enemies reject his claim to be the Messiah and they accuse him of claiming equality with God (5.18; 10.33). Some human beings are unable to recognize Jesus, but others do accept him, and they are given the power to become children of God (1.12). The prologue raises the question of why some women and men believe in Jesus and some reject him. We will examine this question in relation to our study of John's portrayal of women and their roles as disciples. Women feature prominently among those who believe in Jesus, and we will assess their responses to Jesus in the course of our analysis of women in John's Gospel.

The approach of this study

This study includes six chapters which examine the women characters in the following narratives: the mother of Jesus at the wedding in Cana (2.1-11), the Samaritan woman's meeting with Jesus at the well near Sychar (4.1-42), Martha and Mary at Bethany (11.1-44), the anointing of Jesus by Mary of Bethany (12.1-8), the women at the crucifixion (19.25-27) and Mary Magdalene's meeting with the risen Jesus (20.1-18). These chapters will assess John's portrayal of women in the context of the social and historical setting of the first-century Graeco-Roman world.[23] We will examine the ways in which women are introduced and described, the names of women and their family relationships. Most women married at an early age and bore children, and we will explore the autonomy and financial independence of women. We will also analyse John's references to women in relation to their lives at home and their participation in the life of their villages and towns.

---

[21] R. Bultmann (*The Gospel of John*, translated by G. R. Beasley-Murray (Oxford: Blackwell, 1971), 47–8), prefers this translation of καταλαμβάνω, and he notes the parallel use of the verbs οὐκ ἔγνω and οὐ παρέλαβον in the prologue (1.10-11).

[22] A. Reinhartz, *The Word in the World: The Cosmological Tale in the Fourth Gospel*, SBLMS 45 (Atlanta, GA: Scholars Press, 1992), 4–5, 38.

[23] For a study of the lives of Jewish women in Graeco-Roman Palestine, see T. Ilan, *Jewish Women in Greco-Roman Palestine* (Peabody, MA: Hendrickson, 1996) and L. J. Archer, *Her Price Is Beyond Rubies: the Jewish Woman in Graeco-Roman Palestine* (Sheffield: JSOT Press, 1990).

In John's Gospel women confess their faith in Jesus, and he reveals his identity as the Messiah and Son of God to them. We will examine the discipleship roles of women and the question of whether John includes women in Jesus's group of disciples. In this study we will examine John's portrayal of women in relation to his apocalyptic world view. Jesus has come to bring humanity eternal life and to inaugurate the new creation. We will explore the ways in which John associates women with the theme of new creation. Finally, we will assess the extent to which John's accounts of women provide indications of the roles of women in the Johannine community. This study aims to examine John's distinctive portrayal of women and to contribute to a greater understanding of the roles of women in the early church.

A feminist interpretation of John's Gospel

Women in John's Gospel takes a feminist approach to the interpretation of John's portrayal of women in relationship to discipleship and their roles within the Johannine community. Feminist scholars bring new questions to the study of New Testament texts and develop a variety of approaches to their interpretation.[24] They assess the representation of women in the New Testament and the ways in which the texts construct gender.[25] Feminist commentators analyse the extent to which the New Testament writings are inclusive of women and they examine the ways in which the texts challenge or restrict the roles of women in patriarchal society. They also emphasize the ethics of biblical interpretation, including the impact of these interpretations on the church and society.[26] Some feminist scholars assess theological concepts within the New Testament.[27] Dorothy Lee, for example, examines the concept of 'abiding' in John's Gospel, and she explores the ways in which the mutuality within this concept challenges gender polarities.[28] Recent scholars such as Colleen Conway examine the ways in which the New Testament authors engage with Graeco-Roman concepts of masculinity in their portrayal of Jesus.[29] Conway's work raises questions

---

[24] E. Schüssler Fiorenza, *In Memory of Her: A Feminist Theological Reconstruction of Christian Origins*, 2nd edn (New York: Crossroad, 1995), 41–60; L. Schottroff, *Lydia's Impatient Sisters: A Feminist Social History of Early Christianity* (Louisville, KY: Westminster John Knox, 1995).

[25] S. Heine, *Women and Early Christianity: Are the Feminist Scholars Right?* (London: SCM Press, 1987); C. Ricci, *Mary Magdalene and Many Others: Women Who Followed Jesus* (Kent: Burns & Oates, 1994); E. Schüssler Fiorenza (ed.), *Searching the Scriptures: A Feminist Commentary*, vol. 2 (New York: Crossroad, 1994); C. A. Newsom and S. H. Ringe (eds), *Women's Bible Commentary*, exp. edn (Louisville, KY: Westminster John Knox, 1998); R. S Kraemer and M. R. D'Angelo (eds), *Women and Christian Origins* (Oxford: Oxford University Press, 1999), A.-J. Levine (ed.) with M. Blickenstaff, *A Feminist Companion to John*, 2 vols (London: Sheffield Academic Press, 2003).

[26] E. Schüssler Fiorenza, 'The Ethics of Biblical Interpretation: Decentering Biblical Scholarship', *JBL* 107 (1988): 3–17.

[27] M. Grey, *Redeeming the Dream: Feminism, Redemption and Christian Tradition* (London: SPCK, 1989); S. M. Schneiders, *The Revelatory Text: Interpreting the New Testament as Sacred Scripture* (New York: HarperCollins, 1991), 180–99.

[28] D. A. Lee, 'Abiding in the Fourth Gospel: A Case Study in Feminist Biblical Theology', in *A Feminist Companion to John*, edited by A.-J. Levine with M. Blickenstaff, vol. 2 (London: Sheffield Academic Press, 2003), 64–78.

[29] C. M. Conway, *Behold the Man: Jesus and Greco-Roman Masculinity* (Oxford: Oxford University Press, 2008).

about the ways in which the gender roles of women and men in the ancient world develop in relationship with one another. Lynn Cohick points out that the question 'what does it mean to be male and female' was frequently asked in the Graeco-Roman world.[30] She notes that gender was often employed rhetorically in discussions of issues such as government, political corruption and philosophical concepts of virtue. In addition, Susan Hylen points out that there are different understandings of gender in the Graeco-Roman world.[31] She notes that norms for women's behaviour may be interpreted in a variety of ways according to the social and cultural context. As she observes, domestic virtues such as modesty, industry and loyalty to the family may be valued as virtues which support the civic leadership of women.

Our study employs a feminist approach to the analysis of John's portrayal of women since we will assess the extent to which John's portrayal of women challenges or conforms to the patriarchal society of the first-century Graeco-Roman world. We will examine the gospel to discover if there are any indications that John is aware of the issue of gender. We will also determine whether John's presentation of discipleship is inclusive of women. This book will focus on the narratives that feature women in order to determine the characteristic features of the discipleship of women in John's Gospel. We will aim to identify some insights into the historical experience of women in one of the early Christian communities. Feminist scholars wish to recover the forgotten history of the lives of women, and this study seeks to contribute to our knowledge of the role of women in Jesus's mission and the forms of participation of women in the early church.

John's Gospel features a number of extended narratives that feature women, and the synoptic gospels also include a number of narratives featuring women characters. Jesus heals women (Mt. 8.14-15// Mk 1.29-31// Lk. 4.38-39; Mt. 9.18-26// Mk 5.21-43// Lk. 8.40-56) and he speaks of women in his parables (Lk. 15.8-10; Lk. 18.1-8). Women are present in the crowds listening to his teaching (Mt. 12.46-50// Mk 3.31-35// Lk. 8.19-21). Although Jesus does not include a woman in his inner circle of twelve male disciples, women are present in the wider group of disciples who follow him (Mk 15.40-41; Lk. 8.1-3). Women are described at the crucifixion of Jesus (Mt. 27.55-56// Mk 15.40-41// Lk. 23.49// Jn 19.25-27) and they are the first to visit his tomb (Mt. 28.1-10// Mk 16.1-8// Lk. 24.1-10// Jn 20.1-18).

The large number of women in the gospel traditions has encouraged commentators to highlight Jesus's positive attitude towards women.[32] Recent research, however, has emphasized the importance of interpreting Jesus in relation to the social and political context of first-century Judaism. Scholars such as Judith Plaskow argue that the status of women in first-century Palestine has been denigrated in order to demonstrate the

---

[30] L. H. Cohick, *Women in the World of the Earliest Christians: Illuminating Ancient Ways of Life* (Grand Rapids, MI: Baker Academic, 2009), 27–8.

[31] S. E. Hylen, *Women in the New Testament World* (Oxford: Oxford University Press, 2019), 25–41, 160–8.

[32] L. Swidler, *Biblical Affirmations of Women* (Philadelphia, PA: Westminster, 1979); Schüssler Fiorenza, *In Memory*, 105–59, B. Witherington, *Women in the Ministry of Jesus: A Study of Jesus' Attitudes to Women and Their Roles as Reflected in His Earthly Life* (Cambridge: Cambridge University Press, 1984).

liberating practice of Jesus.³³ Plaskow points out that scholars have often contrasted the positive attitude of Jesus towards women with the less favourable attitudes of his contemporaries. She proposes that we may read the sources differently if we interpret the attitude of Jesus in continuity with his Jewish background. In the past, passages from the Mishnah have been employed to reconstruct the lives of women, and on the basis of those reconstructions the suggestion has been made that women were secluded in society whereas most poor women would have worked outside the home. Judith Wegner, however, points out that the Mishnah reflects the ideals of the rabbis rather than the historical experiences of women.³⁴ The Mishnah contains some early traditions but it was not codified until around 200 CE, and it is important to assess the extent to which the regulations of the Mishnah were followed in the first century.

Some scholars such as A.-J. Levine argue that the portrayal of women in texts including *Joseph and Aseneth, the Testament of Job*, Tobit, Judith, *4 Maccabees, Pseudo-Philo*, Philo on the Therapeutrides and Josephus' *War* 2.559-61 suggests that women contributed to religious and public life in many forms of Second Temple Judaism.³⁵ As she points out, these texts provide evidence of the education of women and their leadership roles in public life. In Alexandria, women and men lived in a religious community which engaged in worship and the study of the Law.³⁶ The Babatha archive, moreover, provides examples of the business transactions of Babatha, a Jewish woman from Judea, who conducted her own financial affairs in the second century CE.³⁷ Tal Ilan argues that the lives of Jewish women were diverse, and different groups followed different interpretations of the Law.³⁸ She observes that the author of Sirach, Josephus and the authors of Tannaitic literature represent the views of the upper middle classes and aristocrats, and the wealthy were the only people who could afford to have separate women's quarters in their homes. Ilan rightly emphasizes the variety of forms of Judaism in the first century. Her work stresses the necessity of identifying evidence which illustrates the lives of women in the Johannine community.

This study will also interpret John's presentation of women in relation to the varied roles of women in the early Christian communities. The New Testament writings contain debates over the role of women in the early church. In his letter to the Galatians, Paul includes a baptismal formula which states that there is no longer 'male and female' (3.27-28; cf. 1 Cor. 12.13; Col. 3.11). The use of this baptismal formula in early Christian communities indicates that some groups were concerned about the roles of women in the church and in the wider society.³⁹ The baptismal formula offers

---

³³ J. Plaskow, 'Anti-Judaism in Feminist Christian Interpretation', in *Searching the Scriptures*, edited by E. Schüssler Fiorenza, vol. 1 (New York: Crossroad, 1993), 119-20.
³⁴ J. R. Wegner, *Chattel or Person? The Status of Women in the Mishnah* (Oxford: Oxford University Press, 1988), 4.
³⁵ A.-J. Levine, 'Second Temple Judaism, Jesus and Women: Yeast of Eden', *BibInt* 2 (1994): 8-20.
³⁶ J. Taylor, *Jewish Women Philosophers of First-Century Alexandria – Philo's 'Therapeutae' Reconsidered* (Oxford: Oxford University Press, 2003).
³⁷ For an analysis of Babatha's ketubbah, see Y. Yadin, J. C. Greenfield and A. Yardeni, 'Babatha's *Ketubba*', *IEJ* 44 (1994): 75-101; M. A. Friedmann, 'Babatha's *Ketubba*: Some Preliminary Observations', *IEJ* 46 (1996): 55-76.
³⁸ Ilan, *Jewish Women*, 226-9.
³⁹ For a study of the role of Gal. 3.28 in Early Christianity, see P. N. Hogan, *'No Longer Male and Female': Interpreting Galatians 3.28 in Early Christianity* (London: T&T Clark, 2008).

a new understanding of gender relations which are based on human participation in Christ's death and resurrection. There is also evidence that women held leadership roles in some early Christian communities. Paul refers to women such as Phoebe who had the role of a 'deacon' in Cenchreae (διάκονος, Rom. 16.1). Prisca and Aquila were 'fellow workers' of Paul (τοὺς συνεργούς μου, Rom. 16.3), and Andronicus and Junia are described as 'prominent among the apostles' (ἐπίσημοι ἐν τοῖς ἀποστόλοις, Rom. 16.7). On the other hand some passages in the New Testament seek to restrict the leadership roles of women such as the instructions which state that women are not permitted to speak in church or to teach (1 Cor. 14.33-35; 1 Tim. 2.11-15). The desire to limit the roles of women may be seen in the household codes which advocate the subordination of women to their husbands (Col. 3.18-4.1; Eph. 5.21-6.9; 1 Pet. 2.18-3.7) and in the criteria listed in the pastoral epistles which associate men with positions of authority in the church (1 Tim. 3.1-13; Tit. 1.5-16).

The varied experience of women in the early church raises questions about the factors which encouraged some people to support and others to oppose the leadership roles of women. David Balch proposes that the experience of persecution led some communities to restrict the roles of women to traditional roles within society.[40] He suggests that the author of 1 Peter included the household code which advocated the subordination of women (2.18-3.7) because there were concerns in the wider Graeco-Roman society about the behaviour of women who joined Christian communities, particularly those whose husbands were not Christians. On the other hand Margaret MacDonald examines the process of institutionalization in Pauline communities and argues that the roles of women were restricted as Christianity became more centrally organized and a male hierarchical leadership was established.[41] As Karen King points out, the Gospel of Mary offers an alternative view of the leadership roles of women to the restrictions of 1 Timothy.[42] Women such as Maximilla and Priscilla were leaders of the Montanist movement in the second century CE.[43] The diversity in the leadership roles of women in the early church raises questions about the nature of the roles of women in the Johannine community. In this study we will aim to examine the factors which have influenced the roles of women in the Johannine community.

We will seek to gain an understanding of the roles of women in the Johannine community which may be compared to the roles of women in other early Christian communities. Elisabeth Schüssler Fiorenza argues that Mark and John illustrate the countercultural nature of early Christianity, and women in the Markan and Johannine communities have the roles of leaders and apostles.[44] She points to the foundational role of the Beloved Disciple in John's Gospel and proposes that the Johannine community is 'constituted as the discipleship of equals by the love they have for one another'. On the other hand Turid Karlsen Seim suggests that some members of the

---

[40] D. L. Balch, *Let Wives Be Submissive: The Domestic Code in 1 Peter* (Chico, CA: Scholars Press, 1981).
[41] M. Y. MacDonald, *The Pauline Churches: A Socio-Historical Study of Institutionalization in the Pauline and Deutero-Pauline Writings* (Cambridge: Cambridge University Press, 1988), 235-8.
[42] K. L. King, 'The Gospel of Mary Magdalene', in *Searching the Scriptures*, edited by E. Schüssler Fiorenza, vol. 2 (New York: Crossroad, 1994), 622-5.
[43] R. R. Ruether, *Women and Redemption: A Theological History* (London: SCM Press, 1998), 51-3.
[44] Schüssler Fiorenza, *In Memory*, 323-34.

Johannine community may not support the prominence of women.[45] In her analysis of the meeting of Jesus and the Samaritan woman, she notes that the disciples are surprised to find Jesus talking to a woman but they are afraid to voice any criticism of Jesus (4.27). Seim suggests that the response of the disciples indicates that some members of John's community do not support Jesus's acceptance of the discipleship of women. In this study we will seek to recover the role of women in the Johannine tradition and examine the social and historical factors that have influenced the roles of women in the Johannine community. This research aims to contribute to a wider analysis of the roles of women in the early church and to an assessment of the influence of women in the development of Christianity.

A literary reading of John's Gospel

This study will assess John's portrayal of women in relation to John's Gospel as a literary unity. Some scholars including Raymond Brown note that there are awkward transitions between some passages.[46] In the Farewell Discourse, for example, Jesus announces to his disciples, 'Rise, let us go from here' (14.31) but John continues with two more chapters of Jesus's speech.[47] John Ashton identifies four aporias: Jn 21, 6.1, 10.1 and 20.30-31, and he argues that these passages indicate that the gospel has undergone a period of revision.[48] Most scholars believe that ch. 21 has been added to the original ending of the gospel (20.30-31).[49] The final verses of ch. 20 appear to be the original conclusion to the gospel since they state that the purpose of the gospel is to lead the audience to faith in Jesus as the Messiah and Son of God. In John 20 Jesus appears to his disciples in Jerusalem but in John 21 the disciples return to Galilee and go out fishing. It is strange to find the disciples in Galilee after the account of their meeting with the risen Jesus in Jerusalem. The last chapter may be interpreted as a later addition which assesses the leadership roles of Peter and the Beloved Disciple and the scope of the early Christian mission. The addition of ch. 21 which features the male disciples raises questions about the discipleship role of women since Mary Magdalene is a key witness to the resurrection in ch. 20. We will examine the issue of whether or not her role as a witness is downplayed by the addition of the account of the resurrection appearance of Jesus to the male disciples.

---

[45] T. K. Seim, 'Roles of Women in the Gospel of John', in *Aspects on the Johannine Literature*, edited by L. Hartman and B. Olsson, ConB. 18 (Uppsala: Almqvist & Wiksell International, 1987), 56–73.
[46] R. E. Brown, *The Gospel according to John*, 2 vols, AB 29-29A (Garden City, NY: Doubleday, 1966–70), 1:xxiv–xl.
[47] For an analysis of this passage, see G. L. Parsenios, *Departure and Consolation: The Johannine Farewell Discourses in Light of Greco-Roman Literature*, Supplements to Novum Testamentum 117 (Leiden: Brill, 2005), 49–76. Parsenios proposes that John has employed the literary convention of the dramatic exit in 14.31 in order to halt the narrative and to draw attention to Jesus's departure to his death.
[48] Ashton, *Understanding*, 42–53.
[49] Brown, *John*, 2:1077–82; C. K. Barrett, *The Gospel according to St. John: An Introduction with Commentary and Notes on the Greek Text*, 2nd edn (London: SPCK, 1978), 576–8; B. Lindars, *The Gospel of John*, NCBC (London: Marshall, Morgan & Scott, 1972), 618–22.

John's Gospel, however, has a unity of style and language, and it includes distinctive metaphors of light and darkness, and truth and falsehood. There are carefully developed dialogues and discourses and Jesus characteristically speaks with 'I am' sayings (6.35; 8.12; 10.9, 11; 11.25; 14.6; 15.1). In this study we will primarily focus on the portrayal of women in relation to the final redaction of the gospel, but we will also take some account of the historical development of narratives which feature women. One of the main literary characteristics of John's Gospel is the number of extended narratives which depict conversations between Jesus and characters such as Nicodemus, the Samaritan woman, Martha, the blind man, Mary Magdalene and Thomas. We will assess John's presentation of women in these narratives and examine the ways in which his presentation of women may reflect the roles of women in the Johannine community. The Samaritan woman leads other people from her town to Jesus, and they acclaim him as the 'Saviour of the World' (4.42). Martha confesses her faith in Jesus as the 'Messiah and the Son of God' (11.27) and Mary anoints Jesus as the Messiah (12.1-8). Mary Magdalene passes on the news of the resurrection with the testimony, 'I have seen the Lord' (20.18). In this study we will identify the distinctive features of the discipleship of women. John highlights the faith of women who recognize Jesus as the Messiah and Son of God. We will assess the contribution of the women's confessions of faith to his definition of discipleship and his understanding of the new creation.

John's Gospel and the synoptic gospels

This research aims to assess John's distinctive portrayal of women in relation to the gospel as a literary unity but we will also examine the ways in which he has developed the traditions he has received about women. John's Gospel contains narratives featuring women characters which do not appear in the synoptic gospels such as the account of the mother of Jesus at the wedding at Cana (2.1-11) and the meeting of Jesus and the Samaritan woman (4.1-42). The sisters, Martha and Mary, are mentioned in Luke's Gospel (10.38-42) but there is no description of the raising of Lazarus. The anointing of Jesus by a woman takes place in all four gospels but John's Gospel is the only gospel which identifies the woman who anoints Jesus as Mary of Bethany (12.1-8). Mary Magdalene is a key witness to the death and resurrection of Jesus in every gospel but John is the only gospel which includes an account of the conversation of Mary and the risen Jesus (20.11-18). The similarities and differences between John's Gospel and the synoptic gospels raise the question of whether John knew the synoptic gospels.

The similarities between John's Gospel and the synoptic gospels have led scholars such as C. K. Barrett to argue that John did know the synoptic gospels.[50] Barrett notes that the order of passages in John's Gospel follows the order of passages in Mark's Gospel. Both gospels place the account of John the Baptist, Jesus's departure to

---

[50] Barrett, *St. John*, 42–54. Recent scholars who argue that John knows the synoptic gospels include A. T. Lincoln, *The Gospel according to Saint John*, Black's New Testament Commentaries (London: Continuum, 2005), 26–39 and W. E. S. North, *A Journey Round John: Tradition, Interpretation and Context in the Fourth Gospel*, LNTS 534 (London: T&T Clark, 2015), 207–19.

Galilee, the feeding of the five thousand, Jesus's act of walking on water, the confession of Peter, Jesus's departure to Jerusalem, the Last Supper, the arrest, and the Passion and resurrection in the same order. Mark and John both refer to Jesus's departure to Galilee after the account of the mission of John the Baptist (Mk 1.4-8, 14-15; Jn 1.19-36; 4.3), and they include a reference to the departure to Jerusalem following Peter's confession (Mk 9.30; 10.1, 32, 46; Jn 7.10-14). There are also several examples of verbal agreements between Mark's Gospel and John's Gospel. In the accounts of the feeding of the five thousand, Mark and John both refer to the sum of two hundred denarii (Mk 6.37; Jn 6.7) and five loaves and two fish (Mk 6.38; Jn 6.9). They also mention twelve baskets (Mk 6.43; Jn 6.13) and five thousand men (Mk 6.44; Jn 6.10). In Mark's account of Jesus's act of walking on water Jesus tells the disciples, 'Take heart, it is I; do not be afraid' (θαρσεῖτε, ἐγώ εἰμι μὴ φοβεῖσθε, 6.50) and in John's Gospel he says, 'It is I; do not be afraid' (ἐγώ εἰμι μὴ φοβεῖσθε, 6.20).

On the other hand a number of scholars including Percival Gardner-Smith argue that John did not know the synoptic gospels.[51] Gardner-Smith notes the ways in which supporters of the view that John knew the synoptic gospels emphasize a small number of verbal agreements between the gospels but do not take into account the greater number of differences in the content between the gospels. He proposes that the verbal agreements between John's and Mark's accounts of the feeding of the five thousand may have arisen in the oral tradition. As he observes, the large number of differences in these passages suggest the independent nature of the Johannine tradition. Gardner-Smith highlights the differences between John's account and Mark's account of the anointing of Jesus.[52] In the Johannine account there is no reference to the setting of the house of Simon the leper. John identifies the woman who anoints Jesus as Mary of Bethany, and Judas as the disciple who objects to the expensive perfume.[53]

John's Gospel contains material which is not in the synoptic gospels and material which has similarities with the synoptic tradition. Marianne Thompson argues that the similarities between John and the synoptic gospels suggest that they share some oral or written material.[54] The greatest number of similarities between Mark's Gospel and John's Gospel occurs in the Passion Narrative. The Passion Narrative may have developed at an early stage of the Christian tradition since Christians would wish to give an account of the reasons why Jesus was arrested and put to death by the Roman authorities. John and the other evangelists may have had access to a pre-Marcan passion narrative.[55] It is probable that John is aware of the traditions which appear in the synoptic gospels such as Jesus's prayer in Gethsemane and the tradition that Joseph of Arimathea was forced to carry the cross of Jesus.

---

[51] P. Gardner-Smith, *Saint John and the Synoptic Gospels* (Cambridge: Cambridge University Press, 1938), 88–97.
[52] Gardner-Smith, *Saint John*, 27–33.
[53] Gardner-Smith, *Saint John*, 42–50.
[54] M. M. Thompson, *John: A Commentary* (Louisville, KY: Westminster John Knox, 2015), 2–8.
[55] For a study of the theory of a pre-Marcan passion narrative, see M. L. Soards, 'Appendix IX: The Question of a PreMarcan Passion Narrative', in *The Death of the Messiah. From Gethsemane to the Grave: A Commentary on the Passion Narratives in the Four Gospels*, edited by R. E. Brown, 2 vols, ABRL (Garden City, NY: Doubleday, 1998), 2:1492–1524.

John's sources may include a signs source, a saying source and a pre-Marcan passion narrative. These sources have developed in the Johannine tradition and have been formed into John's Gospel. D. Moody Smith argues that John's Gospel is an 'independent gospel' which represents an 'independent witness' (1.14; 19.35; 21.24).[56] He points out that John's Gospel contains considerable chronological and geographical differences from the synoptic gospels. In John's Gospel Jesus frequently visits Jerusalem over a period of several years, and the Last Supper takes place on the Eve of Passover rather than on Passover. John, however, gives no explanation for these contradictions. As Smith notes, John's Gospel differs from the other gospels in unexpected ways since John makes no reference to Jesus's trial before the Sanhedrin and he does not include any reference to the tearing of the temple veil at the crucifixion of Jesus.

The distinctive language and metaphors of John's Gospel, moreover, suggest that John's Gospel reflects an independent tradition. There are a number of similarities between the imagery of light, life and truth found in the gospel and in the Johannine Epistles. The gospel identifies the Spirit as the Paraclete (14.16, 26; 15.26), and the only other occurrence of this term in the New Testament is the identification of Jesus as the Paraclete who makes intercessions on behalf of the community in 1 Jn 2.1. The similarities between the gospel and the epistles suggest a close relationship between the writings but the theological differences, including the contrast between the realized eschatology of the gospel and the future eschatology of 1 Jn (2.28; 4.17), point to different authors. D. Moody Smith observes that the similarities between John's Gospel and the Johannine Epistles suggest the formation of the Johannine tradition within a particular geographic area.[57] It is possible that the Johannine community consists of several churches in the vicinity of one another who share the Johannine tradition and theological perspective.[58] This study will employ the term 'Johannine community' to refer to a group of churches who share a distinctive tradition and theological language. Raymond Brown notes that 2 John and 3 John address churches in two different locations, and he points out that Gaius and Diotrephes are leaders in different communities.[59] The Johannine Epistles refer to individual Christians and missionaries who travel between these churches. These letters illustrate a recognizable network of early Christian communities.

In this study we will examine each narrative featuring a woman character in order to identify John's distinctive portrayal of women. We will also assess any indications that John has knowledge of the synoptic traditions which feature women. This approach will enable us to discover the characteristics of John's portrayal of women and to examine the extent to which he has developed traditions to reflect the interests and concerns of his community. We will aim to determine the Johannine view of the roles

---

[56] D. M. Smith, *John among the Gospels*, 2nd edn (Columbia: University of South Carolina Press, 2001), 195–212.

[57] D. M. Smith, 'Johannine Christianity: Some Reflections on Its Character and Delineation', *NTS* 21 (1975): 228–48.

[58] G. Stanton (*The Gospels and Jesus*, 2nd edn (Oxford: Oxford University Press, 2002), 56–7) proposes that the gospels were first addressed to groups of house-churches which were located near one another.

[59] R. E. Brown, *The Epistles of John*, AB30 (Garden City, NY: Doubleday, 1982), 101–2.

of women in relation to the historical and social context of the Johannine community and to explore the extent to which his portrayal of women provides evidence of the debates over the roles of women in the early church.

The Johannine community

One of the aims of this research is an analysis of the extent to which John's presentation of women reflects the roles of women in the Johannine community. Richard Bauckham, however, challenges the belief that the gospels are addressed to individual communities, and that the evangelists' selection of material provides indications of the needs and the concerns of their communities.[60] He proposes that missionaries travelled between communities and that the gospels were written for all Christians. On the other hand Philip Esler rightly argues that the evangelists were embedded in a group-orientated culture, and they would have addressed their gospels to their own communities even if they hoped that other communities would also receive their gospels.[61] Bauckham's analysis, moreover, does not take into account the diversity of the early Christian communities who held a range of theological perspectives.[62] David Sim challenges Bauckham's view that the early Christians regarded themselves as members of a worldwide Christian movement, and he notes the gulf between Christians who advocated circumcision and law observance and those who did not.[63] Sim points out that Christian Gnostics and Jewish Christians produced gospels for their own communities which were not accepted throughout the early church. In addition, Margaret Mitchell observes that there is a lack of evidence in patristic writings to suggest that evangelists believed that they were writing 'for all Christians'.[64]

The argument that the gospels are written for different communities is supported by the differences between some passages which feature women in John's Gospel and the synoptic gospels. In Matthew's Gospel Jesus instructs his disciples that they should not go to the gentiles or to a town of the Samaritans (10.5-6). On the other hand John portrays the Samaritan woman positively as an example of faith. The Samaritan woman

---

[60] R. Bauckham (ed.), *The Gospels for All Christians: Rethinking the Gospel Audiences* (Edinburgh: T&T Clark, 1997).
[61] P. F. Esler, 'Community and Gospel in Early Christianity: A Response to Richard Bauckham's *Gospels for All Christians*', *SJT* 51 (1998): 235–48. Richard Bauckham gives his response to Philip Esler in the same journal, 'Response to Philip Esler', *SJT* 51 (1998): 249–53.
[62] R. E. Brown ('Not Jewish Christianity and Gentile Christianity but Types of Jewish/Gentile Christianity', *CBQ* 45 (1983): 74–9) proposes four different types of Jewish/Gentile Christianity. The first group consists of Jewish Christians and their gentile converts who require circumcision and full observance of the Law. The second group refers to Jewish Christians and their gentile converts who do not require circumcision but do observe some Jewish purity laws. The third group consists of Jewish Christians and their gentile converts who do not require circumcision and the observance of purity laws in relation to food, and the final group consists of Jewish Christians and their gentile converts who do not demand circumcision and the observance of food laws and who are critical of the Temple. Brown situates John's Gospel within this type.
[63] D. C. Sim, 'The Gospels for All Christians? A Response to Richard Bauckham', *JSNT* 84 (2001): 3–27.
[64] M. M. Mitchell, 'Patristic Counter-Evidence to the Claim That "The Gospels Were Written for All Christians"', *NTS* 51 (2005): 36–79.

convinces the people in her town to welcome Jesus. The synoptic gospels depict the visit of women to the tomb of Jesus but John's Gospel is the only gospel which includes an account of the visit of Peter and the Beloved Disciple before giving an extended account of the meeting of Mary Magdalene and the risen Jesus. It is probable that John has introduced the Beloved Disciple into the resurrection narrative on account of his role in the Johannine tradition. At the end of the gospel the Beloved Disciple is described as the one who gives authority to the Johannine tradition but he is not named (21.24-25). John's omission of his name suggests that the gospel is addressed to a group who is aware of his identity.

Our analysis of the roles of women in the Johannine community may be assisted by an examination of the possible location of the community. John's Gospel has traditionally been associated with Ephesus on the basis of the writings of Irenaeus (*Adv. Haer.* 3.1.1).[65] The gospel has similarities with the apocalyptic themes of the book of Revelation in its use of dualistic terminology of light and darkness, and truth and falsehood. In John's Gospel Jesus is described as 'the lamb of God' (ὁ ἀμνὸς τοῦ θεοῦ, 1.29, 36), and in Revelation he is frequently identified as the 'lamb' but with a different Greek term (ἀρνίον, Rev. 5.6, 8, 12; 6.1, 16). The author of Revelation addresses the seven churches in Asia Minor. Ignatius of Antioch also shows knowledge of some of the terms used in the gospel including 'the prince of the world' and 'living water' (*Romans* 7). The links between the gospel, the Johannine Epistles and Revelation along with Ignatius's awareness of the gospel point to a location within Asia Minor.

Other features of John's Gospel, however, suggest a possible Palestinian influence upon the gospel traditions. The gospel contains detailed information about locations in Jerusalem (7.2, 37; 10.22; 11.55) which suggests a Judean influence on the development of the Johannine tradition. John devotes a considerable amount of space to the account of the meeting of Jesus and the Samaritan woman, and he situates this narrative in a prominent place (4.1-42). Raymond Brown traces the development of the theology of the Johannine community over a period of time, and he suggests that the mission to the Samaritans has had an impact on the formation of John's Christology.[66] We will explore the ways in which the meeting of Jesus with the Samaritan woman may provide indications of a Samaritan influence upon John's Gospel.

One of the key factors in establishing the social and historical context of the Johannine tradition is the presentation of tense accounts of the conflict between Jesus and the religious authorities, particularly the Pharisees.[67] D. Moody Smith proposes that John's theology has been shaped by the historical experiences of his community.[68] There are many references to 'the Jews' (οἱ Ἰουδαῖοι) who are portrayed as the opponents of Jesus even though Jesus and his disciples are all Jewish. As Urban von Wahlde points out, the term 'the Jews' primarily refers to the religious authorities when it is associated

---

[65] Recent scholars who associate John's Gospel with the setting of Ephesus include Thompson, *John*, 17–22.
[66] Brown, *Community*, 25–91.
[67] For a study of the relationship between John's Gospel and Judaism, see R. A. Culpepper and P. N. Anderson (eds), *John and Judaism: A Contested Relationship in Context* (Atlanta, GA: SBL Press, 2017).
[68] D. M. Smith, *The Theology of the Gospel of John* (Cambridge: Cambridge University Press, 1995).

with hostility towards Jesus.[69] Adele Reinhartz, moreover, observes that the term 'the Jews' is used only once of Jesus (4.9), and it is not applied to anyone who has faith in Jesus.[70] Raymond Brown thus rightly proposes that John is writing at a time when the community of John has left the synagogue, and the term 'the Jews' refers to those who reject Jesus and remain in the synagogue.[71]

The historical circumstances behind the tense debates between Jesus and the religious authorities have been examined by J. Louis Martyn who notes that those who confess that Jesus is the Messiah face exclusion from the synagogue (9.22; 12.42; 16.2).[72] As Martyn points out, there is no evidence of a formal ban to exclude Christians from the synagogue during the lifetime of Jesus, and he argues that the gospel may be read as a two-level narrative which reflects the time of Jesus and also the time of the Johannine community. Martyn's analysis points to the influence of the historical experiences of the Johannine community on John's Gospel. In John 9 the description of the blind man's parents highlights the fear of women and men that they may be excluded from the synagogue. John's portrayal of the man's mother and father raises the question of whether women were caught up in the disruption of family relationships and friendships brought about by the tensions between Jewish Christians and the synagogue authorities.

In recent years, however, some scholars have challenged Martyn's two-level reading of John's Gospel.[73] Adele Reinhartz argues that Martyn's two-level reading is primarily based on John's three references to the exclusion of Jesus's followers from the synagogue (9.22; 12.42; 16.2).[74] She notes that there are other passages in the gospel which depict a good relationship between the Jews who believe in Jesus and their neighbours. In John 11, mourners from Jerusalem come to Bethany to comfort Martha and Mary at the death of their brother. Reinhartz points out that the sisters have not been excluded from the synagogue on account of their faith in Jesus even though they have been friends with Jesus for some time. The narrative, however, concludes with an account

---

[69] U. C. von Wahlde ('"The Johannine Jews": A Critical Survey', *NTS* 28 (1982): 33–60) notes that this term is used in reference to the crowd in Galilee in 6.41 and 6.52 but he argues that this passage contains diverse literary strata and reflects the work of a redactor.

[70] A. Reinhartz, '"Jews" and Jews in the Fourth Gospel', in *Anti-Judaism and the Fourth Gospel*, edited by R. Bieringer, D. Pollefeyt and F. Vandecasteele-Vanneuville (Louisville, KY: Westminster John Knox, 2001), 220–1.

[71] Brown, *John*, 1:lxx–lxxiii.

[72] J. L. Martyn, *History and Theology in the Fourth Gospel*, 2nd edn (New York: Crossroad, 1995), 24–62.

[73] See R. Hakola, *Identity Matters: John, the Jews and Jewishness*, Supplements to Novum Testamentum 118 (Leiden: Brill, 2005), 33–40. Hakola argues that the story world of the gospel does not reflect the historical circumstances at the time of the Johannine community. He proposes that the early Christians developed persecution as a motif in their symbolic universe because Jesus had been persecuted and put to death. Scholars who dispute Hakola's interpretation of John's Gospel include Martinus de Boer in his essay, 'The Johannine Community under Attack in Recent Scholarship', in *The Ways That Often Parted. Essays in Honor of Joel Marcus*, edited by L. Baron, J. Hicks-Keeton and M. Thiessen, Early Christianity and Its Literature 24 (Atlanta, GA: SBL Press, 2018), 215–19. De Boer rightly points out that John's Farewell Discourse gives a detailed account of the persecution of Johannine Christians in the period after Jesus's death. He notes that it is improbable that John would attribute specific prophecies to Jesus such as the exclusion from the synagogue (16.2) if they had not been fulfilled in the lifetime of the members of the Johannine community.

[74] A. Reinhartz, *Befriending the Beloved Disciple: A Jewish Reading of the Gospel of John* (London: Continuum, 2001), 37–9.

of some mourners who go to the Pharisees in order to report Jesus's sign (11.45-46). Their reports lead to the plot of the religious leaders to put Jesus to death. One of the characteristics of John's Gospel is the division in the crowds over the identity of Jesus (7.25-31, 40-44; 10.19-21). Some people in the crowds believe in Jesus but others do not. We will assess Reinhartz's interpretation of the relationship between Martha and Mary and the mourners from Jerusalem in more detail in Chapter 4 of this book. In this study we will seek to determine the extent to which the narratives that feature women reflect the history of the Johannine community.

This study will examine John's portrayal of women in relation to his apocalyptic world view. John's Gospel contains several extended narratives which feature individual women including the mother of Jesus, the Samaritan woman, Martha and Mary of Bethany, and Mary Magdalene. We will assess the characteristics of John's presentation of these women, and we will analyse the question of whether he is aware of the issue of gender. John depicts conversations between women and Jesus in which women recognize Jesus as the Messiah and Son of God. In this study we will assess John's presentation of women in relation to his definition of discipleship. Jesus has come to bring humanity eternal life and to inaugurate the new creation. We will examine John's portrayal of women in relation to the theme of new creation. Finally, we will assess the extent to which the narratives featuring women give indications of the roles of women in the Johannine community. John's Gospel has been described as an egalitarian gospel, and we will examine any indications that women had leadership roles in the Johannine community. In this way our study also seeks to contribute to a wider understanding of the roles of women and the forms of their participation in the early church.

2

The mother of Jesus (2.1-11)

Introduction

The first narrative featuring a woman in John's Gospel is an account of the mother of Jesus who has been invited to a wedding at Cana (2.1-11). She notices that the wedding party has run out of wine, and she informs Jesus. The mother of Jesus is present at Jesus's first sign when he transforms the water in six stone water jars into abundant wine. At the end of the gospel, she is described as a witness to the crucifixion of Jesus (19.25-27). The two narratives form a frame around Jesus's mission. Mary prompts Jesus to carry out his first sign in which he reveals his glory (2.11), and she stands near Jesus's cross at the hour of his glorification (19.27; cf. 17.1-5). The prominent position of the passages featuring the mother of Jesus suggests that she has an influential role in John's Gospel. In this chapter we will analyse John's portrayal of the mother of Jesus in the account of the transformation of water into wine at the wedding at Cana, and in Chapter 6 we will examine the significance of her presence at the crucifixion of Jesus.

Scholars propose different interpretations of John's portrayal of the mother of Jesus at the wedding at Cana. John's association of Mary with Jesus's first sign has led Adeline Fehribach to suggest that Mary is depicted as 'the mother of an important son' character-type from the Old Testament, and she suggests that Mary wishes her son to perform a miracle in order to increase his honour.[1] Other scholars such as Gail O'Day argue that Mary is portrayed as a 'model disciple' because she believes that Jesus will respond to her request.[2] Our interpretation of the role of the mother of Jesus focuses on an analysis of the conversation between Jesus and his mother. Mary brings the lack of wine to Jesus's attention but he addresses her as 'woman' (γύναι, 2.4), and he does not wish to intervene because his 'hour' has not yet come. Mary, however, instructs the servants to do whatever Jesus tells them. Mary's conversation with Jesus leads him to perform his first sign, and he transforms the water in six stone jars into wine. In this chapter we will assess the extent to which John portrays Mary as an example of discipleship. In the Old Testament and early Jewish writings abundant wine is an

---

[1] A. Fehribach, *The Women in the Life of the Bridegroom: A Feminist Historical-Literary Analysis of the Gospel of John* (Collegeville, PA: Liturgical Press, 1998), 42–3.
[2] G. R. O'Day, 'John', in *Women's Bible Commentary*, edited by C. A. Newsom and S. H. Ringe, exp. edn (Louisville, KY: Westminster John Knox, 1998), 383.

image of the fruitfulness of the new creation (Amos 9.13-14; Hos. 14.7; Jer. 31.12; *1 En.* 10.19; *2 Bar.* 29.5). In John's Gospel Jesus comes to bring humanity eternal life and to inaugurate the new creation. We will also analyse John's portrayal of the mother of Jesus in relation to the Johannine theme of new creation.

The account of Jesus's act of transforming water into wine does not appear in the synoptic gospels. Jesus's sign, however, is similar to his miraculous multiplication of loaves which appears in both John's Gospel and the synoptic gospels (Mt. 14.13-21; Mk 6.35-44; Lk. 9.12-17). The accounts of the transformation of water into wine and of the multiplication of loaves may be interpreted as miracles of 'provision'. It is possible that the account of the transformation of water into wine originated in the sayings of Jesus about the new wine of the kingdom of God. In Mark's Gospel Jesus compares the advent of the kingdom to new wine that tears apart old wineskins (2.22; cf. Mt. 9.17; Lk. 5.37-39). On the other hand scholars such as Rudolf Bultmann argue that John's account of this sign has been influenced by Graeco-Roman traditions about Dionysus who is associated with the miraculous transformation of water into wine.[3] C. K. Barrett rightly observes that John's account primarily reflects Jewish eschatological expectations of abundant wine but he points out that the sign may also be intended to appeal to people of a Hellenistic background who have knowledge of the traditions concerning Dionysus.[4]

It is probable that John has employed a pre-existing source of miracles in his account of the wedding at Cana. Bultmann notes that John refers to the account of the wedding at Cana as the 'first' sign (2.11) and the healing of the son of the official as the 'second' sign (4.34).[5] John's numbering of the signs is puzzling because he includes references to other signs which take place between these two signs (2.23; 4.45). Bultmann argues that John's numbering of the signs refers to the first two signs in a Signs-Source. Robert Fortna, moreover, proposes that the mother of Jesus was a central character in the account of the wedding at Cana in the Signs-Source since she is mentioned before Jesus, and she takes the initiative in requesting the sign.[6] Fortna suggests that John is responsible for the addition of Jesus's reply to Mary in v. 4. As Fortna rightly points out, Jesus's reluctance to intervene is an unexpected feature because the mother of Jesus is portrayed positively in the account. In this chapter we will assess John's development of the conversation between Jesus and his mother. John highlights the role of Mary in the account of the first sign of Jesus, and in later church history Mary is venerated as the mother of Jesus (cf. Epiphanius, *Pan.* 78.23; 79).[7] We will seek to determine whether Mary has an honoured position within the Johannine community. We will

---

[3] R. Bultmann, *The Gospel of John*, translated by G. R. Beasley-Murray (Oxford: Blackwell, 1971), 118–19.

[4] C. K. Barrett, *The Gospel according to St John: An Introduction with Commentary and Notes on the Greek Text*, 2nd edn (London: SPCK, 1978), 189.

[5] Bultmann, *Gospel*, 113.

[6] R. Fortna, *The Fourth Gospel and Its Predecessor* (Edinburgh: T&T Clark, 1989), 57.

[7] For an analysis of the role of Mary in the New Testament and in the church, see B. R. Gaventa, *Mary: Glimpses of the Mother of Jesus* (Edinburgh: T&T Clark, 1999); J. Pelikan, *Mary through the Centuries: Her Place in the History of Culture* (New Haven, CT: Yale University Press, 1996) and M. Warner, *Alone of All Her Sex: The Myth and the Cult of the Virgin Mary* (London: Weidenfeld and Nicolson, 1976).

also explore the extent to which John's portrayal of Mary may provide insights into the role of women in the Johannine community.

The portrayal of the mother of Jesus

The mother of Jesus has a prominent role at the beginning and the end of Jesus's mission but John does not include Mary's name. This omission is unexpected because Mary is named in the synoptic gospels, and she is well known in the early church.[8] In a later passage the crowd claims to know Jesus's mother and father, which implies that they would know Mary's name (6.42). John's frequent identification of Mary as 'the mother of Jesus' (2.1, 3, 5, 12; 19.25) draws attention to Mary's unique role as the mother of Jesus. The name 'Mary' is also the most popular Jewish woman's name in Palestine in the Second Temple period.[9] John refers to Mary of Bethany (11.1–12.8), Mary of Clopas (19.25) and Mary Magdalene (19.25; 20.1-18). His identification of Mary as 'the mother of Jesus' thus differentiates her from the other women in the gospel who are named Mary.

Mary is mentioned at the beginning of the narrative before Jesus and his disciples are introduced (2.1). John suggests that she has closer associations with the family who are celebrating the wedding than Jesus and the disciples do. The wedding takes place at Cana in Galilee, and Jesus is known as Jesus of Nazareth (18.5, 7, 8; 19.19) which links him with the town of Nazareth in Galilee. Jesus and his disciples are invited to the wedding, and Jesus's brothers may also be present, since they accompany Jesus, Jesus's mother and the disciples to Capernaum after the wedding (2.12). There is, however, no mention of Jesus's father at the wedding at Cana. Jesus is identified twice as the 'son of Joseph' (1.45; 6.42) but Joseph does not appear in John's Gospel. Joseph is described in the birth narratives of the Gospels of Matthew and Luke but he is not present in the synoptic gospels in the accounts of Jesus's adult life.

It is possible that Joseph died before Jesus began his mission, and Mary was a widow. Widows formed one of the most vulnerable groups in the patriarchal society of the first-century Graeco-Roman world. These women were often unable to support themselves financially, and they lacked the protection of a husband. The Old Testament includes commandments concerning the care of widows and orphans (cf. Isa. 1.23; 10.2; Jer. 22.3; Zech. 7.10), and the synoptic gospels illustrate the precarious nature of the lives of widows in the account of the poor widow who gives her last two coins to the Temple treasury (Mk 12.41-44; Lk. 21.1-4) and the parable of the widow who seeks justice from an unrighteous judge (Lk. 18.1-8). As Tal Ilan notes, the rabbis were aware of the difficult situation of widows, and they encouraged widows to marry again.[10] The

---

[8] T. W. Martin ('Assessing the Johannine Epithet "the Mother of Jesus"', *CBQ* 60 (1998): 63–73) lists examples of writings which refer to a woman as a mother of a prominent son even when the authors are aware of the women's names, for example, Plutarch, *Sol*. 27.7.5; *Mor*. 318F; Dio Chrysostom, *Or*. 10.27.3; 10.29.5; 11.55.3; 11.10.107. Josephus does not record the name of the mother of Herod in *The Jewish War* but he does name her in *Antiquities* 15.6.5.

[9] T. Ilan, 'Notes on the Distribution of Jewish Women's Names in Palestine in the Second Temple and Mishnaic Periods', *JJS* 40 (1989): 186–200.

[10] T. Ilan, *Jewish Women in Greco-Roman Palestine* (Peabody, MA: Hendrickson, 1996), 147–51.

rabbis developed laws which were designed to make remarriage easy for women. Ilan points out that women were only required to have one witness to testify to the death of their husbands, and the witness was permitted to be a woman (*m. Yeb.* 16.5-7; *b. Yeb.* 115a). In John's Gospel, Mary acts with initiative throughout the narrative, and John's presentation of her character as a figure of authority differs from traditional portraits of vulnerable widows.

John mentions the brothers of Jesus at the conclusion to our passage but in Roman Catholic tradition Mary does not have any other children. John's references to the brothers of Jesus are interpreted as Jesus's half-brothers from an earlier marriage of Joseph or as his cousins. The theory that Jesus's brothers are the sons of Joseph, however, first appears in the second-century text the *Protevangelium of James* (9.2; 17.1–18.1). On the other hand the New Testament contains many references to Jesus's 'brothers' (Mt. 12.46; 13.55-56; Lk. 8.19-20; Acts 1.14; 1 Cor. 9.5; Gal. 1.19). In addition, the term ἀνεψιός (cousin, cf. Col. 4.10) is not used in reference to Jesus's brothers. Mark also refers to Jesus's sisters in his account of the comments of the people of Nazareth about Jesus's family (αἱ ἀδελφαὶ αὐτοῦ, 6.3). The numerous references to Jesus's brothers and sisters in the New Testament imply that Mary did have other children.[11] Jesus's brother, James, becomes a leader of the Jerusalem church, and the New Testament contains letters which are attributed to James and to Jude, another brother of Jesus.

In our passage the mother of Jesus plays a leading role, and Jesus's brothers remain in the background. Mary shows concern for the wedding hosts and guests, and she is the one who brings the lack of wine to Jesus's attention. The mother of Jesus takes charge of the situation, and she gives instructions to the servants in a household that is not her own. Urban von Wahlde suggests that her actions imply that she is well known to the family at Cana.[12] It is surprising, however, that she gives commands to the servants without consulting the bridegroom or the steward. In our passage Mary is willing to act independently of Jesus. She expects Jesus to respond to her request even though he is initially reluctant to intervene. John presents the mother of Jesus as a figure of authority who acts decisively throughout the narrative. John's portrayal of Mary at the wedding at Cana indicates that he wishes to emphasize her unique role as the mother of Jesus and to stress her close relationship with Jesus at the beginning of Jesus's mission.

The conversation between Jesus and his mother

Our narrative begins with a joyful celebration of a wedding but the festivities are threatened when the wine runs out. Jesus's mother realizes what has happened, and she brings the situation to Jesus's attention with a simple statement, 'They have no wine' (2.3). Mary is concerned about the hosts and guests, and she acts as an intercessor on

---

[11] For an assessment of the references to Mary's children, see R. E. Brown, K. P. Donfried, J. A. Fitzmyer and J. Reumann (eds), *Mary in the New Testament: A Collaborative Assessment by Protestant and Roman Catholic Scholars* (London: Geoffrey Chapman, 1978), 65–7, 199–201.

[12] U. C. von Wahlde, *The Gospel and Letters of John*, vol. 2 (Grand Rapids, MI: Eerdmans, 2010), 82.

their behalf by bringing their needs to Jesus. Some scholars such as Ernst Haenchen propose that Mary wishes Jesus to carry out a miracle.[13] On the other hand Robert Maccini points out that John makes no reference to Mary's faith in Jesus, and he argues that she does not know about the power of Jesus to transform water into wine.[14] At this stage in the gospel Jesus has not yet carried out any signs. Mary does not make a specific request for a miracle but she brings the lack of wine to Jesus's attention, implying that she does expect Jesus to alleviate the situation.

Jesus, however, replies abruptly, 'Woman, what has this to do with you and me? My hour has not yet come' (2.4). Jesus's response is unexpected because he calls his mother 'woman' (γύναι), and he seems unconcerned about the threat to the wedding celebrations. As Colleen Conway points out, the narrator refers to Mary as the 'mother of Jesus' four times which emphasizes her relation to Jesus (2.1, 3, 5, 12), whereas Jesus speaks to her as 'woman'.[15] The address 'woman' appears impolite and uncaring but it is not disrespectful in a first-century context. Jesus speaks to the Samaritan woman calling her 'woman' (γύναι, 4.21), and the angels and Jesus address Mary Magdalene as 'woman' (γύναι, 20.13, 15). In the synoptic gospels Jesus uses the address 'woman' when he speaks to the Canaanite woman (Mt. 15.28) and to the woman who is crippled (Lk. 13.12). In these passages the address 'woman' is respectful but these women are not members of Jesus's family.

It is possible for the address 'woman' to be used in conversations between family members. George Beasley-Murray cites the example of Pheroras who addresses his wife as 'woman' (ὦ γύναι, Josephus, *Ant.* 17.74).[16] In this passage, however, the address γύναι could also be translated as 'wife'. In the following verse Josephus refers to the instructions of this woman's husband (τοῦ ἀνδρὸς τὰς ἐπιστολάς, *Ant.* 17.76) by using the Greek term for 'man' (ἀνήρ). In our narrative Jesus's address is very unusual because Jesus is speaking to his mother, and there are no other known examples of a son addressing his mother in this way. Jesus addresses his mother as 'woman' again at the crucifixion when he entrusts her to the care of the Beloved Disciple. He announces to his mother, 'Woman, here is your son' and he says to the Beloved Disciple, 'Here is your mother' (γύναι, 19.25-27). In the Passion Narrative the Johannine Jesus employs the address 'woman' in the context of his leave-taking from his mother. In this passage his address is not disrespectful because he is concerned about her future welfare.

In our passage, however, Jesus employs the address 'woman' in a response to Mary which suggests that Jesus is distancing himself from his mother's request. Jesus's reply τί ἐμοὶ καὶ σοί may be translated literally as 'what to me and to you'. This phrase has negative connotations in some Old Testament passages (cf. 1 Kgs 17.18; 2 Kgs 3.13; 2 Sam. 16.10; 19.23; 2 Chron. 35.21; Judg. 11.12), and it is associated with hostility when used by those possessed by demons in exorcism accounts in the New Testament (Mt. 8.29; Mk 1.24; 5.7; Lk. 4.34; 8.28). Raymond Brown translates v. 4 as 'What has

---

[13] E. Haenchen, *John 1* (Philadelphia, PA: Fortress, 1984), 172.
[14] R. G. Maccini, *'Her Testimony Is True': Women as Witnesses according to John*, JSNTSup 125 (Sheffield: Sheffield Academic Press, 1996), 115–17.
[15] C. M. Conway, *Men and Women in the Fourth Gospel: Gender and Johannine Characterization*, SBLDS 167 (Atlanta, GA: Society of Biblical Literature, 1999), 73.
[16] G. R. Beasley-Murray, *John*, WBC 36, 2nd edn (Nashville, TN: Thomas Nelson, 1987), 34.

this concern of yours to do with me?'[17] On the other hand J. Ramsey Michaels points out that Jesus's response may indicate that he does not believe that the lack of wine is a concern of either his mother or himself.[18] Brown's interpretation is more convincing since Jesus states that he does not wish to intervene because his 'hour' has not yet arrived (οὔπω ἥκει ἡ ὥρα μου, 2.4).

In our narrative Jesus's reply indicates that he is unable to act as he wishes since the timing of his mission is constrained by the purposes of God. John's use of the term the 'hour' (ὥρα) has theological significance. John employs the term the 'hour' throughout the gospel to refer to the time of Jesus's Passion (7.30; 8.20; 12.23-24, 27-28; 13.1; 17.1). The term the 'hour' alludes to the culmination of the conflict between Jesus and the power of evil. Jesus has come into the world to reveal God, and the revelation of the glory of Jesus and God takes place at the crucifixion. John's use of the term the 'hour' recalls the use of the term 'hour' in apocalyptic texts as a reference to the end-time crisis (cf. Dan. 10.40, 45 LXX; Mk 14.35, 38, 41; Rev. 3.10). In John's Gospel, Jesus's 'hour' marks the turning point between the present age and the inauguration of the new creation. In our passage Jesus's allusion to 'the hour' reflects his foreknowledge of events and also emphasizes his wish to follow the timing of God.

Jesus's reply to Mary indicates that he does not wish to intervene to alleviate the situation at the wedding at Cana because his 'hour' has not yet arrived. Mary, however, instructs the servants to do whatever Jesus tells them (2.5). Jesus then carries out his first sign, and he transforms water into abundant wine. In our passage Jesus expresses reluctance to intervene, and his performance of the sign is unexpected. John's narrative therefore raises the question of whether Mary changes Jesus's mind. Charles Giblin points out that Jesus's initial delay in responding to Mary's request for his assistance foreshadows several other occasions in the gospel.[19] He compares the response of Jesus in our passage to three similar accounts in John's Gospel: the healing of the official's son (4.46-54), the request of Jesus's brothers (7.2-14), and the request of Martha and Mary (11.1-44). Giblin observes that human beings make a request to Jesus on each occasion. At first Jesus responds negatively but he finally carries out his own independent action which relates to the needs of the situation.

In our passage, however, Jesus states his reluctance to act ahead of his 'hour' but he still responds to Mary's request for his help. John's development of the narrative suggests that Mary does change Jesus's mind. Colleen Conway proposes that the mother of Jesus has a greater understanding of Jesus's mission than he has because she realizes that 'the time for revelation and the movement towards the hour has come'.[20] Conway's analysis, however, downplays the way in which Mary's instructions to the servants point to the authority of Jesus. Mary's instructions to the servants demonstrate her faith and trust in Jesus. John depicts the close relationship between Jesus and his mother, and he emphasizes her influence upon her son. The conversation between

---

[17] R. E. Brown, *The Gospel according to John*, 2 vols, AB29-29A (Garden City, NY: Doubleday, 1966–70), 1:99, 102.

[18] J. Ramsey Michaels, *The Gospel of John*, NICNT (Grand Rapids, MI: Eerdmans, 2010), 143–5.

[19] C. H. Giblin, 'Suggestion, Negative Response, and Positive Action in St John's Portrayal of Jesus (John 2.1-11; 4.46-54; 7.2-14; 11.1-44)', *NTS* 26 (1980): 197–211.

[20] Conway, *Men and Women*, 76–8.

Jesus and his mother illustrates her faith in Jesus's power before his mission begins. Mary is convinced that Jesus will intervene, since she tells the servants to follow Jesus's instructions. Mary's concern for the wedding celebration prompts her to seek Jesus's help, and her request leads Jesus to act ahead of his 'hour'.

In our passage there is a tension between Jesus's reluctance to act before his 'hour' and his performance of the sign in the present. At the wedding at Cana Jesus speaks of his 'hour' as a future event but he proceeds to carry out the sign. John's use of the term 'hour' in our passage may be compared to his references to the 'hour' in similar passages. As George Beasley-Murray observes, John presents other occasions in which Jesus speaks of the arrival of the 'hour' in Jesus's mission (cf. 4.23; 5.25).[21] In the account of the meeting between Jesus and the Samaritan woman, Jesus states that the 'hour is coming and is now here' (ἔρχεται ὥρα καὶ νῦν ἐστιν, 4.23) in which God will be worshipped 'in spirit and in truth'. In John 5, Jesus states that 'the hour is coming and is now here' (ἔρχεται ὥρα καὶ νῦν ἐστιν, 5.25) when the dead will come back to life in response to the voice of the Son of God. In the account of the wedding at Cana, Jesus's act of transforming water into abundant wine indicates that the fruitfulness of the new creation may be experienced in the present world. John's account of the sign indicates that the events which are associated with the eschatological 'hour' are already taking place in the lifetime of Jesus.

Jesus's transformation of the water into wine enables the wedding festivities to continue with a higher quality of wine than the wedding party had previously enjoyed. The positive conclusion to the narrative raises the question of why Jesus was initially unwilling to intervene. John Ashton proposes that Jesus is reluctant to act ahead of his 'hour' because he is afraid that his sign may be understood.[22] In other accounts of the signs of Jesus there are indications that Jesus's enemies oppose him because they are unable to recognize him (9.13-17; 11.45-46; 12.37-43). On the other hand Judith Lieu points out that there is no indication of any threat to Jesus on account of his performance of the sign in our passage.[23] She notes that the question of Jesus's hesitancy is not resolved within the narrative. The Johannine Jesus, however, refers to his forthcoming 'hour' which is a time of conflict between Jesus and his enemies. Jesus's sign also remains concealed from the hosts, the steward and the guests. The steward confirms the quality of the wine but he believes that the wine has been provided by the bridegroom. The hidden nature of Jesus's sign suggests that Jesus's action could arouse opposition.

John, moreover, provides hints that the joy of the wedding feast is linked to Jesus's future suffering. The conversation between Jesus and his mother associates the provision of abundant wine with Jesus's death. Jesus's initial response to Mary, 'My hour has not yet come' (2.4), links the sign to the 'hour' of his Passion. At the end of the gospel the mother of Jesus and the Beloved Disciple will be present at the hour of his death (19.25-27). In this passage the blood and water that flow from Jesus's side recall the presence of wine and water at the wedding at Cana (19.34). Jesus's first sign

---

[21] Beasley-Murray, *John*, 36.
[22] J. Ashton, *Understanding the Fourth Gospel*, 2nd edn (Oxford: Oxford University Press, 2007), 173–4.
[23] J. M. Lieu, 'The Mother of the Son in the Fourth Gospel', *JBL* 117 (1998): 66.

reveals his glory (ἐφανέρωσεν τὴν δόξαν αὐτοῦ, 2.11), and the time of his glorification is linked to his death (ἐδοξάσθη, 13.31-32; δόξασόν, 17.1-5).

In our narrative Mary's intervention leads Jesus to transform the water in six stone jars into abundant wine. In the Old Testament and early Jewish writings abundant wine is often a sign of the new creation (Amos 9.13-14; Hos. 14.7; Jer. 31.12; *1 En.* 10.19; *2 Bar.* 29.5). At the wedding at Cana, Jesus's ability to provide the wine of the new creation points to his identity as the Messiah. In *2 Baruch* there is a description of the events which will take place when 'the Anointed One will begin to be revealed' (29.3). In this passage the appearance of the Messiah at the end of the age is associated with abundant wine, 'And on one vine will be a thousand branches, and one branch will produce a thousand clusters, and one cluster will produce a thousand grapes, and one grape will produce a cor of wine' (29.5). The sign reveals Jesus's identity as Messiah because the abundance of the new creation will come about through Jesus's death and resurrection.

The conversation between Jesus and his mother highlights Mary's role in leading Jesus to carry out his first sign. Mary shows concern for the wedding party, and she expects Jesus to respond to her request for assistance. Although Jesus is reluctant to intervene ahead of his 'hour' she demonstrates her faith by telling the servants to follow Jesus's instructions. Mary overcomes Jesus's reluctance to intervene, and her request leads Jesus to perform his first sign. Jesus transforms water into abundant wine, and this sign looks forward to the fruitfulness of the new creation. Mary's role as 'mother' is emphasized because she is present at the beginning of Jesus's mission. In our narrative Mary is depicted as the mother of Jesus who addresses him on behalf of the hosts and guests at the wedding feast. John associates Mary with the timing of Jesus's first sign which reveals Jesus's glory and points to his identity as the Messiah.

The revelation of the hidden Messiah

John presents Mary as a model of faith because she believes that Jesus is able to alleviate the lack of wine at the wedding at Cana. Her faith serves as an example to John's audience that Jesus will come to their aid even if a situation appears bleak. Mary's request prompts Jesus to perform his first sign which reveals his glory and as a result his disciples believe in him. John emphasizes the faith of Mary and the disciples but most of the other characters are not aware that a miracle has taken place. The servants who have followed Jesus's instructions know what has occurred but the bridegroom, steward and wedding guests share the good wine without realizing that Jesus has performed a sign.

John's portrayal of Mary indicates that she has greater understanding of Jesus than the other characters in the narrative. Mary knows that a miracle has taken place but Jesus does not reveal his identity to others in the course of the narrative. Jesus orchestrates the tasting of the wine by the steward since he instructs the servants to take the wine to the steward. Jesus's action implies that he wishes to demonstrate the superior quality of the new wine but he does not reveal his own role in the miracle. The steward has the task of ensuring that the wine is fit to be served to the wedding guests, and he commends the bridegroom because he has kept the best wine until last (2.10). The steward's praise serves as a confirmation that a miracle has taken place. Nevertheless, the steward does not know where the wine has come from (οὐκ ᾔδει πόθεν ἐστίν, 2.9).

John links the hidden nature of Jesus's identity with questions concerning his origins. The steward's lack of knowledge about the origin of the wine echoes the earlier questioning of the disciples about the origin of Jesus. In the opening chapter Nathanael asks if anything good can come from Nazareth (1.46). Rudolf Schnackenburg notes that human beings question themselves and others repeatedly about where Jesus has come from (7.27; 8.14; 9.29; 19.9).[24] The opponents of Jesus claim to know where he has come from (τοῦτον οἴδαμεν πόθεν ἐστίν, 7.27; cf. 9.29) whereas Jesus tells them that they do not know where he has come from or where he is going (οὐκ οἴδατε πόθεν ἔρχομαι ἢ ποῦ ὑπάγω, 8.14). At the end of the gospel the Roman governor, Pilate, also asks Jesus where he has come from (πόθεν εἶ σύ, 19.9). These statements connect the question of Jesus's identity to his mysterious heavenly origins, and they highlight the difficulties that some human beings find in recognizing Jesus. In our passage the steward's statement raises the question of the origins of Jesus's gift. John's repeated references to the 'mother of Jesus', however, link Jesus's earthly origins with Mary. The presence of the mother of Jesus highlights the humanity of Jesus in the midst of the account of a sign that reveals his glory.

The steward's question about the source of the wine points to the hidden nature of John's Christology. John depicts Jesus as the hidden Messiah who has come from God into the world. Jesus is the Messiah and Son of God but his divine glory will not be fully revealed until the crucifixion (13.31-32). The theme of secrecy relates to the initial response of Jesus to Mary that his 'hour' has not yet come, since the sign is proleptic of the glory that is revealed at the 'hour' of Jesus's death. John associates the theme of secrecy with the identity of Jesus and the purpose of his mission. John's portrayal of the hidden nature of Jesus is introduced in the opening chapters of the gospel. He presents John the Baptist as a witness whose purpose is to reveal Jesus. John the Baptist announces to the crowd who approach him for baptism, 'In your midst stands one whom you do not know' (1.26). In addition, John the Baptist does not recognize Jesus until he sees the Spirit descend on Jesus during his baptism (1.31-34). He has been told that he will recognize the one on whom the Spirit descends and remains as the one who will baptize with the Holy Spirit (1.33). In this passage God is the one who reveals Jesus's identity since Jesus is recognized through the descent of the Spirit upon him.

John's portrayal of Jesus suggests that John has knowledge of the apocalyptic concept of the hidden Messiah.[25] In a later passage Jesus's opponents show their knowledge of the tradition of the hidden Messiah in their statement that they know where Jesus has come from but 'when the Messiah comes no one will know where he

---

[24] R. Schnackenburg, *The Gospel according to St. John*, 3 vols (London: Burns & Oates, 1968–82), 1:333.
[25] Scholars who examine evidence for the apocalyptic concept of the hidden Messiah include S. Mowinckel, *He That Cometh* (Oxford: Blackwell, 1956), 304–8 and M. de Jonge, 'Jewish Expectations about the "Messiah" according to the Fourth Gospel', *NTS* 19 (1973): 246–70.

comes from' (cf. 7.27).[26] As Raymond Brown notes, allusions to a similar tradition may be found in the second-century work of Justin, *Dialogue with Trypho* (8.4; cf. 110.1).[27] Justin states, 'Even if the Messiah is already born and in existence somewhere; he is nevertheless unknown; even he himself does not know about himself, nor does he have any kind of power until Elijah comes and reveals him' (*Dial.* 8.4). John Ashton argues that it is probable that John's community was aware of the apocalyptic concept of the hidden Messiah since Jesus is unrecognized by many characters within the gospel.[28] Nevertheless, Ashton rightly observes that John's portrayal of Jesus differs from Justin's account of the hidden Messiah since Jesus is aware of his heavenly origins. In John's Gospel, Jesus's knowledge of his heavenly origins leads to a conflict with his opponents who are unable to recognize his identity as the Messiah.

The concept of a hidden Messiah may be seen in several apocalyptic texts. Barnabas Lindars suggests that the tradition of the hidden Messiah originally related to the figure of the Son of Man but was then applied to the Messiah.[29] In *1 Enoch* the Son of Man is described as pre-existent, 'For this purpose he became the Chosen One; he was concealed in the presence of the Lord of the Spirits prior to the creation of the world, and for eternity' (48.6). In apocalyptic writings God's purposes are concealed until the time has come for them to be fulfilled. In *4 Ezra* the appearance of the Messiah is associated with the revelation of the secrets of the end-time. The city of Jerusalem and the land which have been kept hidden will be disclosed, and 'the Messiah shall be revealed with those who are with him' (7.26-28). In John's Gospel Jesus's identity is concealed until he accomplishes God's purposes at the time of his death on the cross.

In our passage John portrays the mother of Jesus as a unique character who has faith in Jesus before he begins his mission. Mary recognizes Jesus as the one who may alleviate the situation at the wedding at Cana. Throughout the gospel characters struggle to understand Jesus but Mary already has knowledge of his power. The advent of Jesus provokes a crisis in the world in which some people respond to Jesus and others reject him. Mary has a unique role as the mother of Jesus, and her intervention leads Jesus to carry out his first sign. John establishes the close relationship between Mary and Jesus as mother and son. He demonstrates Mary's influence upon Jesus, and he associates Mary with the purpose of Jesus's mission. Her intervention is also connected to a sign which leads to the faith of the disciples. The disciples recognize Jesus's identity as the Messiah and Son of God but the steward, bridegroom and guests do not know that a miracle has taken place. The mother of Jesus leads Jesus to perform his first sign which looks forward to the abundance of the new creation.

---

[26] For an analysis of John's employment of the tradition of the hidden Messiah in his presentation of Jesus, see S. Miller, '"Among You Stands One Whom You Do Not Know" (John 1:26): The Use of the Tradition of the Hidden Messiah in John's Gospel', in *The Ways That Often Parted: Essays in Honor of Joel Marcus*, edited by L. Baron, J. Hicks-Keeton and M. Thiessen, Early Christianity and Its Literature 24 (Atlanta, GA: SBL Press, 2018), 243–63.

[27] Brown, *John*, 1:53.

[28] Ashton, *Understanding*, 207–11.

[29] B. Lindars, *The Gospel of John*, NCBC (London: Marshall, Morgan & Scott, 1972), 293.

Discipleship and the mother of Jesus

In our passage Mary is instrumental in bringing a request to Jesus which reveals his glory and as a result his disciples believe in him (ἐπίστευσαν εἰς αὐτὸν οἱ μαθηταὶ αὐτοῦ, 2.11). This passage forms the conclusion to a series of scenes which feature the first disciples. Andrew and another disciple are disciples of John the Baptist who follow Jesus. Andrew recognizes Jesus as the Messiah (1.41), and he brings his brother, Simon, to Jesus, and Jesus names him 'Peter' (1.35-42). The next day Jesus calls Philip, and Philip leads Nathanael to Jesus (1.43-51). Nathanael describes Jesus as 'Son of God' and 'King of Israel' (1.49). Jesus, however, teaches his disciples that they will see greater things than these. Richard Lightfoot argues that the transformation of water into wine is a fulfilment of Jesus's promise to his disciples (1.51).[30] In this passage Jesus states that the heavens will open, and the angels will ascend and descend on the Son of Man (1.50-51). Our narrative concludes with an event which is associated with 'the opening of the heavens' since the sign reveals Jesus's divine glory and deepens the faith of the disciples.

John presents Mary as a model of faith since she prompts Jesus to carry out his first sign. She is associated with a sign that reveals Jesus's identity as the Messiah and the Son of God. At the end of the gospel the narrator states that the signs are written in order that those who hear the gospel may believe that Jesus is 'the Messiah, the Son of God' and that through faith they may have life in his name (20.30-31). The signs are intended to lead to faith in those who see them. Mary's intervention concludes with John's description of the faith of the disciples. John associates the figure of Mary with the disciples, since the focus of the account is upon the response of the disciples to the sign. In our narrative the disciples illustrate the correct response to the signs, because they believe in Jesus. In some passages, however, there are concerns about the relationship between signs and faith. Jesus performs signs in Jerusalem, and many who witness the signs believe in his name but he does not put his trust in those who see them because he knows their hearts (2.23-25). In a later passage Nicodemus is identified as a witness to the signs but he does not fully understand Jesus (3.2). This passage raises the question of why some people are able to witness the signs without coming to faith in Jesus.

In John's apocalyptic world view the signs act as parables which conceal and reveal Jesus's identity as the Messiah and Son of God. As Brown observes, the signs of Jesus may be compared to the signs which Moses carried out during the Exodus (cf. Exod. 10.1-2; Num. 14.22; Deut. 7.19).[31] Brown's comparison points to the role of Jesus's signs as demonstrations of God's power. Jesus's signs are proleptic of the abundant life that comes through his death and resurrection. The signs point to Jesus's divine identity, and they create a division among those who witness them (cf. 9.16; 11.45-46). In our passage the mother of Jesus does not require a sign to recognize Jesus. The disciples recognize Jesus's identity, but the steward, bridegroom and guests are unaware of the

---

[30] R. H. Lightfoot, *St. John's Gospel* (Oxford: Clarendon, 1956), 100.
[31] Brown, *John*, 1:525–32.

miracle. Jesus carries out the sign for the benefit of the hosts and all the guests. They are able to share the wine of the new age, but they do not know that Jesus is responsible for the provision of the wine. The transformation of water into wine does not lead to opposition but in our narrative, there are hints of future conflict in Jesus's initial reluctance to intervene because his 'hour' has not yet come.

At the end of our passage Mary accompanies Jesus and his disciples but she is not presented as a member of the discipleship group. John sets Mary apart from the group of disciples since she has the unique role of the mother of Jesus. Mary has greater knowledge of Jesus than his disciples. She is closely aligned with the revelation of Jesus's identity and the purpose of his mission. The steward, the bridegroom and the guests do not know the origin of the wine, but the disciples perceive Jesus's glory, and they believe in him. Unlike the servants, the disciples have a continuous commitment to Jesus, and they accompany Jesus, his mother and his brothers to Capernaum (2.12). Mary prompts Jesus to carry out his first sign and her request leads to the faith of the disciples. She acts as 'mother' to the disciples by leading Jesus to perform a sign that deepens their faith. Jesus's Messiahship remains hidden in the world but his mother and the disciples witness his first sign, and they believe in him.

The mother of Jesus and the new creation

In this section we will assess the role of the mother of Jesus in relation to the Johannine theme of new creation. The mother of Jesus prompts Jesus to carry out the 'first' of his signs at the wedding at Cana (ἀρχὴν τῶν σημείων, 2.11). In this narrative John employs the term ἀρχή 'beginning' instead of the more usual term for 'first' (πρῶτος). John's use of this term recalls the opening of the prologue 'in the beginning' (ἐν ἀρχῇ) and the first verse of Genesis (ἐν ἀρχῇ LXX). John's reference to Jesus's 'first' sign relates Jesus's mission to God's purposes in creation. The prologue situates Jesus's mission in relation to God's creative work in which 'all things come into being through him' (1.3). In our passage John's reference to the 'first' sign indicates that this sign marks the 'beginning' of the new creation.

The mother of Jesus initiates the first sign that takes place at the end of the first week of Jesus's mission. John's reference to the timing of the first sign may also allude to the theme of new creation. In the opening chapters John refers to the first three days of Jesus's mission (1.29, 35, 43), and he states that the wedding at Cana occurs 'on the third day' (2.1). As Barnabas Lindars suggests, John may intend to present this week as a new week which signifies the beginning of a new era, since the number seven alludes to the completion of the creation of the world in seven days (Gen. 1.1–2.3).[32] The opening week of the gospel, moreover, is paralleled at the end of the gospel when John narrates the final seven days of Jesus's life. John's use of the timing of a week in both passages indicates that Jesus has come to bring God's work of creation to completion.

---

[32] Lindars, *John*, 128.

In our passage Mary has the key role of bringing the lack of wine to Jesus's attention. Initially, Jesus is reluctant to intervene, and he distances himself from his mother's request by addressing her as 'woman' (γύναι, 2.4). The unexpected nature of Jesus's response suggests that John may intend this address to be interpreted symbolically. Raymond Brown notes that Jesus also addresses Mary as 'woman' in the Johannine account of the crucifixion (γύναι, 19.26).[33] Brown proposes that John presents the mother of Jesus as a new Eve since Eve is identified as the 'woman' (γυνή) in Gen. 3.16-18. As Brown rightly notes, the mother of Jesus is associated with Eve in Revelation 12 and in early Christian texts (Justin, *Dial.* 100.5; Irenaeus, *Haer.* 3.22.4).

Several scholars such as André Feuillet[34] and John McHugh,[35] moreover, associate the mother of Jesus with the character of Eve. Feuillet argues that the Johannine Jesus's address 'woman' may be compared with the description of the woman clothed with the sun in Revelation 12 (γυνὴ περιβεβλημένη τὸν ἥλιον, 12.1).[36] In Revelation, the woman is portrayed as the mother of the Messiah, and she is threatened by a dragon as she is about to give birth. The dragon is described as the ancient serpent, and this description alludes to the serpent who tempts Eve in Genesis. In Genesis, a conflict is described between the 'woman' and the serpent, 'I will put enmity between you and the woman, and between your offspring and hers' (3.15).[37] In Revelation, the child is taken up to heaven, and the woman flees to the desert while the dragon continues to wage war on the rest of her children (12.7). The association of Mary with Eve in Revelation 12 may suggest a similar background to John's portrayal of Mary in his gospel.

Several features of John's portrayal of the mother of Jesus evoke the description of Eve in Genesis. In our passage John repeatedly identifies Mary as the 'mother' of Jesus (2.1, 3, 5, 12), and in Genesis, Eve is called the 'mother of all that live' (Gen. 3.20). In Genesis, God commands Adam and Eve not to eat from the tree of knowledge of good and evil or they will face death (2.16-17; 3.4). Adam and Eve, however, disobey God, and death enters the world. In John's Gospel Jesus obeys the will of God, and he brings humanity the gift of eternal life. John's association of the mother of Jesus with Eve relates our passage to the creative purposes of God. Mary prompts Jesus to carry out the first of seven signs which point to Jesus's identity as the Messiah and Son of God. John's selection of seven signs may also allude to the theme of new creation since the original creation was completed in seven days in Genesis.

In our narrative John associates the mother of Jesus with the 'hour' of Jesus's Passion (2.4). He depicts the death of Jesus as a conflict between Jesus and the power of evil in which Jesus casts out the 'ruler of the world' (12.31; 14.30; 16.11).[38] John employs apocalyptic language to indicate that Jesus not only brings humanity the gift of eternal life but also overcomes the power of evil. In Genesis, Adam's disobedience has a cosmic

---

[33] Brown, *John*, 1:107-9.
[34] A. Feuillet, *Johannine Studies* (New York: Alba House, 1965), 257-92.
[35] J. McHugh, *The Mother of Jesus in the New Testament* (London: Darton, Longman & Todd, 1975), 373-87.
[36] Feuillet, *Johannine Studies*, 257-92.
[37] McHugh, *Mother*, 373-87.
[38] J. L. Kovacs, '"Now Shall the Ruler of This World Be Driven Out": Jesus' Death as Cosmic Battle in John 12:20-26', *JBL* 114 (1995): 227-47.

impact on creation, and in John's Gospel Jesus's death changes the whole of creation. John links the resurrection of Jesus with the gift of eternal life and the emergence of the new creation. In our passage Jesus's transformation of water into wine takes place on the third day (2.1), and Jesus's resurrection is linked to the third day (2.19-21; 20.1). John's account of the abundant wine looks forward to the fruitfulness of the new creation that comes about through Jesus's death and resurrection.

In our passage John associates Mary with Jesus's first sign which reveals his divine glory (ἐφανέρωσεν τὴν δόξαν αὐτοῦ, 2.11). John's reference to glory (δόξα) may also relate to the theme of new creation. In the Old Testament the term 'glory' refers to the visible presence and power of God (cf. Exod. 16.7-10; 24.17).[39] In Jewish tradition Adam lost his glory when he was cast out of Eden. Joel Marcus notes that several texts refer to the loss of Adam's glory and the eschatological expectation that Adam will recover his glory (cf. Sir. 49.16; *LAE* 11.3; 16.2; *Apoc. Mos.* 20.1-2; 21.2, 6).[40] Marcus also observes that there are references to the hope that the elect will inherit 'the glory of Adam' in the end-time (cf. 1QS 4.20-23; CD 3.18-20; 1QH 1.15). In John's Gospel Jesus shares in the divine glory before the creation of the world (17.1), and he comes into the world to reveal his divine glory (1.14). The glory of Jesus may be glimpsed in his signs (2.11; 4.4, 40) but the full revelation of Jesus's glory takes place at the cross when the Father and Son are glorified (ἐδοξάσθη, 13.31-32). The 'hour' of the glorification of Jesus marks the eschatological turning point in the gospel. Jesus's glorification is the 'hour' of the judgement of the world when the 'ruler of the world' is cast out (12.31). The revelation of Jesus's glory at the wedding at Cana is proleptic of the revelation of his glory at the cross.

John links Mary with the first sign of Jesus which serves as the foundation of his mission. In the Old Testament and other Jewish texts abundant wine is frequently associated with eschatological expectations. In the synoptic tradition Jesus speaks of the kingdom of God in terms of new wine that tears apart old wine skins (Mk 2.22). In our narrative the setting of the wedding is also linked to eschatological expectations of the new age (Isa. 54.4-8; 62.4-5; Mt. 8.11; 22.1-14; Lk. 22.16-18; Rev. 19.9). In John's Gospel the transformation of water into wine implies that the new creation is characterized by abundance. The fruitfulness of the new creation, moreover, surpasses the original creation. John demonstrates the higher quality of the new wine in the statement of the steward. The steward is amazed to discover that the 'good wine' has been served last because it is customary to serve the good wine first and then the inferior wine (2.10).

In our passage John gives a positive portrayal of Mary as a new Eve. Mary informs Jesus that the wedding party has run out of wine. She remains faithful even when Jesus is reluctant to intervene. The mother of Jesus points away from herself since she instructs the servants to do whatever Jesus tells them. She prompts Jesus to carry out a sign which alludes to the abundance of the new creation. In several Jewish and early Christian texts, however, Eve is portrayed in a negative way, and her responsibility for the Fall is emphasized. In the *Life of Adam and Eve*, Eve repeatedly refers to her

---

[39] Brown, *John*, 1:503-4.
[40] J. Marcus, 'Son of Man as Son of Adam', *RB* 110 (2003), 57-9.

responsibility for Adam's failure to obey God (3.1; 5.2; 26.2; 35.3). In the New Testament Paul highlights the way in which Eve was 'deceived' by the serpent (2 Cor. 11.2-3). The author of 1 Timothy also gives a negative interpretation of the character of Eve. This author argues that women should not teach or have authority over men because Adam was created first and he was not deceived. On the other hand he states that Eve was deceived and 'became a transgressor' (1 Tim. 2.8-15).[41] Patricia Cox Miller notes that the negative qualities of Eve are emphasized in some early Christian texts, and Mary is depicted as the 'antitype' to Eve (Justin, *Dial.* 100.4-6; Irenaeus, *Haer.* 5.22.4; Epiphanius, *Pan.* 78.17-19).[42]

In the account of the wedding at Cana, John portrays the mother of Jesus positively as a new Eve. In Genesis, Eve disobeyed God but in our passage Mary is a model of faith. She places her trust in Jesus, and her request leads Jesus to perform his first sign. In Genesis, Eve is present at the beginning of creation, and in John's Gospel Mary is present at the beginning of Jesus's mission. John's allusions to Genesis highlight the presence of Mary at the foundation of Jesus's mission of new creation, and they also point to the cosmic scope of Jesus's mission. Jesus has come to cast out the 'ruler of the world' and to destroy the power of death. The transformation of water into abundant wine points forward to the fruitfulness of the new creation. The intervention of Mary leads to the first sign of Jesus in which the abundant wine of the end-time is experienced in the present. John's portrayal of Mary as a new Eve emphasizes the importance of creation imagery in John's Gospel, since Jesus has come to bring eternal life and to inaugurate the new creation.

The mother of Jesus and the Johannine community

John draws attention to the mother of Jesus by placing narratives which feature Mary at the beginning and the end of Jesus's mission. The unique role of Mary within John's Gospel raises the question of whether Mary has a prominent place in the Johannine community. Rudolf Bultmann proposes that Mary wishes Jesus to carry out a miracle, and he suggests that John's portrayal of Mary reflects circles in which Mary already has a position of authority.[43] His suggestion is supported by John's portrayal of Mary since her intervention leads to the faith of the disciples. In our narrative Mary has a close relationship with Jesus, and she is confident that he will respond to her request for assistance. It is possible that Mary has an honoured position within the Johannine tradition. Patricia Miller points out that Mary becomes the subject of theological speculation in early Christian texts such as the *Protevangelium of James* and the *Oration to the Theotokos* by Proclus of Constantinople.[44] She also observes that a Marian Cult

---

[41] G. A. Anderson, 'The Culpability of Eve: From Genesis to Timothy', in *From Prophecy to Testament: The Function of the Old Testament in the New*, edited by C. A. Evans (Peabody, MA: Hendrickson, 2004), 233–51.

[42] P. C. Miller, ed., *Women in Early Christianity: Translations from Greek Texts* (Washington, DC: Catholic University of America Press, 2005), 289–95. For an analysis of the presentation of Mary as a new Eve in the early church, see Warner, *Alone of All Her Sex*, 50–67.

[43] Bultmann, *John*, 116.

[44] Miller, *Women in Early Christianity*, 295–304.

develops in the early church (cf. Epiphanius, *Pan.* 78.23; 79). John's presentation of the influence of Mary on her son may indicate that Mary is venerated as the mother of Jesus in the Johannine community.

In our passage Mary shows concern for the hosts and the guests, and she brings the situation of need to Jesus's attention. The mother of Jesus demonstrates her faith in Jesus as the one who has power to alleviate the situation. She does not consult the bridegroom or steward but places her trust in Jesus. Mary has a key role in the narrative since she prompts Jesus to transform the water in the stone jars into abundant wine. John states that the water in the stone jars is reserved for the observance of the purity regulations (κατὰ τὸν καθαρισμὸν τῶν Ἰουδαίων, 2.6).[45] The six stone jars of water may be intended to provide water for the practice of handwashing before meals. The presence of these jars at the wedding feast implies that the hosts of the wedding observe the purity regulations. The mother of Jesus, Jesus and the disciples are all Jewish, and as wedding guests they may also have participated in this practice. The sign thus raises the question of Jesus's attitude towards the purity regulations in John's Gospel.

John associates the mother of Jesus with the first sign in which Jesus transforms the water that is intended for the observance of the purity regulations into the abundant wine of the new creation. Jesus's sign looks forward to the Messianic age in which human beings will no longer need to observe the purity regulations. John's situation of this sign in a prominent place at the beginning of his gospel suggests that the members of the Johannine community no longer observe the purity regulations.[46] John wishes to situate the authority for the abandonment of the regulations in the lifetime of Jesus. He locates this sign in the presence of his mother at the wedding at Cana in Galilee near his hometown of Nazareth.

In our passage Mary acts independently because she instructs servants in a household that is not her own. Mary's leadership role may also be suggested by her instructions to the servants 'to do whatever Jesus tells them' (2.5). The term 'servants' (διάκονοι) is frequently employed in reference to the leaders of the early church. Paul refers to himself and other leaders as 'deacons' (διάκονοι, 1 Cor. 3.5; 2 Cor. 3.6; 6.4; 11.23), and he addresses deacons and bishops at the beginning of his letter to the Philippians (διακόνοις, 1.1). In the letter to the Colossians, Tychicus is identified as a 'deacon' (διάκονος, 4.7). The frequent use of this term in the New Testament suggests that John's audience would have been familiar with the role of deacons in the church.

---

[45] R. Deines (*Jüdische Steingefässe und pharisäische Frömmigkeit: ein archäologisch – historischer Beitrag zum Verständnis von Joh 2,6 und jüdischen Reinheitshalacha zur Zeit Jesu* (Tübingen: Mohr Siebeck, 1993), 268–74) identifies archaeological evidence for stone jars in pre-70 CE Palestine, and he argues that the stone jars were used to contain water for the observance of purity regulations. For a study of the archaeological evidence for stone vessels and miqwaoth from the first century in Galilee and Judea, see J. L. Reed, *Archaeology and the Galilean Jesus: A Re-examination of the Evidence* (Harrisburg: Trinity Press, 2000), 41–51, 56–7.

[46] W. Loader ('Jesus and the Law in John', in *Theology and Christology in the Fourth Gospel*, edited by G. Van Belle, J. G. Van der Watt and P. Maritz (Leuven: Leuven University Press, 2005), 149–54) argues that the advent of Jesus has brought about a change in the Johannine Christians' attitude towards the Law (cf. 1.17-18). Loader proposes that John presents the Law as an 'interim measure' until the arrival of Christ.

In the New Testament women have the role of deacon as in the example of Phoebe who is described as a deacon of the church at Cenchreae (διάκονος, Rom. 16.1). In some later texts, however, there are attempts to restrict the role of women deacons. Women deacons are not permitted to conduct baptisms (*Didascalia apostolorum* 3.9; *Apostolic Constitutions* 3.9.1-4; Epiphanius, *Pan.* 79.2.3-4.1) but they have the role of anointing other women at baptism, teaching women and visiting them in their homes (*Didascalia apostolorum* 3.12; *Apostolic Constitutions* 3.16.1-2).[47] As Charlotte Methuen notes, there were also attempts to restrict the role of female deacons by placing them under the authority of a male bishop.[48] In John's Gospel the servants have the role of serving wine to the wedding guests. It is possible that deacons are responsible for serving wine at the Lord's Supper in the first century. In the early church there is evidence in several texts that deacons had the role of serving wine at the Eucharist (*Did.* 14.1-3; *1 Clem.* 42.4; Ignatius, *Trall.* 2; Justin, *1 Apol.* 1.65.5). The mother of Jesus instructs the servants in this account, and they distribute the wine among the guests. John's portrayal of Mary in our passage suggests that she is regarded as a figure of authority within the Johannine community. The distinctive features of John's presentation of Mary may reflect the leadership roles of women within the worship of the church, and the provision of wine may allude to the celebration of the Eucharist. John's portrayal of the leading role of Mary in the account of Jesus's first sign suggests that she may be venerated in the Johannine community.

Conclusion

The mother of Jesus appears in the account of Jesus's first sign at the wedding at Cana, and she informs Jesus that the wine has run out. Mary shows her concern for the hosts and guests, and she intercedes on their behalf. At first Jesus is reluctant to intervene because his 'hour' has not yet come. Mary remains confident that Jesus is able to assist the wedding party, and she instructs the servants to do whatever he tells them. She overcomes Jesus's reluctance to intervene, and her request prompts Jesus to carry out the first of a series of signs that point to his identity as the Messiah and Son of God. John depicts the close relationship between Jesus and his mother, and the account demonstrates the influence of Mary upon Jesus at the start of his mission. John's account of the transformation of water into wine looks forward to the Messianic age that comes about through Jesus's death and resurrection.

---

[47] Miller, *Women in Early Christianity*, 7-8, 62-8. For an analysis of the office of female deacon in the early church, see U. E. Eisen, *Women Officeholders in Early Christianity: Epigraphical and Literary Studies* (Collegeville, PA: Liturgical Press, 2000), 158-98; K. Madigan and C. Osiek (eds), *Ordained Women in the Early Church: A Documentary History* (Baltimore, MD: John Hopkins University Press, 2005), 11-24.

[48] C. Methuen ('Widows, Bishops and the Struggle for Authority in the *Didascalia Apostolorum*', *JEH* 46 (1995): 197-213) points out that the author of the *Didascalia Apostolorum* seeks to restrict the leadership roles of the group of widows by developing the role of female deacons who are placed under the authority of a bishop.

John links his portrayal of Mary with the theme of new creation. He portrays Mary as a new Eve who is present at the beginning of Jesus's mission. In Genesis, Adam and Eve disobeyed God, and death entered the world. In John's Gospel Jesus has come to bring eternal life and to inaugurate the new creation. John's portrayal of Mary as a new Eve reflects his realized eschatology. The abundant wine of the new creation may be experienced in the present world. Mary's request initiates Jesus's first sign that leads to the revelation of Jesus's glory and the faith of his disciples. Mary is present at the time when Jesus begins his mission, and she will also be present at the crucifixion, the hour of his glorification. The prominent location of the passages that feature Mary suggests that she is venerated as the mother of Jesus in the Johannine tradition. Mary acts with independence and authority at the wedding at Cana. John's account of the faith of the mother of Jesus at the wedding at Cana suggests that she acts as a model of discipleship for the Johannine community.

3

The Samaritan woman (4.1-42)

Introduction

At the beginning of ch. 4 Jesus travels to Samaria, and he meets a Samaritan woman at a well near Sychar. Jesus is tired from his journey, and he requests a drink of water from the woman. She is surprised that a Jewish man would like a drink from the water jar of a Samaritan woman, but she responds positively to his offer of living water (4.10). In the course of their conversation she recognizes Jesus as a prophet, and she asks others in her town if he could be the Messiah (4.29). Some scholars such as Raymond Brown argue that the woman's question indicates that she does not fully believe that Jesus is the Messiah.[1] Other commentators, including Elisabeth Schüssler Fiorenza, rightly interpret the Samaritan woman as an example of faith because she progresses from misunderstanding to knowledge of Jesus's identity.[2] The Samaritan woman, moreover, has the role of a disciple since she tells the people in her town about Jesus. Many Samaritans believe in Jesus on account of her testimony, and he stays in their town for two days. More Samaritans believe through their own meeting with Jesus, and they express their faith that Jesus is the 'Saviour of the World' (4.42).

John presents an extended conversation between the Samaritan woman and Jesus which explores the relations between Samaritans and Jews. John Meier notes that the Samaritans may be defined in terms of their geographical region, in terms of their physical descent or in terms of their religious identity.[3] As Meier points out, most references to the Samaritans in the gospels including our passage regard Samaritans in relation to their religious identity. Jews and Samaritans view Abraham as their ancestor, and Samaritans trace their descent from the tribes of Manasseh and Ephraim (cf. Josephus, *Ant.* 9.201; 11.340-41).[4] Ingrid Hjelm notes that the origins of the conflict

---

[1] R. E. Brown, *The Gospel according to John*, 2 vols, AB 29-29A (Garden City NY: Doubleday, 1966–70), 1:173.
[2] E. Schüssler Fiorenza, *In Memory of Her: A Feminist Theological Reconstruction of Christian Origins*, 2nd edn (New York: Crossroad, 1995), 327.
[3] J. P. Meier ('The Historical Jesus and the Historical Samaritans: What Can Be Said?' *Bib* 81 (2000): 2045) notes that the inhabitants of Samaria included Jews, other indigenous Semitic groups and descendants of the Assyrians, Babylonians, Persians and Greeks.
[4] For an analysis of Samaritan beliefs and practices, see R. Pummer, *The Samaritans. A Profile* (Grand Rapids, MI: Eerdmans, 2016), 1–25 and T. Wardle, 'Samaritans, Jews, and Christians: Multiple Partings and Multiple Ways', in *The Ways That Often Parted. Essays in Honor of Joel Marcus*, edited

between Jews and Samaritans are difficult to determine since Jews and Samaritans hold different views of their histories.[5] In 2 Kings 17 the Assyrians took the Israelites into exile, and they settled people from five nations in Samaria. In this passage the new nations were accused of developing a syncretistic religion by worshipping their own gods and the God of Israel. On the other hand Samaritans dated the beginning of the conflict to the period when the priest Eli moved the location of the Temple to Jerusalem, and the two groups disagreed over whether the Temple should be located in Jerusalem or on Mount Gerizim.[6] Tensions between Jews and Samaritans, however, increased during the Second Temple period (cf. Sir. 50.25-26; *T. Levi*), and the Samaritan Temple was destroyed by John Hyrcanus in a military campaign during 128 BCE. Josephus gives a negative interpretation of the account of the Samaritans in 2 Kgs 17.30-32 by arguing that they only claimed to be the descendants of the tribes of Ephraim and Manasseh when the Jews were prospering but that they denied shared descent when the Jews were in trouble (*Ant.* 9.291; 11.340).

It is difficult to determine John's source for the account of the meeting between Jesus and the Samaritan woman since this passage only appears in John's Gospel. John's portrayal of the faith of the Samaritan woman and of the people in her town differs from the presentation of Samaritans in the synoptic gospels. The Gospel of Mark does not contain any references to Samaritans, and in Matthew's Gospel Jesus instructs his disciples not to go to gentiles or to visit a town of the Samaritans (10.5-6). Luke includes positive accounts of Samaritans in the parable of the good Samaritan (10.29-37) and the account of the Samaritan who returns to thank Jesus after he has been healed of leprosy (17.11-19). In Acts, the mission to the Samaritans, however, does not take place until after the death of Jesus. Philip conducts the first mission in Samaria, and his work is later supported by Peter and John (Acts 8.4-25). John's account of the positive response of a Samaritan town to Jesus raises the question of whether Jesus's mission included Samaritans. To what extent is John's account of the Samaritan woman historical? Are there any indications that John has developed the narrative as a means of supporting the later mission of the Johannine community to Samaritans?

John's account of the Samaritan woman, moreover, includes some detailed knowledge of Samaritan beliefs and traditions. The Samaritan woman claims descent from Jacob, and the Samaritans regarded themselves as the descendants of Manasseh and Ephraim. She recognizes Jesus as a prophet, and Samaritans expected an eschatological prophet based on their reading of Deuteronomy 18. In the course of the conversation the Samaritan woman and Jesus discuss the correct location of the Temple and the nature of true worship. Samaritans believed that the Temple should be

---

by L. Baron, J. Hicks-Keeton and M. Thiessen, Early Christianity and Its Literature 24 (Atlanta, GA: SBL Press, 2018), 15–39.

[5] For an assessment of the origins of the Samaritans, see I. Hjelm, *The Samaritans and Early Judaism*, JSNTSup 303 (Sheffield: Sheffield Academic Press, 2000), 13–75.

[6] For an analysis of the archaeological excavations at the site of the Samaritan Temple on Mount Gerizim, see Y. Magen, 'Mount Gerizim and the Samaritans', in *Early Christianity in Context. Monuments and Documents*, edited by F. Manns and E. Alliata (Jerusalem: Franciscan Printing Press, 1993), 134–48, and the articles by R. J. Bull, 'An Archaeological Context for Understanding John 4.20', *BA* 38 (1975): 54–9 and 'An Archaeological Footnote to "Our Fathers Worshipped on This Mountain" John IV.20', *NTS* 23 (1977): 460–2.

located on Mount Gerizim whereas Jews worshipped in the Temple in Jerusalem. John's presentation of the Samaritan woman suggests that his audience has some knowledge of Samaritan beliefs and the key features of the conflict between Jews and Samaritans.

In this chapter we will examine John's portrayal of the Samaritan woman in relation to the social and historical setting of the first-century Graeco-Roman world. The Samaritan woman has been married five times, and she is not married to her present partner. We will assess John's presentation of the Samaritan woman's personal life and the function of John's references to her marriages within his narrative. In our passage the Samaritan woman recognizes Jesus as a prophet, and she wonders if he could be the Messiah. Her recognition of Jesus raises the question of whether John portrays her as a model of faith. We will analyse the extent to which John's account of the Samaritan woman illustrates his understanding of discipleship. We will also examine John's portrayal of the Samaritan woman in relation to the theme of new creation. The conversation between Jesus and the Samaritan woman contains several eschatological features. Jesus offers the woman the gift of 'living water', and he speaks to her about the 'hour' in which worshippers will worship God 'in spirit and in truth' (4.23). John's positive presentation of the faith of the Samaritan woman suggests that he depicts her as a representative of Samaritans who are attracted to Christianity. In this chapter we will assess the extent to which John employs the account of the meeting between the Samaritan woman and Jesus to support the mission of the Johannine community to Samaritans.

The portrayal of the Samaritan woman

The Samaritan woman is anonymous, and she is introduced into the narrative as she carries out her daily task of walking to Jacob's well to draw water. John's setting of the conversation between Jesus and the Samaritan woman at a well recalls the location of several betrothal narratives in the Old Testament such as the meeting of Abraham's servant and Rebekah (Gen. 24.10-61), the meeting of Jacob and Rachel (Gen. 29.1-20), and the meeting of Moses and Zipporah (Exod. 2.15-21). In these narratives Abraham's servant finds a wife for Isaac, and Jacob and Moses meet their future wives. Jocelyn McWhirter points out that John's presentation of the hidden identity of Jesus is reminiscent of the hidden identity of Abraham's servant and Jacob in the Old Testament.[7] In Genesis, Abraham's servant reveals his identity after Rebekah has given him a drink and watered the camels (24.22-27), and Jacob waters Laban's flock before he reveals his identity to Rachel (29.10-12). In John's Gospel Jesus asks the Samaritan woman for a drink of water, and she discovers his identity in the course of their conversation about 'living water'.

John's portrayal of the Samaritan woman, however, differs in several ways from the presentation of women in the Old Testament betrothal narratives. In the betrothal narratives the women are young and unmarried whereas the Samaritan woman has

---

[7] J. McWhirter, *The Bridegroom Messiah and the People of God* (Cambridge: Cambridge University Press, 2006), 61.

been married five times, and her current partner is not her husband. In our passage Jesus asks the Samaritan woman for a drink of water but she acts differently from the women in the betrothal narratives since she expresses her surprise that a Jewish man requests a drink of water from a Samaritan woman (4.9). John implies that there are some tensions between the woman and her neighbours because she visits the well at midday whereas it is customary for women to go to a well to draw water in the early morning or at dusk. She also travels alone even though women usually walk to wells in a group. Some scholars such as Barnabas Lindars argue that the number of her past relationships suggests that she may be viewed as disreputable.[8] Nevertheless, Lindars also notes that John's references to the Samaritan woman's husbands demonstrate Jesus's divine knowledge of the woman's life.

Some feminist scholars, however, take issue with the tendency of scholars to give negative interpretations of the woman's past life. Gail O'Day rightly points out that John does not give any explanation for the number of the woman's marriages.[9] In the first century women married at a young age, and their marriages were frequently arranged by their parents.[10] Women were not able to divorce their husbands, and it is possible that the women's husbands have died or they have abandoned her. O'Day suggests that the Samaritan woman may have been in a similar situation to that of Tamar in Genesis 38, and her five marriages may reflect the practice of Levirate marriage.[11] She refers to the dispute between Jesus and the Sadducees over his belief in the resurrection in the synoptic gospels. The Sadducees cite the example of a woman who has been married seven times to seven brothers in accordance with the laws of Levirate marriage (Mt. 22.23-33; Mk 12.18-27; Lk. 20.27-40). The Sadducees' reference to Levirate marriage, however, is employed as an illustration to counter Jesus's belief in the resurrection, and there is no evidence that Levirate marriage was carried out in the first century.

There are indications, moreover, that the woman is aware of the potential criticism of her past life. When Jesus asks her to call her husband, she replies that she has no husband and she says nothing about her current partner (4.17). Jesus, then, reveals his knowledge of her past relationships and her current partner but he does not criticize the woman. As Ulrich Wilckens notes, the woman's past life is characterized by distress and difficulties, and she no longer has the protection of marriage in her relationship with her current partner.[12] The woman may be marginalized within her town on account of her relationships but Jesus shows compassion for the woman by offering her the gift of 'living water'.

In our narrative Jesus does not directly criticize the Samaritan woman's relationships. His reference to her husband leads to the revelation of his divine knowledge of her personal life. As Teresa Okure observes, Jesus's knowledge of the past life of the woman is reminiscent of Jesus's divine knowledge of Nathanael at the beginning of the gospel

---

[8] B. Lindars, *The Gospel of John*, NCBC (London: Marshall, Morgan & Scott, 1972), 185–7.
[9] G. R. O'Day, 'John', in *Women's Bible Commentary*, edited by C. A. Newsom and S. H. Ringe, exp. edn (Louisville, KY: Westminster John Knox, 1998), 384.
[10] T. Ilan, *Jewish Women in Greco-Roman Palestine* (Peabody, MA: Hendrickson, 1996), 65–9, 79–83.
[11] O'Day, 'John', 384.
[12] U. Wilckens, *Das Evangelium nach Johannes* (Göttingen: Vandenhoeck and Ruprecht, 1998), 83.

(1.47-51).¹³ Jesus tells Nathanael that he saw him sitting under a fig tree before he was called by Philip. Nathanael responds to Jesus by addressing him as the 'Son of God' and 'King of Israel' (1.49). In our passage the woman is amazed that Jesus knows about her past life. Nevertheless, the Samaritan woman's response suggests that she is concerned about her past and current relationships. When she tells others in her village about Jesus, she describes him as the one who told her everything that she has ever done (4.29). Her reply suggests that she equates Jesus's knowledge of everything that she has ever done with his knowledge of her relationships.

The Samaritan woman's five marriages, however, may also have symbolic significance within the narrative. Andrew Lincoln proposes that John's reference to the woman's five husbands may allude to the account of the Samaritans in 2 Kings 17.¹⁴ The Assyrians settled five new nations in the land who worshipped seven gods. John may intend his reference to the woman's five husbands to allude to these gods. As Raymond Brown points out, the term 'ba'al' may be translated as 'husband' or 'lord', and may also be applied to gods.¹⁵ On the other hand Ernst Haenchen argues against an allegorical interpretation of the five husbands because the account in 2 Kings 17 refers to seven gods rather than five.¹⁶ Josephus, however, refers to five gods of the Samaritans in his account of the narrative of 2 Kings 17 (*Ant.* 9.288). John may thus include a reference to the woman's five husbands in order to allude to the charge that Samaritans followed a syncretistic religion.

Jesus's meeting with the Samaritan woman demonstrates the positive response of a Samaritan to his teaching but the woman's past life suggests that she is an unlikely choice of a model disciple. It is possible that John refers to the woman's five husbands as a way of engaging with the views of some members of his audience who are aware of the criticism that Samaritans have developed a syncretistic religion. In the Old Testament God is often presented as a bridegroom, and Israel is depicted as a bride (cf. Isa. 54.4-5; 62.5; Jer. 2.2-3). Adeline Fehribach argues that Jesus is portrayed as the Messianic bridegroom, and the Samaritan woman represents the Samaritan people with whom God wishes to renew 'familial relations'.¹⁷ We have noted the association of wedding imagery with the joy and celebration of the end-time in the account of the wedding at Cana (2.1-11). Several of Jesus's parables employ the setting of a wedding as an image of the fulfilment and celebration of the kingdom of God (cf. Mt. 22.1-14; 25.1-13; Lk. 14.7-11).

In the Old Testament marriage is concerned not only with the union of two individuals but it is also the means of bringing together two families and households. In the ancient world marriages are frequently employed to form alliances between two nations, and in our passage the meeting of Jesus and the Samaritan woman creates the opportunity of a new discipleship community of Jews and Samaritans. In

---

[13] T. Okure, *The Johannine Approach to Mission: A Contextual Study of John 4:1-42* (Tübingen: Mohr Siebeck, 1988), 108.
[14] A. T. Lincoln, *The Gospel according to Saint John*, BNTC (London: Continuum, 2005), 175.
[15] Brown, *John*, 1:171.
[16] E. Haenchen, *John 1* (Philadelphia, PA: Fortress, 1984), 221.
[17] A. Fehribach, *The Women in the Life of the Bridegroom: A Feminist Historical-Literary Analysis of the Gospel of John* (Collegeville, PA: Liturgical Press, 1998), 80.

the Old Testament there are some hopes of the union of the northern and southern kingdoms (Ezek. 37.15-23; Zech. 9.13; 10.6-7).[18] In John's Gospel, Jesus is depicted as the bridegroom who is able to include Samaritans and Jews in a new understanding of the people of God.

In our narrative John presents the Samaritan woman as a representative of Samaritans who are attracted to Christianity. His setting of the narrative at Jacob's well highlights the common traditions of Jews and Samaritans because both groups are descendants of Jacob. Ellen Aitken notes that John alludes to Jacob traditions in the setting of Jacob's well (4.5-6) and the comparison between Jesus and Jacob (4,12).[19] As she points out, Jacob is the father of Joseph, the ancestor of the Samaritan tribes, and she argues that these allusions are intended to support the mission to the Samaritans. John may therefore develop his account of the meeting of the Samaritan woman and Jesus to allude to the prophetic expectations of the restoration of Israel.

John presents a positive account of the response of the people of a Samaritan town to Jesus. On the other hand the negative attitude towards Samaritans in Matthew's Gospel suggests that some objections to the Samaritan mission existed within first-century Christianity. The Matthean Jesus sends his twelve disciples out on mission but warns them to avoid the gentiles and any town of the Samaritans (10.5-6). In Matthew's Gospel Samaritans are not included within the 'lost sheep of the house of Israel' but in our passage John alludes to the shared descent of Jews and Samaritans. It is possible that John is aware of the criticism of Samaritans on account of the charges that they have intermarried with gentile nations and worshipped their gods. John shapes his account of the meeting between Jesus and the Samaritan woman in order to address these criticisms. In our passage Jesus is aware of the woman's previous relationships, and he is sympathetic to the hardship of her life. His knowledge of her life leads her to recognize him as a prophet and to seek to discover more about his identity as the Messiah. The woman's past becomes an opportunity for her to communicate her faith. Instead of calling her husband, this woman brings her whole town to Jesus. The meeting between the woman and Jesus shows the ways in which the tensions between Jews and Samaritans are overcome, and in the next section we will explore the portrayal of the woman as an example of faith.

The conversation between the Samaritan woman and Jesus

In Chapter 2 we examined the conversation between Mary and Jesus at the wedding at Cana (2.1-11), and in this section we will analyse the longer conversation between

---

[18] M. L. Coloe ('The Woman of Samaria: Her Characterization, Narrative, and Theological Significance', in *Characters and Characterization in the Gospel of John*, edited by C. W. Skinner; LNTS 461 (London: T&T Clark, 2012), 195-6) proposes that John develops the account of the meeting of the Samaritan woman and Jesus to allude to the reunion of Samaria and Judea.

[19] E. B. Aitken, 'At the Well of Living Water: Jacob Traditions in John 4', in *From Prophecy to Testament. The Function of the Old Testament in the New*, edited by C. A. Evans (Peabody, MA: Hendrickson, 2004), 342–52.

the Samaritan woman and Jesus. In our narrative John highlights the differences between the Samaritan woman and Jesus in terms of gender and race since the woman is identified three times as a Samaritan woman (4.7-9). Jesus initiates the conversation by requesting a drink of water from the Samaritan woman (4.7) but she replies by asking him how it is that he, a Jew, asks for a drink from her, a Samaritan woman (ἡ Σαμαρῖτις, 4.9).[20] The narrator adds the explanation that Jews do not share vessels with Samaritans (οὐ γὰρ συγχρῶνται Ἰουδαῖοι Σαμαρίταις, 4.9).[21] The verb συγχράομαι has been translated as 'to have dealings with' but David Daube points out that this verb may be better translated as 'to use together' since the woman refers to the sharing of her water jar.[22] Barrett argues that the verb should be translated as 'to use together with', and he notes a regulation from the Mishnah which states that 'the daughters of the Samaritans are menstruants from their cradle' (*m. Nid.* 4.1).[23] He proposes that this regulation dates from 66–67 CE, and he argues that John has added the explanation to his source. Barrett, however, also cites a regulation from the Mishnah which states that two men who eat with a Samaritan must say the grace (*m. Ber.* 7.1). This regulation implies that Jews were not prohibited from sharing meals with Samaritans. It is possible that the verb συγχράομαι not only refers to the tense relations between Jews and Samaritans but also indicates concerns about ritual purity. There is no bucket at the well, and Jesus's request implies that he wishes to drink from the woman's water jar.

The Johannine Jesus responds to the Samaritan woman's concerns by offering her 'living water' (ὕδωρ ζῶν, 4.10) and referring to his ability to bring her 'the gift of God' (τὴν δωρεὰν τοῦ θεοῦ, 4.10). Jesus has asked the woman for water but as Dorothy Lee observes, Jesus reverses the initial situation, since the woman is now portrayed as the person in need of water.[24] Jesus uses figurative language, claiming that he is able to give the woman 'living water' (ὕδωρ ζῶν, 4.10). He contrasts the water that lies at the bottom of the well with the fresh running water that is found in springs. Jesus's phrase 'living water' has rich symbolic associations within the Old Testament and Jewish writings. 'Living water' has been associated with revelation, since water is linked with wisdom (Prov. 13.14; 16.22; 18.4; Sir. 15.3; 24.21; *1 En.* 48.1; 49.1), and in some texts the term 'living water' refers to the wisdom in the Law (Sir. 24.23-29; CD 3.16; 6.4-11; 19.34).[25] Jesus's reference to 'living water' also has associations with purity since the term 'living

---

[20] H. Thyen (*Das Johannesevangelium* (Tübingen: Mohr Siebeck, 2005), 246) rightly observes that John tends to present Jesus as the one who initiates conversations, whereas individuals in the synoptic gospels approach Jesus with a question or a request.

[21] B. M. Metzger (*A Textual Commentary on the Greek New Testament: A Companion Volume to the United Bible Societies' Greek New Testament*, 3rd edn (London: United Bible Societies, 1975)) notes that this verse is omitted by several witnesses (ℵ* D a b e). It is accepted by the UBS text because asides are a characteristic feature of John's Gospel and some scribes may have omitted the verse because they did not consider it to be an accurate account of the relations between Jews and Samaritans.

[22] D. Daube, 'Jesus and the Samaritan Woman: The Meaning of συγχράομαι', *JBL* 69 (1950): 137–47.

[23] C. K. Barrett, *The Gospel according to St. John: An Introduction with Commentary and Notes on the Greek Text*, 2nd edn (London: SPCK, 1978), 232–3.

[24] D. A. Lee, *The Symbolic Narratives of the Fourth Gospel: The Interplay of Form and Meaning*, JSNTSup 95 (Sheffield: JSOT, 1994), 71.

[25] For an analysis of the interpretation of 'living water' as Jesus's revelation or teaching, see Brown, *John*, 1:178–9.

water' is used to describe the running water which is required to cleanse objects that have contracted impurity (Lev. 14.5-6, 50-52; 15.13; Num. 19.17). Jews and Samaritans both accepted the authority of the Pentateuch but followed different interpretations of the purity regulations and therefore questioned one another's state of purity.[26]

Water, however, is also frequently employed as a metaphor for the Spirit (Isa. 32.15; 44.3; Ezek. 11.19; 36.25-27; 1QS 3.6-9; 4.20-26). In John's Gospel the phrase 'living water' (ὕδατος ζῶντος, 7.38) is associated with the gift of the Spirit to those who believe in Jesus, and the water which Jesus brings is thus aligned with the Spirit that will be given at his death (7.37-39). In our passage Jesus offers the woman 'living water' which 'wells up to eternal life' (ἁλλομένου εἰς ζωὴν αἰώνιον, 4.14). In the Old Testament the verb ἅλλομαι (leap, well up) is linked with the Spirit (cf. Judg. 14.6, 19; 15.14; 1 Sam. 10.10; 17.13 LXX). The conversation between the Samaritan woman and Jesus has an eschatological focus, since the Spirit is identified as the gift of the new age in the Old Testament and in Jewish writings (Isa. 44.3; Joel 2.28-29; Ezek. 36.25-27; 1QS 4.20-22).

Jesus's figurative language encourages the Samaritan woman to seek an explanation of the 'living water' which he is offering to her. John employs an 'incongruity or absurdity' in the literal level of Jesus's speech which encourages a search for a symbolic meaning.[27] Initially, the woman believes that Jesus's offer of 'living water' refers to the fresh running water which is found in springs. She interprets his offer of 'living water' in a material sense, and she points out that he has no bucket and the well is deep (4.11). Jesus moves the discussion from the material significance of 'living water' to its spiritual significance by telling her that those who drink the water which he offers will not thirst again, since it will become a spring within an individual welling up to eternal life (4.13-14).

The Samaritan woman is aware of her desire for 'living water'. She recognizes her thirst and the burden of travelling daily to the well to draw water, and she asks Jesus for some 'living water'. In response Jesus asks the woman to call her husband which creates an abrupt change in the direction of their conversation. As Rudolf Schnackenburg argues, the woman's marriages are presented as a means of bringing the woman to faith in Jesus.[28] Francis Moloney rightly notes that Jesus's knowledge about the woman's life acts as a turning point in the story.[29] Jesus's knowledge of the woman's life leads her to recognize him as a prophet (4.19), and she introduces the discussion about the correct location of the Temple. Jesus prophesizes that the time is coming when Jews and Samaritans will worship neither in Jerusalem nor on Mount Gerizim, but he still acknowledges the priority of Israel with the statements, 'we worship what we know' and 'salvation comes from the Jews' (4.22). Jesus argues that God is Spirit, and true worshippers must worship 'in spirit and in truth' (4.24). It is no longer necessary to

---

[26] Y. Magen ('The Ritual Baths (Miqva'ot) at Qedumim and the Observance of Ritual Purity among the Samaritans', in *Early Christianity in Context. Monuments and Documents*, edited by F. Manns and E. Alliata (Jerusalem: Franciscan Printing Press, 1993), 181–2) examines the archaeological evidence for the observance of purity regulations by Samaritans in the first century.

[27] C. R. Koester, *Symbolism in the Fourth Gospel. Meaning, Mystery, Community* (Minneapolis, MN: Fortress, 2003), 8.

[28] R. Schnackenburg, *The Gospel according to St. John*, 3 vols (London: Burns & Oates, 1968–82), 1:432.

[29] F. J. Moloney, *The Gospel of John*, Sacra Pagina Vol. 4 (Collegeville, PA: Liturgical Press, 1998), 127.

worship God in the Temple in Jerusalem or on Mount Gerizim because Jesus is the one who brings the Spirit which wells up in each individual. Jesus looks forward to a situation in which one of the sources of conflict between Jews and Samaritans is removed, since both groups may worship God together 'in spirit and in truth'.

John portrays the Samaritan woman as a skilful debater who is able to respond to Jesus's figurative language. The conversation between the woman and Jesus enables them to find common ground in the human need for water. Jesus is thirsty, and the woman acknowledges the necessity of visiting the well each day to draw water. John's development of the conversation enables the woman and Jesus to move beyond a discussion about natural water to an account of the spiritual gift of 'living water'. She replies to Jesus's remarks with humour and also with boldness. The Samaritan woman takes a pragmatic approach to the situation by saying that she does not like to have to come to the well to draw water but her appreciation of the necessity of water to sustain life enables her to grasp the deeper spiritual meaning of 'living water'. The Samaritan woman is an unlikely choice of character to represent the Samaritans, since she appears to be an outsider in her community. Nevertheless, Jesus's acceptance of the woman overcomes any criticism of her life. John's portrayal of the woman as an 'outsider' may enable her to respond positively to a stranger who is also an 'outsider' to her community. John develops the conversation between the Samaritan woman and Jesus to support the mission of the Johannine community to Samaritans.

The revelation of the hidden Messiah

The Samaritan woman is willing to engage in a conversation with Jesus, and she responds positively to his offer of 'living water'. She recognizes Jesus as a prophet, and she wonders if he could be the Messiah. John demonstrates the growth of the woman's recognition of Jesus in the course of their conversation. The woman's use of the term 'Messiah', however, is unexpected because the Samaritans did not expect a Davidic Messiah. Brown notes that the Samaritans expected a prophetic figure called the Taheb which may be translated as 'the one who returns'.[30] The Samaritans' beliefs were based on the prophecy of Deut. 18.15-18 which states that a prophet like Moses will arise. As Brown observes, the Samaritan Pentateuch contains a reference to the eschatological prophet (cf. Deut. 18.15) in the tenth commandment (Exod. 20.17b). Edwin Freed, moreover, points out that the Taheb was expected to restore true worship.[31] In our passage John connects these expectations to a discussion about the location of the Temple. The Samaritan Temple was destroyed by John Hyrcanus in 128 BCE but the Samaritans still looked for the restoration of their Temple.

It is difficult to determine the beliefs of the Samaritans in the first century because there are no surviving Samaritan writings from that time. There is a reference to Samaritan beliefs in Josephus's account of a first-century Samaritan movement which centred on a prophetic figure. Josephus describes a Samaritan prophet who led crowds

---

[30] Brown, *John*, 1:171-2.
[31] E. D. Freed, 'Did John Write His Gospel Partly to Win Samaritan Converts?' *NovT* 12 (1970): 250.

up Mount Gerizim in order to find the Temple vessels. Pilate responded violently by attacking the prophet and putting his followers to death (*Ant.* 18.85-89). Hopes of an eschatological prophet may also be seen in Qumran texts (cf. 1QS 9.11; 4Q Testamonia). The title 'prophet' may thus form common ground between the eschatological beliefs of some Jews and Samaritans.

The hope that an eschatological prophet will arise is a distinctive feature of the Christology of John's Gospel. In the synoptic gospels some people believe that Jesus is one of the prophets (cf. Mt. 16.14; Mk 8.28; Lk. 9.19) but the title 'the prophet' occurs several times in John's Gospel. John the Baptist is asked if he is 'the prophet' (1.21), and after the feeding of the five thousand Jesus is identified by the crowd as 'the prophet' who is to come into the world (οὗτός ἐστιν ἀληθῶς ὁ προφήτης ὁ ἐρχόμενος εἰς τὸν κόσμον, 6.14-15). The crowd wishes to make Jesus their king but he resists this attempt by withdrawing from them. In a later passage the religious leaders state that they oppose Jesus because they believe that 'no prophet' will come from Galilee (7.52).

In our passage, however, the Samaritan woman says that she believes that Jesus is a prophet rather than 'the prophet'. In a later passage the blind man also describes Jesus as 'a prophet' (9.17). In these narratives John depicts the growing understanding of the characters of Jesus's identity. The characters recognize Jesus as a prophet at an initial stage of their conversations with Jesus. They then develop their understanding, since the Samaritan woman wonders if Jesus is the Messiah (4.29). The blind man recognizes Jesus as the Son of Man, and he confesses his faith in Jesus with the statement, 'Lord, I believe' (9.38). John's audience, however, may relate the recognition of Jesus as a prophet by the Samaritan woman and by the blind man to their eschatological hopes for a prophet like Moses. John employs the title 'the prophet' to express continuity between Moses and Jesus but he also points forward to the ways in which Jesus goes beyond Moses.

In our narrative the Samaritan woman expresses her belief that the Messiah is coming who 'will announce to us all things' (ἀναγγελεῖ ἡμῖν ἅπαντα, 4.25). It is possible that the Samaritan woman's statement associates the title 'Messiah' with Samaritan beliefs. Schnackenburg notes that the *Memar Marqah*, a Samaritan text of the third or fourth century CE, states that the Taheb will reveal the truth (cf. *Memar Marqah* 4.1) and in our passage Jesus brings revelation (4.25).[32] There is also evidence of first-century Jewish expectations of a Messiah who is linked with the figure of the prophet like Moses. Dale Allison points out that Peter's speech in Acts 3 associates the Messiah with a prophet like Moses (3.17), and he proposes that this speech implies that a Jewish-Christian audience would have known a Messianic interpretation of Deuteronomy 18.[33] Allison also observes that several rabbinic texts link eschatological hopes for the Messiah with the figure of Moses (*Eccl. Rab.* 1.28; *Exod. Rab.* 1.26; *Ruth Rab.* 5.6; *Tg.Cant.* on 4.5). These examples indicate that the Samaritans and the rabbis identified the Deuteronomic hopes for a prophet like Moses with expectations of the Messiah.

---

[32] Schnackenburg, *St. John*, 1:441.
[33] D. C. Allison, *The New Moses: A Matthean Typology* (Edinburgh: T&T Clark, 1993), 85-90.

The Samaritan woman's determination to question Jesus leads him to reveal his identity as the Messiah with an 'I am' saying (ἐγώ εἰμι, ὁ λαλῶν σοι, 4.26). Jesus's reply 'I am' may be interpreted as an ordinary response of identification but at a deeper level this phrase is linked to the high Christology of the gospel. This verse is the first example of the 'I am' sayings which are associated with the revelation of Jesus's identity throughout the gospel. Some stand alone (cf. 6.20; 8.24, 28, 58; 13.19; 18.5, 6, 8), and others have a predicate (6.35; 8.12; 10.7, 9; 11.25).[34] John employs the 'I am' sayings to point to the divinity of Jesus because God's name is revealed to Moses as 'I am' in Exod. 3.14 LXX. This identification is also used of God in the revelation formulas in the Old Testament (ἐγώ εἰμι αὐτὸς λαλῶν, Deut. 32.39; Isa. 41.4; 43.10; 46.4). As Andrew Lincoln observes, Jesus's reply 'I am the one who is speaking to you' recalls the statements of God 'I am the one who speaks' (Isa. 45.19; 52.6 LXX).[35] John's use of this formula alludes to the role of Jesus as the divine revealer, and it reflects Jesus's purpose of coming into the world in order to make God known (1.18).[36]

John presents the Samaritan woman as a recipient of the revelation of Jesus's identity, and she asks the people from her town, 'Could this man be the Messiah?' (μήτι οὗτός ἐτιν ὁ χριστός, 4.29). Raymond Brown argues that the woman expresses doubt over Jesus's identity because the term μήτι is usually employed to introduce questions that expect a negative response.[37] The woman, however, leaves her water jar behind because she is so eager to tell others about Jesus (4.28). Her water jar is an important possession that is necessary for the woman to carry the water which she needs to sustain life. On a symbolic level she has no concern for the water from the well after having met someone who offers her 'living water'. At the same time her action emphasizes the theme of reciprocity in the narrative. At the beginning of the account Jesus is thirsty, and he may now drink from the jar which she has left behind. The Samaritan woman has recognized her need for spiritual water, and Jesus has offered her the 'living water' of the Spirit.

John reveals the identity of Jesus in the course of the conversation between the Samaritan woman and Jesus. The Samaritan woman meets a stranger at Jacob's well, and he turns out to be the one who offers 'living water' to both Jews and Samaritans. John's revelation may be compared with the motif of the hidden Messiah which we discussed in Chapter 2. In our passage the Samaritan woman asks Jesus where this 'living water' comes from (πόθεν οὖν ἔχεις τὸ ὕδωρ τὸ ζῶν, 4.11), and in the account of the wedding at Cana the steward did not know the source of the wine (οὐκ ᾔδει πόθεν ἐστίν, 2.9). In John's Gospel Jesus's signs point to his identity as the Messiah, since they illustrate the gifts which the Messiah brings humanity. In our passage John connects the gift of 'living water' to the identity of Jesus as the Messiah and Son of God.

The Johannine Jesus reveals his identity to a woman who is outwith the recognized structures of authority in her town. The Samaritan woman is not a respected leader

---

[34] Brown, 'Appendix IV: Egō Eimi', in *John*, 1:533–8.
[35] Lincoln, *Saint John*, 69, 178.
[36] For an analysis of the theological significance of the 'I am' sayings, see C. H. Williams, *I Am He: The Interpretation of 'Anî Hû' in Jewish and Early Christian Literature*, WUNT 113 (Tübingen: Mohr Siebeck, 2000).
[37] Brown, *John*, 1:173.

of her community, and she appears to be marginalized on account of her past relationships. Initially, she interprets Jesus's offer of 'living water' on a material level but her desire for water enables her to grasp the spiritual nature of his gift of 'living water'. Jesus's knowledge of the woman's past life leads her to recognize him as a prophet, and she questions him about the correct location for worship. In our passage the Samaritan woman progresses from her recognition of Jesus as a prophet to her belief that he is the Messiah. Samaritans expected the arrival of an eschatological prophet but John presents Jesus as a prophet-Messiah. John associates the Samaritan woman with a growing understanding of Jesus's identity, and she is the first person to whom Jesus addresses an 'I am' saying (4.26).

Discipleship and the Samaritan woman

John's portrayal of the Samaritan woman is reminiscent of the accounts of traditional wise women in biblical texts and rabbinic writings (cf. 2 Sam. 14.1-20; Lk. 18.1-8; *b. 'Erub*. 53b). In these texts women with low social status challenge the authority of powerful men. In our passage the Samaritan woman is not afraid to challenge Jesus, and she demonstrates skill in her ability to respond to his figurative language. She shows courage, and she takes risks in speaking to a man whom she does not know in an isolated location. Her frank recognition of the hardship of her life encourages her to respond favourably to Jesus's offer of 'living water'. John portrays the Samaritan woman as an example of faith, since she recognizes Jesus as a prophet (4.19), and she asks the people in her town, 'Could this man be the Messiah?' (4.29). The terms 'prophet' and 'Messiah' represent stages in the development of her understanding. Jesus then reveals his identity to her with an 'I am' saying (ἐγώ εἰμι, ὁ λαλῶν σοι, 4.26). The male disciples have recognized Jesus's identity as the Messiah and as the Son of God at an earlier stage in the gospel (1.41, 49) but the Samaritan woman is the first person who is not Jewish to recognize Jesus.

In John's Gospel discipleship is concerned with the recognition of Jesus's identity. In the opening chapters the disciples recognized Jesus as the Messiah and Son of God. At the wedding in Cana, Mary's request led to the first sign of Jesus which deepened the faith of the disciples (2.11). In John 4 Jesus alludes to his divine identity with the words 'I am' when he replies to the Samaritan woman's question of whether he is the Messiah. John's definition of discipleship is also concerned with the act of leading others to Jesus. John associates the Samaritan woman with discipleship, since Jesus asks her to call her husband as a witness (φώνησον, 4.16). The verb φωνέω (call) occurs in discipleship accounts in which one person leads another to faith. At the beginning of the gospel Jesus told Nathanael that he saw him before Philip called him (πρὸ τοῦ σε Φίλιππον φωνῆσαι, 1.48). John depicts the Samaritan woman in the role of a disciple, since she summons her whole town to come out to meet him. Her words 'come, see' (δεῦτε ἴδετε, 4.29) are reminiscent of the earlier accounts of the call of Jesus's first disciples. Jesus told the disciples of John the Baptist to 'come and see' (ἔρχεσθε καὶ ὄψεσθε, 1.39), and Philip told Nathanael to 'come and see' Jesus (ἔρχου καὶ ἴδε, 1.46). John associates his understanding of discipleship with a meeting between Jesus and an individual. In our passage John emphasizes the desire of the Samaritans to come and see Jesus for themselves. He gives the Samaritan woman a discipleship role since she convinces the people of her town to approach Jesus.

The Samaritan woman also acts in the role of a disciple, since she bears witness to Jesus (μαρτυρούσης, 4.39). John employs the language of testimony in relation to Jesus's act of bearing witness to God and also in relation to God's witness to Jesus (ὁ μαρτυρῶν, μαρτυρεῖ, 8.18).[38] The verb μαρτυρέω (bear witness) is employed in the conclusion to the gospel in which the Beloved Disciple is identified as the one who bears witness to the traditions in the gospel (ὁ μαρτυρῶν περὶ τούτων, 21.24). In his Farewell Discourse Jesus teaches his disciples that they have the role of witnesses because they have been with him from the beginning (καὶ ὑμεῖς δὲ μαρτυρεῖτε, ὅτι ἀπ' ἀρχῆς μετ' ἐμοῦ ἐστε, 15.27). Jesus has been sent into the world to reveal God. John associates the terminology of witness with the purpose of Jesus and the mission of the Johannine community. The gospel's emphasis on the act of bearing witness to Jesus is connected to the portrayal of Jesus as the hidden Messiah. The disciples' act of bearing witness involves revealing the identity of Jesus to others. Those who discover Jesus's identity are given the task of bearing witness to him in the world.

John states that many Samaritans believe in Jesus 'on account of the woman's word' (διὰ τὸν λόγον τῆς γυναικὸς, 4.39). This verse suggests that the woman acts as a role model for the disciples. In ch. 17 Jesus prays that others may believe through the 'word' of his disciples (διὰ τοῦ λόγου αὐτῶν, 17.20).[39] John's use of the term λόγος (word) in the singular may allude to the 'message' of the gospel. In response to the woman's word the Samaritans invite Jesus to stay with them, and he remains there for two days. Many more Samaritans believe in Jesus as a result of their meeting with him. These Samaritans, however, claim that they do not believe on account of the word of the Samaritan woman but on account of Jesus's word (διὰ τὸν λόγον αὐτοῦ, 4.41). The claim of the Samaritans implies that they regard the woman as an inferior witness. On the other hand their claim is not a negative assessment of the Samaritan woman because the Samaritans would not have met Jesus without her testimony. John emphasizes the significance of each disciple's personal relationship with Jesus. Disciples have the task of bringing others to Jesus, and those who encounter Jesus develop their own relationship with him.

In this account the Samaritans who encounter Jesus for themselves develop a greater understanding of his identity. The Samaritans go beyond the woman's recognition of Jesus as a prophet and her belief that Jesus could be the Messiah. They describe Jesus as the 'Saviour of the World' (ὁ σωτὴρ τοῦ κόσμου, 4.42). This title echoes the earlier statement of Jesus that 'salvation comes from the Jews' (ἡ σωτηρία ἐκ τῶν Ἰουδαίων ἐστίν, 4.22). The Samaritans' confession of faith combines an acceptance of the Jewish origins of salvation with a belief that the scope of salvation encompasses the

---

[38] Lincoln (*John*, 100) argues that John's terminology of 'witness' forms part of the prominent motif of the trial or lawsuit which may be seen throughout the gospel. Lincoln's examination of the lawsuit motif forms the subject of his book, *Truth on Trial: the Lawsuit Motif in the Fourth Gospel* (Peabody, MA: Hendrickson, 2000).

[39] R. E. Brown, *The Community of the Beloved Disciple: The Life, Loves, and Hates of an Individual Church in New Testament Times* (New York: Paulist Press, 1979), 187.

whole world. Our narrative is reminiscent of the earlier conversation between Jesus and Nicodemus in which the purpose of Jesus is defined in terms of his mission to bring salvation to the world (ἵνα σωθῇ ὁ κόσμος δι' αὐτοῦ, 3.17). John's use of the title 'Saviour of the World' may also allude to the divinity of Jesus because God is portrayed as 'Saviour' in the Old Testament (cf. Isa. 43.3, 11; 45.15, 21; 49.26; 60.16; Jer. 14.8; Hos. 13.4).

In our narrative John gives a positive account of the faith of the Samaritan woman but he raises questions about the understanding of the disciples. John states that the disciples are amazed to find Jesus talking to a Samaritan woman (ἐθαύμαζον, 4.27). Gail O'Day argues that the disciples' response represents conventional attitudes in which a male teacher is not expected to converse alone with a woman.[40] It is possible that the disciples are surprised that Jesus is breaking social conventions by speaking to a woman alone in a public place. Tal Ilan refers to several examples of later rabbinic texts in which rabbis warn disciples that they should not engage in conversations with women (*m. Abot* 1.5; *b. Ned.* 20a; *b. Ber.* 43b; *b. 'Erub.* 53b).[41] The gospels, however, contain frequent accounts of the meetings between Jesus and women but they do not include any criticism of these conversations. John's account of the response of the disciples raises the question of why his gospel is the only gospel to refer to the negative attitude of the disciples. Turid Karlsen Seim notes the complex nature of this verse since the disciples are surprised but do not voice their concern to Jesus.[42] The attitude of the disciples is thus contrasted with the behaviour of Jesus who shows no concerns about his conversation with the woman.

Some scholars suggest that John's portrayal of the disciples represents contemporary concerns of some members of John's audience. Sandra Schneiders argues that the disciples are probably male, and she proposes that they represent the attitudes of male Christians in the Johannine community who object to the apostolic role of women.[43] She rightly argues that the account of the Samaritan woman has the function of vindicating the discipleship role of women. Martinus de Boer proposes that Jn 4.7 indicates that Johannine Christianity is moving away from an earlier 'androcentric understanding of discipleship and mission'. He argues that the response of the disciples represents the views of men and also of women in John's community who oppose the equality of men and women in the mission of the church.[44] John's portrayal of the male disciples is intriguing, and it points to different perspectives on the roles of women in the early church. In our passage the disciples may represent later Christians who do not support the roles of women in the early church. John depicts other characters who show insight into Jesus's mission such as the Samaritan

---

[40] O'Day, 'John', 383.
[41] Ilan, *Jewish Women*, 126–7.
[42] T. K. Seim, 'Roles of Women in the Gospel of John', in *Aspects on the Johannine Literature*, edited by L. Hartman and B. Olsson, ConB. 18 (Uppsala: Almqvist & Wiksell International, 1987), 56–73.
[43] S. M. Schneiders, 'Women in the Fourth Gospel and the Role of Women in the Contemporary Church', *BTB* 12 (1982): 40.
[44] M. C. de Boer, 'John 4.27 – Women (and Men) in the Gospel and Community of John', in *Women in the Biblical Tradition*, edited by G. J. Brooke, Studies in Women and Religion 31 (Lewiston: Edwin Mellen Press, 1992), 208–30.

woman. It is probable that John employs the account of Jesus's acceptance of the Samaritan woman in order to challenge the views of later Christians who do not accept the leadership of women.

In some Johannine passages, moreover, women characters are portrayed more favourably than the male disciples. The mother of Jesus has greater understanding of Jesus's identity than the disciples in the account of the wedding at Cana (2.1-11). In our passage the Samaritan woman has more perception of Jesus's intentions than the male disciples. The disciples wish to know what Jesus 'seeks' from the woman, and why he is talking to her but they are afraid to ask him (τί ζητεῖς ἢ τί λαλεῖς μετ' αὐτῆς, 4.27). They are surprised at the prospect that Jesus 'seeks' something from her. The disciples' response reflects their belief that the Samaritan woman has little to offer Jesus or to teach them. John's portrayal of the disciples also raises the question of what Jesus does 'seek' from the woman. In John 4 Jesus refers to God as one who 'seeks' true worshippers (ζητεῖ, 4.23), and his statement suggests that God 'seeks' Samaritans along with all other ethnic groups as true worshippers.

John does not include the disciples in his account of the conversation of Jesus and the Samaritan woman, and the disciples play no part in the mission to the Samaritan town. As D. Moody Smith notes, the disciples do not understand the scope of Jesus's mission.[45] Gail O'Day observes that the disciples do not express their surprise whereas the Samaritan woman openly states her opinions, and she is willing to show her doubts and scepticism.[46] In this way the woman engages with Jesus and develops faith in him. John may portray the disciples as representatives of later Christians who are critical of the Samaritan mission. John seeks to counter his opponents' views in his positive account of the faith of the Samaritan woman. John's account demonstrates that outsiders such as the Samaritan woman are able to understand Jesus and to respond positively to his teaching.

The following conversation between Jesus and the disciples is concerned with the direction of Jesus's mission. The disciples offer Jesus food but he replies that he has food to eat which they do not know (4.32), since his food is to do the will of God and to bring his work to completion (4.33). Jesus points out that the fields are ripe for harvest (4.35), which suggests that the Samaritans are ready to respond to his mission. Jesus's saying recalls his teaching about the need for labourers to collect the abundant harvest in Matthew and Luke (Mt. 9.37-38; Lk. 10.12). In our passage Jesus tells his disciples that he will send them to harvest crops that 'others' have sown (4.38). John wishes to link Jesus and the woman with the act of sowing whereas the term 'others' refers to the missionaries of the future. Oscar Cullmann proposes that the reference to 'others' alludes to the mission of Philip and the Hellenists to the Samaritans in Acts 8, and he associates the Hellenists with the members of the Johannine community.[47] In Acts, the leaders of the Jerusalem church did not initiate the Samaritan mission but at a later

---

[45] D. M. Smith, *John* (Nashville, TN: Abingdon Press, 1999), 119.
[46] G. R. O'Day, *Revelation in the Fourth Gospel: Narrative Mode and Theological Claim* (Philadelphia, PA: Fortress, 1986), 74–5.
[47] O. Cullmann, *The Johannine Circle: Its Place in Judaism among the Disciples of Jesus and Early Christianity* (London: SCM, 1956), 49.

stage Peter and John visit Samaria to uphold the mission of Philip. It is possible that the leaders of the Jerusalem church did not initially support the mission to Samaria, and Luke seeks to downplay their reservation since he wishes to promote unity in the church. John may thus intend his account of the Samaritan woman to counter the views of those who oppose the Samaritan mission and to support the inclusion of Samaritans within the Johannine community.

John portrays the Samaritan woman as an outsider in her community but he demonstrates that she still has the courage to communicate with the people of her town. The strength of her testimony is evident in her ability to convince others about Jesus. John's portrayal of the Samaritan woman in the role of a missionary raises the question of whether or not other women in the Johannine community have this role. In the early church there is evidence that some women had the role of missionaries. Paul states that some apostles, including the brothers of Jesus and Peter, were accompanied by their wives (1 Cor. 9.5). There are also accounts of couples who travel together on mission such as Prisca and Aquila (Rom. 16.3), and Andronicus and Junia are described as 'prominent among the apostles' (Rom. 16.7). The Samaritan woman, however, does not travel on a formal mission. She leads people from her own town to Jesus, and her story acts as a model of an informal type of mission. John's account of the Samaritan woman is an example of the way in which Christianity may spread through personal contact between friends and neighbours. His presentation of the Samaritan woman and the people of her town suggests that Christianity developed in John's community through the informal witness of women and men to neighbours rather than through the formal mission of the church.

The Samaritan woman and the new creation

In this section we will examine John's portrayal of the Samaritan woman in relation to the theme of new creation. Jesus meets the Samaritan woman at the well at Sychar, and he offers her 'living water'. The conversation has an eschatological focus since Jesus's gift of 'living water' wells up within a person, leading to eternal life (4.14). The 'living water' which Jesus brings is of a different quality to the ordinary water that may be found in the well at Sychar. Anyone who drinks the water from the well will thirst again, whereas the person who drinks 'living water' will receive a constant source of refreshment. Jesus offers the woman the gift of 'living water' which corresponds to the eschatological gift of the Spirit.

John's account of the meeting between Jesus and the Samaritan woman focuses on water which is one of the main elements of the natural world. Jesus defines the gifts that he brings human beings in terms of the natural resources of the world. Human beings require water to sustain life, and Jesus has come to bring women and men 'abundant life' (ζωὴν ἔχωσιν καὶ περισσὸν ἔχωσιν, 10.10). In John's Gospel Jesus's gifts are frequently associated with life. He is 'the bread of life' (ὁ ἄρτος τῆς ζωῆς, 6.35) and he is 'the way, the truth, and the life' (ζωή, 14.6). In our passage John associates the term 'living water' (ὕδωρ ζῶν, 4.10) with Jesus's gift of eternal life since it wells up to eternal life (εἰς ζωὴν αἰώνιον, 4.14). Jeannine Brown rightly notes that John frequently links the motif of life with the theme of the renewal of creation.[48] In our passage John's use of the term 'living water' links the gift of the Spirit with the theme of new creation. In Genesis, the Spirit is present with God at the beginning of creation (1.2), and in John's Gospel the Spirit is depicted as the power of the new creation. The gift of the Spirit is not only associated with the gift of eternal life to human beings but is also linked with the emergence of a new world.

John's account of the meeting between Jesus and the Samaritan woman has several similarities with the earlier account of the mother of Jesus at the wedding at Cana (2.1-11). In both accounts the gifts of Jesus are linked to his identity. The Samaritan woman asks Jesus where he has found 'living water' (πόθεν οὖν ἔχεις τὸ ὕδωρ τὸ ζῶν, 4.11). Her question echoes the question of the steward at the wedding at Cana since he does not know the source of the wine (οὐκ ᾔδει πόθεν ἐστίν, 2.9). Jesus has come from the heavenly realm, and his gifts reflect that divine reality. His gifts are of a different quality from the material water and wine that are experienced in the earthly realm. John's account indicates that Jesus is able to bring these gifts on account of his divine identity.

In the course of the conversation, moreover, Jesus addresses the Samaritan woman as 'woman' (γύναι, 4.21). This address recalls the account of the wedding at Cana in which Jesus addressed his mother as 'woman' (γύναι, 2.4). Jesus's address to his mother alluded to the portrayal of Eve as the 'woman' in the creation account of Genesis (γύναι, 2.22-23; 3.1-22 LXX). John portrays Mary as a new Eve who was present at the first sign which marked the beginning of Jesus's mission. In the account of the wedding at Cana John's portrayal of Mary as a new Eve associated her with the purpose of Jesus's mission to bring humanity eternal life and to inaugurate the new creation. In the account of the wedding at Cana, Jesus's address 'woman' was unexpected because Jesus was speaking to his mother. In our narrative Jesus is speaking to a Samaritan woman, and the address 'woman' may be interpreted as a respectful address to a woman whose name he does not know.

John's audience, however, may be aware of the theological associations of this address. John has already associated the address 'woman' with the theme of new creation in the account of the wedding at Cana. In our narrative John links the Samaritan woman with the gift of 'living water' which is the eschatological gift of the Spirit. John employs the address 'woman' on occasions when Jesus brings revelation about the end-time. It is significant that Jesus uses the address 'woman' when he speaks to the Samaritan woman about the forthcoming 'hour'. He tells the Samaritan woman that the 'hour' is coming when people will not worship God on Mount Gerizim or Jerusalem (4.21). Jesus prophesies that the 'hour' is coming and is now present when true worshippers will worship in spirit and in truth (4.23). Jesus's reference to the imminence of his 'hour' recalls the account of the wedding at Cana in which Jesus was reluctant to intervene because his 'hour' had not yet come (2.4). Mary's request, however, prompted Jesus to perform his first sign and his act of transforming water into wine revealed his glory. John associates the women characters in both passages with Jesus's 'hour'. The abundant wine of the

---

[48] J. K. Brown, 'Creation's Renewal in the Gospel of John', *CBQ* 72 (2010): 277-8.

new creation and the new worship in spirit and in truth are both linked to the 'hour' of Jesus's death.

John not only links the account of the Samaritan woman to Jesus's 'hour', but he also alludes in several ways to the account of the crucifixion of Jesus. The Samaritan woman meets Jesus at midday, the sixth hour (4.6), and Jesus is condemned to crucifixion at the sixth hour (19.14). Richard Lightfoot compares the weariness of Jesus (4.6) with his physical suffering in the Passion Narrative (19.1-2), and the thirst of Jesus (4.7) with his statement at the crucifixion, 'I am thirsty' (διψῶ, 19.28).[49] As Lightfoot proposes, these correspondences point forward to the cost to Jesus of his mission. In addition, both accounts focus on the role of the Spirit and on the gift of eternal life. Jesus offers the Samaritan woman 'living water' which alludes to the gift of the Spirit (7.37-39), and Jesus dies, giving up the Spirit (παρέδωκεν τὸ πνεῦμα, 19.30). The correspondences between the two passages highlight the association of the gift of the Spirit with the death of Jesus.

Jesus, however, tells the Samaritan woman that the 'hour' is coming, and is already present when true worshippers will worship 'in spirit and in truth'. Jesus speaks of the 'hour' as a future event, but it is also present in his mission. In our passage the Johannine Jesus alludes to the future worship of God in the period after the destruction of the Temple.[50] In Jewish writings hopes and expectations of the new age are frequently concerned with the restoration of the Jerusalem Temple (cf. Tob. 14.5; *1 En.* 90.28-29; *Jub.* 1.17; *T. Benj.* 9.2; 11QT 29.8-10). In John's Gospel there is no reference to the hope for a new temple. In John 2, Jesus challenges his opponents to put him to death by saying, 'Destroy this Temple and I will raise it again in three days' (2.19). Jesus's enemies believe that he is talking about the Temple whereas he refers to his body. His reference to three days, moreover, alludes to his resurrection in three days (2.19-21). In John's Gospel Jesus replaces the Temple as the means of access to the presence of God, and he is depicted as the one who brings revelation of God.

John's account of the conversation between the Samaritan woman and Jesus illustrates several features of the theme of new creation. Jesus offers the woman the gift of 'living water' which is associated with the Spirit. Jesus's gift of the Spirit is offered to Jews and Samaritans, and the Spirit breaks down the boundaries between the two groups. The Samaritan woman points out that Jews worship in the Temple in Jerusalem whereas Samaritans believe God should be worshipped on Mount Gerizim. The Johannine Jesus, however, speaks of the 'hour' when true worshippers will worship God 'in spirit and in truth'. John suggests that those who worship 'in spirit and in truth' no longer require a Temple because Jesus replaces the Temple as the means of access to God. Jesus's prophecy thus removes one of the barriers between the joint worship of Jews and Samaritans. In our passage the Spirit is given to both Jews and Samaritans, and the gift of the Spirit forms a new unity between these groups in the Johannine community.

---

[49] R. H. Lightfoot, *St. John's Gospel* (Oxford: Clarendon, 1956), 122.
[50] For an analysis of John's attitude to the Temple, see M. L. Coloe, *God Dwells with Us: Temple Symbolism in the Fourth Gospel* (Collegeville, PA: Liturgical Press, 2001).

The Samaritan woman and the Johannine community

John has placed the account of the Samaritan woman in a prominent position near the beginning of his gospel. John's location of the account indicates that the mission to Samaritans is a key issue for John's community. His portrayal of the faith of the Samaritan woman suggests that she is a representative of the Samaritans who believe in Jesus. The Samaritan woman leads many people in her town to Jesus, and they confess their faith in him as the 'Saviour of the World' (4.42). Several scholars such as Raymond Brown argue that the Samaritans have joined the Johannine community and influenced the development of John's theology.[51] The account of the Samaritan woman is the only narrative in which Samaritans appear in John's Gospel but in a later passage Jesus's opponents accuse him of being a Samaritan and demon-possessed (8.48). At the time of this controversy Jesus has only visited one Samaritan town, and the accusation that he is a Samaritan may reflect a later period in the history of the Johannine community when Samaritans have joined the community. In our passage the disciples are surprised to find Jesus in conversation with the Samaritan woman. Our analysis of the disciples, however, suggests that some early Christians may be suspicious of the Johannine mission to Samaritans. In this section we will examine the extent to which John may have developed the account of the Samaritan woman in order to support the mission of his community to the Samaritans.

There are few sources about the Samaritans in the New Testament. Mark makes no reference to the Samaritans. Matthew contains the prohibition of Jesus against going to the gentiles or to a town of the Samaritans (10.5), and the mission of Jesus is focused on the 'lost sheep of the house of Israel' (10.6; 15.24). Luke contains the parable of the good Samaritan (10.29-37), and he also includes an account of the healing of ten lepers (17.11-19) in which the Samaritan is the only healed person to return to thank Jesus. The Samaritan is described as a 'stranger' (ἀλλογενὴς, 17.18) which suggests that he is regarded as a gentile. Richard Coggins notes that the term 'stranger' is used in the inscription in the Temple which forbids non-Jews to go further into the Temple court (*Ant.* 9.291).[52] Jesus is rejected by a Samaritan village because his face is set towards Jerusalem (9.51-56) but he ignores James and John's proposal to take vengeance on the village, and they move on to another Samaritan village. As Meier points out, the evidence from Luke and John suggests that the historical Jesus had a positive attitude towards Samaritans and had good relations with individual Samaritans but he did not engage in a mission to the Samaritans as a group.[53]

John's account of the faith of the Samaritan woman and the people of her town differs from Matthew's presentation of Samaritans. In Matthew's Gospel Jesus's instruction to the disciples to avoid entering a Samaritan town is the only reference to the Samaritans in the gospel. W. D. Davies and Dale Allison propose that this verse may be intended to answer any questions concerning the mission to the Samaritans since the status

---

[51] Brown, *Community*, 36–40.
[52] R. J. Coggins, 'The Samaritans and Acts', *NTS* 28 (1982): 423–34.
[53] Meier, 'Historical Jesus', 231–2.

of the Samaritans was unclear (cf. *m. Qidd.* 4.3).[54] As they note, the ancestors of the Samaritans were Jewish but they were considered to be racially mixed (*Ant.* 9.277-91; *b. Qidd.* 75a-6a). The textual evidence indicates that there may have been some debate over whether the Samaritans were regarded as Jews or as gentiles. In Matthew's Gospel Jesus's prohibition places Samaritans in the same category as gentiles, and it may reflect the views of some early Christians who opposed a mission to the Samaritans. At the end of Matthew's gospel Jesus commands his disciples to carry out a mission to all nations, and this mission would probably include Samaritans and gentiles (28.19).

It is possible that some members of John's community regard Samaritans in the same category as gentiles. John's account of the meeting between the Samaritan woman and Jesus, however, emphasizes the shared traditions of Samaritans and Jews. The Samaritan woman and Jesus share the ancestor, Jacob. Our analysis of the conversation between the Samaritan woman and Jesus points to some of the reasons why Samaritans may have responded positively to Christianity. Jesus's knowledge of the Samaritan woman's life leads her to recognize him as a prophet and as the Messiah. In this passage the Jewish expectations concerning the Messiah are linked with the Samaritan hopes for an eschatological prophet. Wayne Meeks notes the correspondences between John's association of Jesus with prophet-king traditions (cf. 6.14-15) and Samaritan beliefs concerning the enthronement of Moses when he ascends Mount Sinai to receive the Law (*Memar Marqah* ii.12, iv.6, vi.2).[55] In Samaritan traditions Moses receives heavenly secrets from God when he ascends Mount Sinai. Meeks, moreover, observes that the prophet-royal traditions concerning the figure of Moses occurs in Jewish texts including Philo's *Life of Moses* and the Tanḥuma collection of Jewish midrashim.[56] Meeks proposes that there are 'overlapping traditions and mutual influence' in Samaritan and Jewish sources in Palestine even in the first century.[57] His work demonstrates the close connections between John's Christology and Samaritan beliefs concerning Moses. John's portrayal of Jesus as the prophet and king may therefore appeal to Samaritans who have joined the Johannine community.

The woman and Jesus meet at Jacob's well, and Jacob is the father of the twelve tribes of Israel. Samaritans and Jews both claimed descent from Jacob since Samaritans believed themselves to be descendants of Manasseh and Ephraim, the sons of Joseph. Several Old Testament references allude to the restoration of the twelve tribes in the end-time (Isa. 27.12-13; Hos. 11.11; 2 Macc. 1.27), and prophetic texts look forward to the reunion of the northern and southern kingdoms (Ezek. 37.15-23; Zech. 9.13; 10.6-7). The Samaritans may have responded to Jesus's mission because they looked forward to the restoration of Israel.[58] In our passage Jesus offers the Samaritan woman

---

[54] W. D. Davies and D. C. Allison, *The Gospel according to Saint Matthew*, 3 vols (Edinburgh: T&T Clark, 1991), 2:166.

[55] W. A. Meeks, *The Prophet-King: Moses Tradition and the Johannine Christology* (Leiden: Brill, 1967), 216–57, 318–19.

[56] Meeks, *The Prophet-King*, 107–17, 192–5.

[57] Meeks, *The Prophet-King*, 256–7.

[58] S. Miller, 'The Woman at the Well: John's Portrayal of the Samaritan Mission', in *John, Jesus, and History, Volume 2: Aspects of Historicity in the Fourth Gospel*, edited by P. N. Anderson, F. Just and T. Thatcher (Atlanta, GA: Society of Biblical Literature, 2009), 73–81.

the 'living water' of the Spirit, and he prophesies that the time is coming when true worshippers will worship God 'in spirit and in truth'. In the new age it will no longer be necessary to worship in the Temple in Jerusalem nor on Mount Gerizim because Jesus brings the Spirit which wells up in each person. Jesus's gift of the Spirit breaks down the boundaries between Jews and Samaritans and enables a new community to form from the two groups.

John's placement of the meeting between the Samaritan woman and Jesus in a key position within the gospel suggests that the mission to Samaritans is a subject of importance to his audience. The woman's favourable response to Jesus presents her as a model of faith who represents the discipleship of Samaritans. James Purvis proposes that some of the traditions of John's Gospel developed in Samaria or Samaria-Galilee since John portrays Jesus as the prophet-Messiah and he has a negative attitude towards the Temple in Jerusalem.[59] Early Christians outwith these areas, however, may have held hopes of an eschatological prophet and they may also have rejected the Temple in Jerusalem. Many Samaritans had left Samaria and settled in the major cities of the Graeco-Roman world.[60] John's positive portrayal of the Samaritan woman suggests that some Samaritans may have lived in the vicinity of the Johannine Christians and that they may have become members of the Johannine community.

Conclusion

John portrays the Samaritan woman as an example of faith and discipleship who is willing to ignore social and religious boundaries in order to engage in conversation with Jesus at the well at Sychar. Initially, she does not understand Jesus but she recognizes Jesus's identity in the course of their conversation. She responds positively to Jesus's offer of 'living water' by pointing out the hardship of her life and the necessity of her frequent journeys to the well to draw water. In the course of the conversation, Jesus reveals his knowledge of her past marriages and her current relationship. The Samaritan woman recognizes Jesus as a prophet, and she then wonders if Jesus could be the Messiah. John depicts the Samaritan woman as the first person to whom Jesus reveals his identity with an 'I am' saying (4.26). The woman is portrayed in the role of a missionary, since she encourages other people from her town to believe in Jesus.

In the course of the conversation between the Samaritan woman and Jesus, the woman grows in her understanding of Jesus's identity and the scope of his mission. John portrays the Samaritan woman as a representative of Samaritans who are attracted to Christianity. Jesus seeks Samaritans as true worshippers of God, and his gift of 'living water' alludes to the Spirit which is the eschatological gift of the new creation. The account of the Samaritan woman suggests that Samaritans have joined

---

[59] J. D. Purvis, 'The Fourth Gospel and the Samaritans', *NovT* 17 (1975): 161–98.
[60] B. Lifshitz and J. Schiby ('Une Synagogue Samaritaine à Thessalonique', *RB* 75 (1968): 268–78) note that Samaritans moved to Alexandria in the time of Pompey, and a large Samaritan community developed in that city. A Samaritan community was located in Rome, and there is evidence of distinctive Samaritan communities in Asia Minor and Greece.

the Johannine community. The conversation between the woman and Jesus draws attention to the shared descent of Jesus and the Samaritan woman, and it examines the question of the correct location of the Temple. Jesus prophesies that a time is coming when true worshippers will no longer worship on Mount Gerizim or in Jerusalem but will worship 'in spirit and in truth' (4.21-24).

John's account of the meeting between the Samaritan woman and Jesus also indicates that John is aware of the issue of gender within the early church. At the beginning of the passage John draws attention to the differences between the Samaritan woman and Jesus in terms of gender and race (4.2-9). The Samaritan woman, moreover, shows greater understanding of Jesus's mission than the male disciples who are surprised to find Jesus talking to a woman (4.27). It is possible that the disciples represent some early Christians who are critical of the community's mission to Samaritans. John may be aware of the criticism of the Samaritan mission in some Jewish-Christian communities (cf. Mt. 10.5-6). Some Jewish Christians may have regarded Samaritans as gentiles whereas the conversation between the Samaritan woman and Jesus focuses on the shared traditions of Samaritans and Jews. Jesus, moreover, takes the opportunity of the woman's return to her town to discuss the Samaritan mission. The Samaritan woman has a role in the initiation of the mission to the people of her town but the disciples will also have a role in bringing the mission to completion. John's account of the meeting of Jesus and the Samaritan woman serves to give authority to the mission of the Johannine community to Samaritans.

4

Martha and Mary of Bethany (11.1-44)

Introduction

The third account featuring women in John's Gospel is concerned with two sisters, Martha and Mary of Bethany. These women are friends of Jesus, and they send word to him when their brother, Lazarus, falls ill. Jesus, however, delays his journey to Bethany, and by the time he arrives Lazarus has been dead for four days. Nevertheless, the sisters remain faithful to Jesus, and they express their belief that if he had been present Lazarus would not have died. Martha confesses her faith in Jesus as 'the Messiah, the Son of God, the one coming into the world' (11.27). Mary, moreover, leads other mourners to Jesus, and they witness the raising of Lazarus from death. Many believe in Jesus, but some go to the Pharisees to let them know about Jesus's miracle and on the basis of this report the religious authorities decide to arrest Jesus and put him to death. The raising of Lazarus is the final sign of Jesus, and it foreshadows his own death and resurrection. Martha and Mary's message to Jesus initiates this sign, and their presence at Lazarus's tomb looks forward to the prominent role of women as witnesses to the events of the Passion Narrative.

Martha and Mary are not unique to John's Gospel, since they also feature in a narrative in Luke's Gospel in which Martha complains to Jesus that she has all the work to do while her sister Mary sits at the feet of Jesus listening to his teaching (10.38-42). John's portrayal of Martha and Mary shares some similarities with Luke's account of the two sisters. In Luke's Gospel Martha is distracted by 'much serving' (πολλὴν διακονίαν, 10.40), and in John's Gospel Martha 'serves' at a dinner for Jesus in Bethany (διηκόνει, 12.2). Luke presents Martha as the more active sister who is busy serving, and John depicts her as the first sister to leave the house to approach Jesus while Mary remains at home. In Luke's Gospel Mary sits at the feet of Jesus (10.39), and in John's Gospel Mary sits at home with the mourners (11.20). When Mary meets Jesus, she falls at his feet (11.32), and she later anoints Jesus's feet with expensive perfume (12.1-8). The similarities between the gospels raise the question of whether John has knowledge of Luke's Gospel.[1] There are, however, a greater number of differences between the descriptions of Martha and Mary in the two gospels. In Luke's Gospel Martha protests

---

[1] C. K. Barrett (*The Gospel according to St. John: An Introduction with Commentary and Notes on the Greek Text*, 2nd edn (London: SPCK, 1978), 46) suggests that John has read Luke's Gospel.

that she has been left with all the work, but Jesus replies that Mary has chosen the better part, which will not be taken away from her (10.42). Martha is criticized for her household concerns whereas Mary is depicted in a discipleship role since she listens to Jesus's teaching.[2] On the other hand John does not portray one sister more favourably than the other, and he presents both women as models of discipleship. John highlights the Christological confession of Martha, but Mary also has a discipleship role because she anoints Jesus as the Messiah (12.1-8). John's presentation of the women contains considerable differences from that of Luke, and it is probable that his account reflects the independent Johannine tradition.

John's narrative also differs from the account of Martha and Mary in Luke's Gospel since Luke contains no reference to the women's brother, Lazarus. Barnabas Lindars, however, proposes that John is responsible for the addition of the account of the raising of Lazarus to the tradition about the two sisters.[3] Lindars notes that Luke contains a parable which compares the fate of a rich man to that of a beggar called Lazarus (16.19-31). In this parable Lazarus dies, and he is taken to be with Abraham in heaven whereas the rich man suffers in Hades. The rich man asks Abraham to permit Lazarus to return from the dead to warn his brothers of their fate. Lazarus, however, is a popular name in the first century, and there are no clear connections between the parable and John's narrative, since Lazarus is not a beggar and he does not describe his experience of death. The different presentations of Lazarus in the two gospels suggest that John has not been influenced by Luke's parable.

John's account focuses on the conversation between Martha and Jesus but the narrative begins with a description of Mary as the woman who anoints Jesus's feet with perfume and dries them with her hair (11.2). This reference is puzzling because Mary does not anoint Jesus until after the raising of Lazarus. Raymond Brown argues that this verse has been added by an editor because John elsewhere does not use the term 'Lord' of Jesus in third person narrative.[4] As Ernst Haenchen notes, however, John has a tendency to introduce characters with a description of an action that they are known for as in the portrayal of Nicodemus (7.50; 19.34), Caiaphas (11.49; 18.14), Judas (6.71) and 'the disciple whom Jesus loved' (13.23).[5] On the other hand John's reference to Mary has led Richard Bauckham to propose that John expects his audience to know Mark's account of an anonymous woman who anoints Jesus in Bethany (Mk 14.3-9). He suggests that John has added a reference to Mary in order to provide the identity of the woman.[6] Bauckham's argument is not convincing since John's reference to Mary

---

[2] For a more positive interpretation of the role of Martha, see L. Alexander, 'Sisters in Adversity: Retelling Martha's Story', in *Women in the Biblical Tradition*, edited by G. J. Brooke, Studies in Women & Religion 31 (Lewiston: Edwin Mellen Press, 1992), 167–86. Alexander points out that Luke includes a critical interpretation of the service of Martha but he gives a positive presentation of the service of the women who follow Jesus (8.2-3). As Alexander observes, Martha provides a meal which is needed for the well-being of Jesus and his disciples.

[3] B. Lindars, *The Gospel of John*, NCBC (London: Marshall, Morgan & Scott, 1972), 385.

[4] R. E. Brown, *The Gospel according to John*, 2 vols, AB29-29A (Garden City, NY: Doubleday, 1966–70), 1:423.

[5] E. Haenchen, *John 2* (Philadelphia, PA: Fortress, 1984), 57.

[6] R. Bauckham, 'John for Readers of Mark', in *The Gospels for All Christians: Rethinking the Gospel Audiences*, edited by R. Bauckham (Edinburgh: T&T Clark, 1997), 161–9.

of Bethany describes her act of anointing Jesus and then drying his feet with her hair (11.2), whereas Mark refers to an anonymous woman who anoints Jesus's head. If John wished to remind his audience of Mark's narrative, there would have been no need for him to mention the differences between the accounts.

It is more probable that John has added a reference to Mary of Bethany before the raising of Lazarus in order to draw attention to her role as the one who anoints Jesus. John's references to Mary's act of anointing Jesus create a frame around the account of the raising of Lazarus. This literary technique may be seen in Mark's Gospel which includes several examples of intercalation (3.20-35; 5.21-43; 11.12-25; 14.1-11). In these examples the outer verses frequently shed light on the interpretation of the inner narrative, and in our passage the references to Mary's act of anointing Jesus point to his identity as the Messiah. John places the references to the anointing of Jesus around the account of Martha's confession of faith in Jesus as the Messiah and Son of God. John's account of the raising of Lazarus thus associates Jesus's identity as the Messiah with his power to overcome death. John portrays Mary's act of anointing as a dramatization of Martha's confession that Jesus is the Messiah and Son of God.

John develops his narrative in a series of scenes which conclude with the anointing of Jesus by Mary of Bethany. John's presentation of the conversations between the sisters and Jesus is reminiscent of the earlier conversations between women and Jesus in the account of the mother of Jesus at the wedding at Cana (2.1-11) and the meeting between the Samaritan woman and Jesus (4.1-42). These conversations illustrate the faith of women and their understanding of Jesus's identity. In this chapter we will examine John's portrayal of Martha and Mary in relation to his understanding of discipleship. John gives an extended conversation between Jesus and Martha in which she recognizes Jesus as the Messiah and Son of God. In an earlier account Peter has recognized Jesus as 'the Holy One of God' (6.69) but Martha expresses her faith in Jesus as 'the Messiah, the Son of God, the one coming into the world' (11.27). In the synoptic tradition the confession of Peter that Jesus is the Messiah has a central place (Mt. 16.13-20; Mk 8.27-30; Lk. 9.18-20), but in John's Gospel Martha's confession of faith shows greater insight into Jesus's identity than that of Peter. John's presentation of Martha thus raises the question of why John places more emphasis on her confession than on Peter's confession. In the course of this chapter we will examine the role of Martha's confession of faith within John's Gospel. The request of Martha and Mary, moreover, prompts Jesus to carry out his final sign. The raising of Lazarus illustrates the power of Jesus over death, and it looks forward to the resurrection of the dead at the end of the age. We will assess the role of Martha and Mary in relation to the Johannine theme of new creation. Finally, we will examine the significance of John's portrayal of Martha and Mary for our understanding of the role of women in the Johannine community.

The portrayal of Martha and Mary

Martha, Mary and Lazarus are described as friends of Jesus but John does not say how they met him or the length of time that they have been his friends. In the synoptic gospels Jesus visits Bethany on his way to Jerusalem to celebrate Passover. Jesus is facing danger, and he stays in Bethany in order to avoid arrest (Mt. 26.6; Mk 14.3). In John's Gospel Martha, Mary and Lazarus may provide hospitality to Jesus and his disciples during their visits to Jerusalem. The sisters and brother live together, and there is no reference to their parents. The women do not appear to be married, and they have no children. This situation is unusual since women usually married at a young age, and men were expected to marry when they could provide for a wife and family.[7]

There is evidence, however, that some of the women who followed Jesus were not married. In the gospels there are no references to the husbands of Mary Magdalene (Mk 15.40), Salome (Mk 15.40) and Susanna (Lk. 8.3). John the Baptist, Jesus and Paul also do not appear to have married. On the other hand some of Jesus's disciples such as Peter were married, and we have an account of the healing of Peter's mother-in-law in the synoptic gospels (Mt. 8.14-15; Mk 1.29-31; Lk. 4.38-39). Paul mentions that Peter and Jesus's brothers travelled on mission with their wives (1 Cor. 9.5). We have only a few sources which refer to celibate groups at this time including the Qumran community, and the Therapeutae, a male and a female celibate community in Egypt, which is described by Philo (*Vit. Cont.* 68-69). Martha, Mary and Lazarus, however, live together as a family in the village of Bethany rather than as members of a community who are secluded from the world.

At the beginning of the narrative Martha and Mary are in a vulnerable situation because their brother has died. The women do not appear to have any other male relatives since they are comforted only by mourners from Jerusalem. In patriarchal society women frequently depend on male relatives for financial support and social protection. In our passage Martha and Mary seek out the help of Jesus who takes the place of a male relative in patriarchal society. The women are portrayed in the midst of their grief but they demonstrate initiative in contacting Jesus. John depicts the independence of Martha who leaves the house and who confesses her faith in Jesus. In John 12, Mary also shows courage since she breaks social conventions in order to anoint Jesus's feet at the dinner in Bethany. John presents women who overcome difficult situations and who are willing to break social conventions.

John portrays Martha, Mary and Lazarus as disciples who live in one place and who are not part of Jesus's itinerant mission. His account explores the discipleship of women whose faith in Jesus is expressed in the midst of their daily lives. This situation differs from the emphasis on the itinerant mission of Jesus in the synoptic gospels. In the synoptic gospels Jesus calls twelve male disciples to accompany him on his mission (Mt. 10.1-4; Mk 3.13-19; Lk. 6.12-16) but John places less emphasis on the twelve disciples chosen by Jesus. Many people who demonstrate faith in Jesus are not members of the Twelve such as Nathanael (1.43-51), the Samaritan woman (4.1-42), Martha and Mary, and the blind man (9.1-41). In the synoptic gospels women are

---

[7] T. Ilan (*Jewish Women in Greco-Roman Palestine* (Peabody, MA: Hendrickson, 1996), 64–5) has found only one reference to an unmarried woman in her analysis of inscriptions which relate to Jewish women in Graeco-Roman Palestine. This reference may be found in a reconstructed Greek funeral inscription from Tiberias (CII no. 984) which describes a seventy-five-year-old woman as unmarried (ἄγα(μον)). The date of this inscription, however, is uncertain.

members of the group of disciples who follow Jesus on his mission (Mt. 27.55-56; Mk 15.40-41; Lk. 8.1-3) but John highlights the roles of the women who meet Jesus in the villages where they live. In his study of the Jesus movement Gerd Theissen separates the early church into wandering charismatics and settled supporters.[8] Martha, Mary and Lazarus are depicted as a group of supporters of Jesus who live in one place. John's presentation of the faith of women who live in Bethany may reflect his own experience of members of a community who are located in a specific area.

John's concern for the development of the faith of the women who live within local communities may also be seen in the account of the meeting of Jesus with the Samaritan woman. The Samaritans who come to faith in Jesus remain in their own town, and Jesus spends some time with them there. Martha and Mary are able to represent members of John's community who live in a settled community. In our account John focuses on the portrayal of Martha and Mary who act independently without the support of male relatives. John's presentation does not depict women in subordinate roles to men. In our narrative women are the main characters, and Lazarus has a minor role. The sisters initiate Jesus's final sign by sending word to him about Lazarus's illness, and we are not told anything about Lazarus's experience of being raised to life. John emphasizes the faith of Martha and Mary, and their discipleship role in initiating the final sign of Jesus in which he raises their brother from death.

The conversation between Martha and Jesus

At the beginning of the narrative Martha and Mary speak with one voice by sending word to Jesus to let him know that their brother is ill (κύριε, ἴδε ὃν φιλεῖς ἀσθενεῖ, 11.3). The sisters do not make a direct request to Jesus to heal Lazarus but there is an implicit expectation that Jesus will intervene. John's account of their indirect request is reminiscent of his portrayal of the mother of Jesus who pointed out that there was no wine left at the wedding at Cana (2.3). The women bring situations of human need to Jesus's attention and display faith that he will intervene. In both accounts Jesus does not immediately respond to the women's requests but he later assists them. Jesus has already healed the son of the royal official (4.46-54), the man at the pool of Bethesda (5.1-9) and the blind man (9.1-12). John's presentation of these healing accounts raises the audience's expectations that Jesus will also heal Lazarus. The previous narratives, moreover, feature the healing of people whom Jesus did not know, whereas Martha, Mary and Lazarus are his friends, and Lazarus is described as 'one whom Jesus loves' (11.3).

John does not begin his narrative with an account of the meeting between Jesus and Martha. He prepares his audience for this meeting by narrating an account of a conversation between Jesus and the disciples in which Jesus expresses his understanding of the events. Jesus does not respond at once to the sisters' request for his help, and he stays two days longer before leaving for Bethany. His reluctance to

---

[8] G. Theissen, *The First Followers of Jesus: A Sociological Analysis of the Earliest Christianity* (London: SCM, 1978).

visit Lazarus immediately is surprising because of his friendship with the family. Jesus tells his disciples that Lazarus's illness will not end in death since it is 'for the glory of God so that the Son of God may be glorified through it' (11.4). John's presentation of Jesus's speech places the account of the raising of Lazarus in the context of the revelation of God's glory. His account of the conversation between Jesus and his disciples draws attention to the danger that Jesus faces by returning to Jerusalem. Thomas's willingness to die with Jesus points to the mounting tensions between Jesus and the religious leaders. Their opposition to Jesus has increased throughout the gospel, and plans have been made to arrest Jesus (7.32; 10.39). In ch. 9 the blind man and his parents were questioned by the Pharisees, and the man's parents were afraid that they would be excluded from the synagogue (9.22). At the beginning of ch. 11, John relates the account of the raising of Lazarus to the increasing tensions between Jesus and his opponents, since Jesus can only go to Bethany by placing his own life in danger.

After the account of the conversation between Jesus and his disciples, John focuses on the conversation between Jesus and Martha (11.17-27). John does not refer to the presence of the disciples during Jesus's conversation with Martha. This conversation is reminiscent of the earlier meeting between Jesus and the Samaritan woman in which the disciples had gone away to buy food, and Jesus met the woman alone. In this way John focuses on the conversations between Jesus and individual women. In our passage John depicts the development of Martha's understanding of Jesus in the course of their conversation. When Martha first meets Jesus, she addresses him, 'Lord, if you had been here, my brother would not have died' (11.21). John's account of Martha's speech echoes his presentation of the earlier conversation between Jesus and his disciples. In this conversation Jesus said that he was glad for the sake of his disciples that 'he was not there' so that they may believe (11.15). Martha's words contain an implicit reproach that Jesus has not arrived in time to heal Lazarus. Nevertheless, she expresses her belief in the power of Jesus to help her. Martha does not directly ask Jesus for help but she expresses her faith that God will grant Jesus whatever he asks (11.22). The phrase 'whatever you ask' suggests that she still has hopes that Jesus is able to intervene in some way.

John develops the conversation between Jesus and Martha by employing ambiguous language. Jesus replies to Martha with an ambiguous statement, 'Your brother will rise again' (11.23). Martha interprets Jesus's statement as a reference to the raising of Lazarus at the time of the general resurrection of the dead, 'I know that he will rise in the resurrection on the last day' (11.24). The phrase 'the last day' recalls the eschatological expectations of the last days in the Old Testament (ἐν ἐσχάταις ἡμέραις, cf. Isa. 2.2; Mic. 4.1). Martha's response reflects the traditional Jewish belief in the resurrection at the end of the age. Jesus, however, has the power to raise Lazarus in the present. Martha does not fully understand Jesus's saying because she does not know that Jesus intends to raise her brother from death. John's portrayal of Martha's response is similar to his account of the initial response of the Samaritan woman to Jesus (4.7-26). At first the Samaritan woman did not understand the significance of Jesus's offer of 'living water' but her need for water led her to respond positively to Jesus. In our passage Martha's loss of her brother leads her to recognize Jesus's identity.

John, moreover, depicts Martha as a recipient of Jesus's revelation of his divine identity with the use of an 'I am' saying. Jesus's revelatory statement, 'I am the resurrection and the life' (11.25) alludes to his own role as the agent of the resurrection. In Jewish tradition God raises the dead, and the Messiah is not expected to raise the dead. The Qumran text 4Q451, however, associates an anointed prophet with the resurrection of the dead in the end-time. John Collins notes that this text combines a description of the anointed prophet in Isaiah 61 with a reference to the raising of the dead.[9] Collins proposes that God raises the dead through the agency of an anointed eschatological prophet who is either Elijah or like Elijah. He rightly observes that Jesus links his ability to raise the dead with his identity as the Messiah in the synoptic gospels (cf. Mt. 11.2-6; Lk. 7.18-23). In our narrative the events of the end-time break into the present world through the life-giving power of Jesus.

In Jewish tradition God has the power to raise the dead, and in our passage Jesus is the one who raises Lazarus from death. John presents a unity of action between Jesus and the Father which is illustrated by Jesus's later saying, 'I and the Father are one' (10.30).[10] The 'I am' sayings express the divinity of Jesus (6.35; 8.12; 10.9, 11; 14.6; 15.1), and in our account Jesus's divinity is revealed by his act of raising Lazarus. As Brown notes, the predicates of the 'I am' sayings express the gifts which Jesus brings humanity.[11] In earlier passages Jesus brings 'living water' (ὕδωρ ζῶν, 4.10), and he identifies himself as 'the bread of life' (ὁ ἄρτος τῆς ζωῆς, 6.35). These terms express the nature of the abundant life that Jesus offers humanity (ἵνα ζωὴν ἔχωσιν καὶ περισσὸν ἔχωσιν, 10.10). Jesus brings living water, bread, light and life, and in our passage he is identified with the resurrection on account of his power to raise the dead.

John, moreover, employs questions to focus the attention of the audience on the issue of Jesus's identity. In our narrative Jesus directly addresses Martha and asks her if she believes that whoever has faith in him will never die (11.26). His question recalls his question to the blind man, 'Do you believe in the Son of Man?' (9.35). The Johannine Jesus not only addresses Martha but also speaks to the members of John's audience. Jesus's question is directed to all women and men who are confronted with a decision whether or not to confess their faith in him. Martha is an example of discipleship since she makes a full confession of faith, 'Yes Lord, I believe that you are the Messiah, the Son of God, the one coming into the world' (11.27).

Not all commentators, however, regard Martha as an example of faith. Francis Moloney proposes that Martha's use of the perfect tense of the verb πιστεύω (believe) indicates that she had come to faith before the revelation of Jesus in vv. 25-26.[12] Moloney argues that Martha has always believed that Jesus is the Messiah and Son of God, and he interprets her statement of faith as a reflection of her view of Jesus as a miracle-worker and her belief in the resurrection on the last

---

[9] J. J. Collins, *The Scepter and the Star: The Messiahs of the Dead Sea Scrolls and Other Ancient Literature* (Garden City, NY: Doubleday, 1995), 117–23.

[10] M. W. G. Stibbe, 'A Tomb with a View: John 11.1-44 in Narrative-Critical Perspective', *NTS* 40 (1994): 45.

[11] Brown, *John*, 1:434.

[12] F. J. Moloney, 'Can Everyone Be Wrong? A Reading of John 11.1-12.8', *NTS* 49 (2003): 513–14.

day. On the other hand C. K. Barrett points out that the use of the perfect tense of πιστεύω (believe) is a characteristic feature of John's gospel (3.18; 6.69; 16.27; 20.29).[13] As Barrett argues, this verb implies that an individual has responded to revelation and is in a state of faith. He rightly observes that Martha's response has the grammatical form of a credal confession.[14] John portrays Martha as a representative of a disciple who is challenged to confess her own faith in Jesus. The conversation between Martha and Jesus concludes with her confession of faith.[15] John presents Martha's confession of faith as a direct response to Jesus's revelation that he is the resurrection and the life.

Martha's confession, moreover, recalls earlier confessions of faith which are associated with the male disciples. At the beginning of the gospel Andrew recognized Jesus as the Messiah (1.41), and Nathanael described Jesus as the Son of God (1.49). Moloney proposes that the titles used by the disciples (1.41, 49) express 'limited faith'.[16] He notes that Jesus prophesies that Nathanael will see greater things such as the angels ascending and descending on the Son of Man (1.51). Contrary to Moloney, however, the titles 'Messiah' and 'Son of God' are portrayed as correct understandings of Jesus's identity. At the end of ch. 20 John states that these things have been written in order that the audience may believe that Jesus is 'the Messiah, the Son of God', and as a result receive life in his name (20.31). John's association of the title 'Messiah' with the title 'Son of God' indicates the divinity of the Messiah.[17] Martha thus expresses a statement of faith which reflects the purposes of the gospel.

Martha's confession of Jesus as 'the Messiah, the Son of God, the one coming into the world' defines the nature of Jesus's identity as the Messiah. As Martinus de Boer argues, the title 'Son of God' was initially regarded as a designation for a royal Messiah in Johannine thought but later became associated with the divinity of Jesus as the Christology of the community developed.[18] The titles 'Messiah' and 'Son of God' also appear together in the trial of Jesus before the Sanhedrin in the synoptic gospels (Mt. 26.63; Mk 14.61; Lk. 22.67-70) but the title 'the one coming into the world' is particularly associated with John's Gospel. After the feeding of the five thousand the people acclaimed Jesus as 'the prophet the one coming into the world' (ὁ προφήτης ὁ ἐρχόμενος εἰς τὸν κόσμον, 6.14). This verse suggests that the title 'the one coming into

---

[13] Barrett, *St. John*, 306–7.
[14] Barrett, *St. John*, 397.
[15] D. A. Lee ('Martha and Mary: Levels of Characterization in Luke and John', in *Characters and Characterization in the Gospel of John*, edited by C. W. Skinner; LNTS 461 (London: T&T Clark, 2012), 205) argues that Martha does grow in her understanding of Jesus. Lee points out that characters who engage in conversations with Jesus tend to move 'towards either a deeper understanding or an increasing alienation'.
[16] Moloney, 'Can Everyone Be Wrong?' 514.
[17] J. Ashton (*Understanding the Fourth Gospel*, 2nd edn (Oxford: Oxford University Press, 2007), 147–50) argues that the title 'Messiah' does not engage John's theological interest to the same extent as the themes of Jesus's relationship with God, judgement and revelation. Ashton interprets the title 'Messiah' in relation to the early stage of the Johannine mission, and he interprets the divinity of Jesus in relation to the concept of divine agency. The importance of the title 'Messiah', however, is indicated in the references to the synagogue ban (9.22; 12.42; 16.2), and in the statement that belief in Jesus as Messiah and Son of God brings life to human beings (20.31).
[18] M. C. de Boer, *Johannine Perspectives on the Death of Jesus* (Kampen: Kok Pharos, 1996), 90, 113–16.

the world' is connected with expectations of the appearance of a prophet like Moses (cf. Deut. 18.15, 18). As D. Moody Smith observes, this title may also be linked to expectations of the Messiah.[19] In the synoptic gospels the disciples of John the Baptist asked Jesus if he is 'the one who is to come' (σὺ εἶ ὁ ἐρχόμενος, Mt. 11.3; Lk. 7.19). In John's Gospel the Samaritan woman referred to a Messiah who 'is coming' (οἶδα ὅτι Μεσσίας ἔρχεται, 4.25), and at the entry of Jesus into Jerusalem he was acclaimed as 'the one who comes in the name of the Lord' in the words of Ps. 118.26 (εὐλογημένος ὁ ἐρχόμενος ἐν ὀνόματι κυρίου, 12.13; cf. Mt. 21.9; Mk 11.9; Lk. 19.38).

In John's Gospel, moreover, Jesus is described as the one who has been sent by God into the world, and he identifies himself as the one who comes from above or from heaven (ὁ ἄνωθεν ἐρχόμενος, ὁ ἐκ τοῦ οὐρανοῦ ἐρχόμενος, 3.31). This title points to the pre-existence of Jesus and the distinctive Christology of John's Gospel. In the prologue John identifies Jesus with the light that is 'coming into the world' (ἐρχόμενον εἰς τὸν κόσμον, 1.9). This description expresses the cosmic dimension of the role of Jesus. The love of God for the world initiates the sending of Jesus into the world, and Jesus is identified as the one who comes to bring salvation to the world (cf. 3.16-17). John associates the title 'the one who comes into the world' with the origin of Jesus in heaven. He draws attention to Jesus's purpose in coming into the world by Jesus's use of 'I have come' statements (ἐγὼ ἦλθον ἵνα ζωὴν ἔχωσιν καὶ περισσὸν ἔχωσιν, 10.10; cf. 9.39; 12.27, 47; 18.37).

Martha's confession of faith expresses the Johannine understanding of Jesus's identity. Her confession consists of three titles, 'Messiah', 'Son of God' and 'the one coming into the world', which combine to express John's Christology. Martha's confession defines the title 'Messiah' in relation to Jesus's divine identity as the Son of God. John's use of the title 'the one coming into the world' relates the Messiahship of Jesus to the incarnation and to the cosmic conflict at the heart of the gospel. Jesus has come to cast out the 'ruler of the world' (12.31; 14.30; 16.11).[20] John associates Martha's confession of faith with the faith of the Johannine community. He is writing to encourage his audience to believe in Jesus as the Messiah and Son of God with the result that those who believe may 'receive life in his name' (20.31). The conversation between Jesus and Martha concludes with Martha's statement of faith. As Colleen Conway rightly observes, John's account of Martha's confession of faith recalls the account of the conversation between Jesus and the Samaritan woman which concluded with the confession of the Samaritan townspeople who called Jesus 'the Saviour of the World' (4.42).[21] In our narrative John depicts Martha as an example of faith since she confesses her faith in Jesus as the Messiah and Son of God before his act of raising Lazarus from death. John presents Martha's confession before the raising of Lazarus because he wishes to demonstrate that those who believe in Jesus do not need to fear death.

---

[19] D. M. Smith, *John* (Nashville, TN: Abingdon, 1999), 223.
[20] For an analysis of the cosmic conflict within John's Gospel, see J. L. Kovacs, '"Now Shall the Ruler of This World Be Driven Out": Jesus' Death as Cosmic Battle in John 12:20-36', *JBL* 114 (1995): 227–47.
[21] C. M. Conway, *Men and Women in the Fourth Gospel: Gender and Johannine Characterization*, SBLDS 167 (Atlanta, GA: Society of Biblical Literature, 1999), 143.

The conversation between Mary and Jesus

After Martha's conversation with Jesus, she returns to her sister, Mary, to tell her that Jesus is calling her, and Mary now comes out to meet Jesus. John situates the conversation between Mary and Jesus (11.28-37) in the same location as the conversation between Martha and Jesus. The skilful literary structure of this narrative is stressed by Mary's repetition of the words which were previously spoken by Martha, 'Lord, if you had been here, my brother would not have died' (Κύριε, εἰ ἦς ὧδε οὐκ ἄν μου ἀπέθανεν ὁ ἀδελφός, 11.32). Mary repeats Martha's speech with the exception of the change of the position of the pronoun 'my' (μου). In Mary's speech the pronoun is placed before the verb 'he died' (ἀπέθανεν) rather than after 'brother' (Κύριε, εἰ ἦς ὧδε οὐκ ἄν ἀπέθανεν ὁ ἀδελφός μου, 11.21). John's placement of the pronoun stresses Mary's close relationship with Lazarus and her grief at the loss of his life.

John's repetition of the sisters' speech and his placement of the two conversations in the same location encourage his audience to compare the responses of each woman to the arrival of Jesus. Raymond Brown proposes that John places greater emphasis on Martha's meeting with Jesus than that of Mary, and he suggests that the character of Mary does not add much to the narrative.[22] On the other hand Francis Moloney argues that Mary is portrayed as the more faithful sister since she is the one who anoints Jesus.[23] Moloney suggests that the reference to Mary at the beginning of ch. 11 is intended to encourage John's audience to look forward to the appearance of Mary. He rightly interprets Mary's act of falling at Jesus's feet as an expression of worship. Mary makes no further request to Jesus whereas Martha and Jesus continue their conversation. Nevertheless, Mary's silence does not indicate that she is less faithful than her sister. The meeting of Martha and Jesus focuses on Martha's recognition of Jesus's identity and her confession of faith. The account featuring Mary centres on the expression of her emotions, and Mary demonstrates her devotion to Jesus by her action of falling at his feet, weeping.

In the course of the narrative Jesus responds in different ways to the speech and actions of the sisters. Martha's speech leads Jesus to reveal his identity with an 'I am' saying whereas Mary's expression of grief prompts an emotional reaction in Jesus. When Jesus sees Mary and the mourners weep, he becomes 'deeply moved in spirit and troubled' (ἐνεβριμήσατο τῷ πνεύματι καὶ ἐτάραξεν ἑαυτόν, 11.33). John's use of the verb ἐμβριμάομαι (deeply moved) associates Jesus's strong emotions with anger. In Mark's Gospel this verb occurs in the description of the people who criticize the woman who anoints Jesus with expensive perfume (ἐνεβριμῶντο αὐτῇ, 14.5). Barnabas Lindars proposes that this verb indicates anger because it is used in the account of the healing of the leper in which the healed man is sternly sent away (ἐμβριμησάμενος αὐτῷ, Mk 1.43; cf. Mt. 9.30).[24] In addition, Rudolf Schnackenburg suggests that Jesus is angry at the lack of faith of Mary and of the mourners.[25] On the other hand Raymond

---

[22] Brown, *John*, 1:433.
[23] F. J. Moloney, *Signs and Shadows: Reading John 5-12* (Minneapolis, MN: Fortress, 1996), 166.
[24] B. Lindars, 'Rebuking the Spirit: A New Analysis of the Lazarus Story of John 11', *NTS* 38 (1992): 89–104.
[25] R. Schnackenburg, *The Gospel according to St. John*, 3 vols (London: Burns & Oates, 1968–82), 2:336.

Brown argues that Jesus is angry at the presence of disease which he associates with the power of Satan.[26] Brown's interpretation is more convincing because Jesus shares the grief of Mary and the mourners. John's presentation of Jesus's anger reflects the apocalyptic world view of the gospel. Jesus is engaged in a conflict with the 'ruler of the world' (12.31; 14.30; 16.11), and he has come to conquer the power of death.

John's use of the second verb ταράσσω (trouble, disturb), however, suggests that Jesus is greatly distressed. John employs this verb in several passages which describe intense emotions. In John 12 Jesus cites one of the Psalms of the Righteous Sufferer 'my soul is troubled' (ἡ ψυχή μου τετάρακται, 12.27; cf. Ps. 42.5), and in his Farewell Discourse Jesus is described as 'troubled in spirit' (ἐταράχθη τῷ πνεύματι, 13.21). In the Farewell Discourse, John employs the same verb in the exhortation of Jesus to his disciples that they should not be distressed by his departure from the world (μὴ ταρασσέσθω ὑμῶν ἡ καρδία, 14.1, 27). These passages suggest that Jesus's strong emotions reflect his compassion at the suffering of human beings who are subject to the forces of death.

In our passage, moreover, Jesus breaks down and cries when he sees Mary and the other mourners weep. The sight of their grief leads Jesus to share their sorrow, and his response aligns him with human suffering. John depicts a progression in Jesus's emotional response from anger at the power of disease to anguish at the suffering of human beings. John's portrayal of Jesus in our narrative differs from his characteristic presentation of Jesus as someone who is in control of his emotions. Throughout the gospel Jesus heals individuals, and he is able to raise Lazarus from the dead but in this account his grief hints at his powerlessness. As William Temple suggests, Jesus's signs are not performed without a cost to him.[27] Human beings suffer from illnesses and face death, and the transience of life is overcome only through the death and resurrection of Jesus. John's presentation of this narrative recalls the transformation of water into wine at the wedding at Cana in which Jesus's reference to his 'hour' (2.4) points forward to his passion, and the imagery of wine foreshadows the blood which will flow from his side at the time of his death (19.34). John emphasizes that Jesus's gift of eternal life comes about through the suffering of Jesus and the loss of his life.

In our narrative Mary expresses her devotion to Jesus in the time of her grief at her brother's death. She acts as a representative of those who place their trust in Jesus in times of suffering. Mary's grief prompts the expression of Jesus's own sorrow at the suffering in the world. Jesus's response to Mary demonstrates his compassion and his willingness to share in the suffering of humanity. John portrays Mary as a model of discipleship since her example encourages the members of John's audience to share their own suffering with Jesus. Mary also has a discipleship role because she is instrumental in leading the mourners to Jesus. When the mourners see her leave the house, they believe that she is going to the tomb to weep there, and they set out to accompany her (11.31). John's presentation of Mary may be compared to his portrayal of the Samaritan woman who led the people of her town to Jesus (4.39-42). Mary, however, does not intend to lead the mourners to Jesus whereas the Samaritan woman

---

[26] Brown, *John*, 1:425–6, 435.
[27] W. Temple, *Readings in St. John's Gospel* (London: Macmillan, 1941), 184.

wanted to tell everyone about her meeting with Jesus. Jesus asks the mourners where they have placed Lazarus, and they reply, 'Lord, come and see' (κύριε, ἔρχου καὶ ἴδε, 11.34). Their words echo the language of the discipleship accounts in which Jesus called his disciples to 'come and see' Jesus (ἔρχεσθε καὶ ὄψεσθε, 1.39), and in which Philip told Nathanael to 'come and see' Jesus (ἔρχου καὶ ἴδε, 1.46). On this occasion the roles of the caller and the called are reversed, since Jesus journeys to the place of death and he weeps there (11.35). Some mourners interpret Jesus's weeping as an indication of the love which Jesus had for Lazarus but others wonder why Jesus could not have prevented Lazarus's death. The mourners believe that Jesus is able to heal but they do not expect him to be able to raise the dead.

In this section of the narrative Mary is portrayed more positively than Martha, since Martha appears to doubt Jesus's actions. When Jesus instructs the mourners to remove the stone from the tomb, Martha points out that there will be an odour because Lazarus has been dead for four days (11.39). Dorothy Lee argues that this verse is evidence that Martha does not fully believe in Jesus because she doubts the ability of Jesus to raise Lazarus from the dead.[28] Ruben Zimmermann, moreover, proposes that Martha's objection indicates that her confession of faith is incomplete because she has not accepted the necessity of death.[29] Zimmermann argues that John wishes to emphasize that the glorification of Jesus comes about through his death (cf. 12.24). Martha's objection, however, is a natural human response, and it highlights the miraculous ability of Jesus. Her doubts also give Jesus the opportunity to emphasize the importance of faith in his statement, 'Did I not say to you that if you believe you will see the glory of God' (11.40). As Conway points out, Jesus's question places the raising of Lazarus within the context of Jesus's earlier conversation with Martha and his declaration that he is the resurrection and the life (11.25).[30]

Martha has already confessed her faith in Jesus, and she continues to place her trust in him. In our passage Martha's initial faith is vindicated when Jesus raises Lazarus to life. In other narratives signs lead some characters to faith. Udo Schnelle rightly argues that the revelation of Jesus's glory in his signs has the power to evoke faith in the human beings who witness them.[31] At the wedding at Cana the glory of Jesus was revealed, and his disciples believed in him (2.11). The raising of Lazarus is also associated with revelation of the glory of Jesus and the human response of faith (11.40-42). Many people believe in Jesus, and these people are specifically linked to Mary (οἱ ἐλθόντες πρὸς τὴν Μαριάμ, 11.45). Jesus's sign, however, provokes a characteristic division in the crowd (cf. 7.31, 43; 8.40; 9.16; 10.19, 42), and some people go to the Pharisees to report what has happened. Throughout the gospel Jesus's signs reveal his identity to some people and conceal his identity from others. At the wedding at Cana

---

[28] D. A. Lee, *The Symbolic Narratives of the Fourth Gospel: The Interplay of Form and Meaning*, JSNTSup 95 (Sheffield: JSOT, 1994), 205–6.

[29] R. Zimmermann, 'The Narrative Hermeneutics in John 11. Learning with Lazarus How to Understand Death, Life, and Resurrection', in *The Resurrection of Jesus in the Gospel of John*, edited by C. R. Koester and R. Bieringer, WUNT 222 (Tübingen: Mohr Siebeck, 2008), 90–3.

[30] Conway, *Men and Women*, 150.

[31] U. Schnelle, *Antidocetic Christology in the Gospel of John: An Investigation of the Place of the Fourth Gospel in the Johannine School*, translated by L. M. Maloney (Minneapolis, MN: Fortress, 1992), 80–2.

the disciples witnessed the revelation of Jesus's glory but others were unaware that a sign had taken place. In John's Gospel the signs provide glimpses of Jesus's glory which looks forward to the final revelation of his glory at the crucifixion.

John's presentation of the two sisters highlights the suffering which is experienced by human beings when a loved one dies. The structure of the narrative encourages the members of John's audience to identify with the women in order to deepen their faith in the power of Jesus over death. Martha is an example of faith since she places her trust in Jesus, and he subsequently raises her brother from death. Mary's devotion to Jesus is indicated by the expression of her grief and her act of falling at Jesus's feet. John does not downplay the stark nature of human grief since Jesus also weeps when he sees Mary and the mourners crying. John depicts the faith of both women since Martha's confession of faith points to the divinity of Jesus, and Mary remains devoted to Jesus at the time of her grief at her brother's death. Martha's confession of faith illustrates the high Christology of the gospel, and Mary's grief prompts Jesus to reveal his emotions. In the following section we will assess the role of Martha's confession of faith within John's Gospel.

Martha's confession of faith

In John's Gospel Martha's confession of faith in Jesus as 'the Messiah, the Son of God, the one coming into the world' has a central position as the highest Christological confession which a human being expresses during Jesus's lifetime. At the end of the gospel Thomas confesses his faith in the risen Jesus as 'My Lord and my God' (20.28) but Martha expresses faith in Jesus before the resurrection. Martha's confession of faith takes place before the raising of Lazarus, and John thus associates Martha's confession with a sign that reveals Jesus's divinity. Martha's confession may be compared to the confession of Peter that Jesus is the Messiah in the synoptic tradition (Mt. 16.13-20; Mk 8.27-30; Lk. 9.18-20). Peter is regarded as the leading disciple of the twelve male disciples chosen by Jesus, and he is well known as a leader of the early church (Acts 2.14-42; 8.14-25; 11.1-18; 12.1-19; Gal. 2.11-14). The prominent role of Peter in early Christian tradition raises the question of why John places greater emphasis on the confession of Martha in his gospel.

In the synoptic gospels Peter's confession is presented as a turning point in the mission of Jesus. In Mark's Gospel, Jesus asks the disciples who they think he is, and Peter acts as the spokesperson for the disciples in his response, 'You are the Messiah' (8.29). In Matthew's Gospel, Peter recognizes Jesus as the 'Messiah, the Son of the living God' (Mt. 16.16), and in Luke's Gospel, Peter confesses Jesus as the 'Messiah of God' (Lk. 9.20). In each gospel, Peter's confession is followed by Jesus's predictions of his Passion (Mt. 16.21-23; Mk 8.31-33; Lk. 9.21-22). Matthew, however, develops the role of Peter, and he associates the confession of Peter with the ecclesiology of his gospel (16.13-20). In Matthew's Gospel, Jesus blesses Peter, and addresses him directly, stating that God has revealed this knowledge to Peter. Jesus calls Peter a 'rock', and Jesus prophesies that he will build his church on this rock (σὺ εἶ Πέτρος, καὶ ἐπὶ ταύτῃ τῇ πέτρᾳ οἰκοδομήσω μου τὴν ἐκκλησίαν, 16.18). In this saying the name 'Peter'

(Πέτρος) is highlighted as a cognate of the term 'rock' (πέτρα). Matthew emphasizes the future leadership role of Peter since Jesus tells Peter that he will be given the keys of the kingdom of heaven (16.19). As David Sim argues, Matthew's emphasis on the role of Peter links his gospel to the Petrine tradition, and Peter's position as a disciple gives authority to the teaching of Matthew's church.[32] Peter's confession of faith is the foundational confession of faith for Matthew's community.

The prominent role of Peter in the synoptic gospels raises the question of whether John downplays the role of Peter in his own gospel. In the synoptic gospels Peter recognizes Jesus as the Messiah but in John's Gospel he uses the title 'the Holy One of God' (6.69). The title 'the Holy One of God' only occurs in the Johannine account of the confession of Peter and in the synoptic account of the healing of a man with an unclean spirit who recognizes Jesus as 'the Holy One of God' (Mk 1.24; Lk. 4.34). C. K. Barrett argues that 'the Holy One of God' is a Messianic title, and he notes that Jesus addresses God as 'holy Father' (17.11).[33] It is probable, however, that John intends this title to have less Christological significance than the title, 'Messiah'. The title 'Messiah' is the title which is most frequently given to Jesus in John's Gospel. At the beginning of the gospel the disciples recognize Jesus as the Messiah (1.41). The question of whether Jesus is the Messiah is also one of the key issues in the conflicts between Jesus and his opponents (cf. 9.22; 12.42; 16.1-2). The end of the gospel emphasizes that those who believe that Jesus is the Messiah and Son of God receive life in his name (20.31).

In John's Gospel Martha's confession of faith contains higher Christology than the confession of Peter in the synoptic tradition. In the synoptic tradition Peter recognizes Jesus as the Messiah but Martha's confession defines the Messiahship of Jesus in terms of his incarnation (11.27). As Elisabeth Schüssler Fiorenza notes, Martha expresses the faith of the Johannine community whereas Peter confesses the faith of the Matthean community.[34] Martha's confession reflects the high Christology of John's Gospel. The synoptic gospels link the title 'Messiah' to the title 'Son of God'. John, however, goes further in associating both of these titles with the incarnation.

John's placement of Martha's confession in the account of Jesus's final sign draws attention to the importance of her confession. The raising of Lazarus is the culmination of Jesus's signs, and it reveals Jesus's power over death. Jesus's demonstration of his power to raise the dead is connected to his arrest and execution. This sign leads many people to believe in Jesus, and it prompts the plot of the religious leaders to put Jesus to death. On the other hand John places Peter's confession at an early stage of Jesus's mission. John's account of Peter's confession occurs after the account of the feeding of the five thousand and Jesus's act of walking on water (6.1-71). By the time John is writing, Peter has been martyred, and Petrine Christianity has developed in communities such as Matthew's community. The Johannine tradition has developed a higher Christology than that of Matthew's Gospel. John wishes to define Jesus's identity

---

[32] D. C. Sim, *The Gospel of Matthew and Christian Judaism: The History and Social Setting of the Matthean Community* (Edinburgh: T&T Clark, 1998), 196–9.

[33] Barrett, *St. John*, 307.

[34] E. Schüssler Fiorenza, *In Memory of Her: A Feminist Theological Reconstruction of Christian Origins*, 2nd edn (New York: Crossroad, 1995), 329–30.

as the Messiah in terms of his ability to raise the dead. Jesus is the Messiah and Son of God because he shares the power of God to bring life out of death.

John locates the confession of Martha in the midst of a family group of two sisters and a brother whereas Peter belongs to the group of twelve disciples. Martha, Mary and Lazarus represent the discipleship community who are known as sisters and brothers of Jesus. John thus wishes to associate his community's confession of faith within a settled community of women and men with whom his audience may identify. In the synoptic gospels Peter's confession is depicted as the confession of the twelve male disciples. In John's Gospel this confession is made by a woman which points to the importance of the faith of women within the Johannine tradition. Martha's confession of faith points forward beyond the time of the twelve disciples to the later faith of the women and men in the Johannine community.

Discipleship and Martha and Mary of Bethany

Martha and Mary demonstrate their trust in Jesus by sending word to him when their brother falls ill. John's presentation of Martha and Mary may encourage members of the Johannine community to identify with the family at Bethany. Martha and Mary are present at the raising of Lazarus, and they act as witnesses to the power of Jesus to bring life out of death. Gail O'Day points out that the narrative focuses on the conversations between Jesus and each sister.[35] As she observes, these conversations illustrate the human struggle to maintain faith in Jesus during a time of bereavement. Philip Esler and Ronald Piper, moreover, propose that Martha, Mary and Lazarus act as prototypes for the discipleship community, since this group demonstrates the identity and destiny of those who follow Jesus.[36] The sisters represent disciples who rely on Jesus's assistance and trust in his power to bring life out of death.

At the beginning of the narrative John establishes the close relationship between Jesus and the family at Bethany. John states that Jesus loved Martha, her sister and Lazarus (ἠγάπα δὲ ὁ Ἰησοῦς τὴν Μάρθαν καὶ τὴν ἀδελφὴν αὐτῆς καὶ τὸν Λάζαρον, 11.5). Jesus refers to Lazarus as 'our friend' (ὁ φίλος ἡμῶν, 11.11), thus linking him to the disciples who follow Jesus on his mission. The term 'friends' is a discipleship term within the Johannine tradition since Jesus calls the disciples his 'friends' in the Farewell Discourse (ὑμᾶς δὲ εἴρηκα φίλους, 15.15), and the members of the church are addressed as 'friends' in a later Johannine writing (ἀσπάζου τοὺς φίλους, 3 John 15). Wendy Sproston North notes that Jesus defines his commandment to his disciples to love one another in terms of his willingness to give his life for them (15.12-14).[37] As she points out, Jesus teaches his disciples that they must literally lay down their lives for one another as he lays down his life for his friends.

---

[35] G. R. O'Day, 'John', in *Women's Bible Commentary*, edited by C. A. Newsom and S. H. Ringe, exp. edn (Louisville, KY: Westminster John Knox, 1998), 387.
[36] P. F. Esler and R. Piper, *Lazarus, Mary and Martha: Social Scientific Approaches to the Gospel of John* (Minneapolis, MN: Fortress, 2006), 129–30.
[37] W. E. S. North, *The Lazarus Story within the Johannine Tradition*, JSNTSup 212 (Sheffield: Sheffield Academic Press, 2001), 49–57.

One of the puzzling features of the narrative is the description of Jesus's delay in going to help Lazarus. Jesus is unable to return to Judea immediately because he is constrained by God's timing. Nevertheless, the illness of Lazarus will not end in death but in the 'glory of God' (11.4). The conversation of Jesus and the disciples enables John to draw attention to the theological significance of this sign. After Lazarus has died, Jesus tells his disciples that he is glad for their sake that he was not there so that they may believe (11.14-15). John's account juxtaposes the glory of God with the experience of human suffering. Martha and Mary are distraught at the death of their brother but they must wait for Jesus to arrive. Jesus demonstrates that God has power over death, and the experience of suffering may be transformed into glory. The account of the raising of Lazarus connects faith in Jesus to the gift of eternal life and emphasizes that the disciples do not need to fear death.

Martha and Mary wait for Jesus to come to their assistance, and the account demonstrates that Jesus has the power to help those who place their trust in him. It is also possible that John relates the death of Jesus to questions of early Christians about the timing of the *parousia*. In several early Christian texts there are questions over the time when Jesus will return to earth. Some Christians worry about the fate of those who have died before the *parousia* as in 1 Thess. 4.13-18. At the beginning of our account, Jesus waits for two days before he goes to assist Martha and Mary (11.6). James Martin notes that the delay of Jesus in our passage may be interpreted as an allusion to his absence from his followers in the period following his death (11.21, 32, 37).[38] As Martin points out, the necessity of Jesus's departure is a key theme in his Farewell Discourse (cf. 16.7, 28). On the other hand Sandra Schneiders argues that John does not focus on the delay of the *parousia* but on the way that disciples are able to reconcile the gift of eternal life with the fact that members of the community die.[39] She proposes that the account is intended to strengthen the faith of the Johannine community who are concerned about the death of their members. Schneiders's argument is convincing because John's portrayal of Martha and Mary illustrates the importance of faith at the time of the death of a beloved brother.

In several respects Martha and Mary represent all those who lose a loved one through illness. John's account illustrates Jesus's gift of life which is experienced in the present and which will continue beyond death. It also highlights Jesus's compassion for the women and his distress at the grief of the mourners from Jerusalem. As Susan Hylen notes, Jesus's saying that he is the resurrection and the life indicates that the life which Jesus brings in the present is the same as the gift of eternal life which is traditionally associated with the end-time.[40] In other narratives Jesus offered the Samaritan woman 'living water' (4.10), and he identified himself as 'the bread of life' (6.35). He is portrayed as 'the light of the world' (8.12; 9.5) and 'the true vine' (15.1). In our passage Jesus identifies himself as 'the resurrection

---

[38] J. P. Martin, 'History and Eschatology in the Lazarus Narrative in John 11:1-44', *SJT* 17 (1964): 337–40.
[39] S. M. Schneiders, 'Death in the Community of Eternal Life: History, Theology, and Spirituality in John 11', *Int* 41 (1987): 44–56.
[40] S. E. Hylen, *Imperfect Believers: Ambiguous Characters in the Gospel of John* (Louisville, KY: Westminster John Knox, 2009), 80.

and the life' (11.25), and he reveals his role as the agent of resurrection by raising Lazarus to life.

Jesus demonstrates his power to raise the dead but his actions lead to the increasing opposition of his enemies. The hostility of Jesus's enemies has deepened in the course of his mission. Wendy Sproston North observes that Jesus's enemies seek to stone him for blasphemy on account of his claim, 'I and the Father are one', at the Feast of Dedication in Jerusalem (10.22-42).[41] They also attempted to arrest him but he withdrew to safety to a place across the Jordan. At the beginning of ch. 11 Jesus faces persecution if he returns to Judea, and Thomas speaks for the disciples when he expresses his willingness to go there to die with Jesus (11.16). In earlier narratives hostile debates have taken place between Jesus and the authorities, and the followers of Jesus also faced questioning. In John 5 the lame man was questioned because he had been healed by Jesus on the Sabbath, and Jesus told him to carry his mat. In John 9 women faced questioning since the mother and father of the blind man were asked questions about Jesus. The man's parents were aware that those who confessed their faith in Jesus faced exclusion from the synagogue (9.22). The man's mother and father were afraid of the Pharisees, and they attempted to deflect the attention of the authorities towards their son. The raising of Lazarus not only prompts many people to believe in Jesus but also leads to the decision of the council to arrest Jesus and hand him over to the Romans (11.45-53). When Jesus enters Jerusalem, the crowd wants to see Lazarus because Jesus has raised him from death (12.12-19).

In our narrative Martha and Mary request the help of Jesus when their brother becomes ill. Their request prompts Jesus to carry out a sign which leads to his death and results in a plot to kill Lazarus. John links Mary with the mourners who report the sign to the Pharisees. The family at Bethany remains faithful to Jesus since he will visit them prior to his entry of Jerusalem. They provide a place of refuge while the authorities are searching for him. Martha and Mary are examples of discipleship to the women and men in John's community who face tensions with the leaders of the synagogue in their locality. John's narrative highlights the power of Jesus to overcome death and promises the gift of eternal life to those who have faith in Jesus.

Martha and Mary and the new creation

John associates Martha and Mary with the final sign of Jesus which reveals his glory. John's Gospel contains seven signs which illustrate Jesus's gift of abundant life. The raising of Lazarus is the culmination of the series of signs since it illustrates Jesus's power over death. At the beginning of our passage Martha and Mary send word to Jesus when their brother falls ill. The women remain faithful even when their brother dies, and Jesus raises Lazarus to life. John's account of the raising of Lazarus, moreover, looks forward to Jesus's own death and resurrection. Lazarus has been brought back to life but he will die again. On the other hand Jesus's death and resurrection mark the

---

[41] North, *The Lazarus Story*, 49–50.

turning point between the old age and the inauguration of the new creation. Jesus casts out the ruler of the present world, and he brings humanity the gift of eternal life.

In our narrative the conversation between Martha and Jesus focuses on the power of Jesus to raise the dead. The belief in the resurrection originated in the second century BCE, and it is first seen in Dan. 12.2 in which those who are oppressed on account of their faith are vindicated at the time of the resurrection of the dead. In Daniel, the resurrection of the dead involves the judgement of humanity, since some people will awake to everlasting life, and some to shame and everlasting contempt. The belief in the resurrection developed in intertestamental literature such as *2 Maccabees* and the *Psalms of Solomon*, and it is a prominent feature of apocalyptic writings including *1 Enoch*, *4 Ezra* and *2 Baruch*. The Pharisees believed in the resurrection of the dead but the Sadducees did not (cf. Josephus, *War* 2.162-163; *Ant.* 18.14; Mt. 22.23-33; Mk 12.18-27; Lk. 20.27-40; Acts 23.8). As Raymond Brown observes, belief in life after death was a popular belief in the first century, and it was included in the second benediction of the daily prayer the *Eighteen Benedictions*, 'You, O Lord, are mighty forever for you give life to the dead.'[42]

Martha and Mary's request for Jesus's assistance leads to John's presentation of Jesus as the agent of resurrection. In the Old Testament God gives the prophets Elijah (1 Kgs 17.17-24) and Elisha (2 Kgs 4.32-37) the power to raise the dead but in John's Gospel Jesus becomes the agent of the resurrection when he raises Lazarus from death. John presents Lazarus as the representative of all Christians who die in hope of receiving eternal life. Jesus is identified with the resurrection because he will overcome the power of death, and he is the first to rise from the dead. In Genesis, Adam and Eve disobeyed God, and death entered the world (3.22-24). In John's Gospel Jesus comes to bring humanity the gift of eternal life. The conversation between Jesus and Martha emphasizes that the gift of eternal life is offered in the present. Those who believe in Jesus are no longer subject to the power of death.

In our narrative Martha looks forward to the resurrection on the last day (11.24) but Jesus speaks of eternal life in the present. John's account of the raising of Lazarus contains features of both present and future eschatology. Tensions between present and future eschatology may be seen in other passages in John's Gospel. In ch. 5 Jesus said that whoever listens to his word and believes in the one who sent him has eternal life (5.24). In this passage faith in Jesus enables human beings to pass from death to life, and death no longer has any power over humanity. Jesus continued by saying that 'an hour is coming and is now here when the dead will hear the voice of the Son of God, and those who hear will live' (5.25). In our narrative Martha affirms her belief in the resurrection of the dead on the last day, and there are additional references to the last day in Jesus's teaching on the bread of life (6.39, 40, 44, 54). James Martin explores the relationship between John's realized eschatology and traditional beliefs in the resurrection on 'the last day' (cf. 5.29; 6.39, 40, 44).[43] He proposes that the future elements of John's eschatology should not be downplayed. Jesus is identified with the resurrection because he has power to raise the dead. Nevertheless, Lazarus will die

---

[42] Brown, *John*, 1:434.
[43] Martin, 'History and Eschatology', 337–40.

again, and Jesus's sign is thus proleptic of the power of Jesus to raise the dead at the end of the age.

John, moreover, draws out correspondences between the account of the raising of Lazarus and Jesus's own resurrection. He describes the raising of Lazarus in physical terms, and Lazarus comes out of the tomb with his hands bound and a cloth over his face (11.44). John's reference to the linen cloths and the face covering foreshadows the description of the resurrection of Jesus. After the resurrection, Jesus's linen wrappings are left behind in the tomb, and the cloth that covered his face is rolled up in a separate place (20.6-7). Lazarus returns to life but he remains subject to the constraints of the present world. Lazarus will grow old and die whereas Jesus's death and resurrection is a unique event which inaugurates the new creation.

John's account focuses on the faith of Martha and Mary, and their request to Jesus results in the raising of Lazarus. Marianne Thompson notes that John does not make any references to the faith of Lazarus in the narrative.[44] As Thompson points out, John frequently does not mention the faith of people who are the recipients of Jesus's signs as in the account of the wedding at Cana and the feeding of the five thousand. John's focus on Martha and Mary, however, indicates that the raising of Lazarus involves the restoration of a brother to two sisters. John's account of the raising of Lazarus demonstrates the impact of Jesus's gift of eternal life upon a community. Mourners have come from Jerusalem to comfort the women, and they are witnesses to the sign. Jesus's gift of eternal life is concerned not only with the resurrection of an individual but also with the restoration of relationships within a community.

Jesus's final sign is concerned with the abundant life of the new creation, and Jesus reveals his identity to Martha with an 'I am' saying, 'I am the resurrection and the life' (11.25). This saying defines Jesus's identity in terms of his power over death. In the account of the healing of the blind man, Jesus comes into the world as light (9.39), and in our passage Jesus is identified with life (11.25). The association of Jesus with light and life recalls the opening of the prologue in which Jesus is identified with life and with the true light coming into the world (1.4, 5, 9).[45] The raising of Lazarus is related to the struggle between light and darkness which begins in the prologue (1.5). Jesus is identified as the 'light of the world' (8.12), and he is 'the resurrection and the life' (11.25). Light and life are associated with the creation account of Genesis. God separates light from darkness and breathes life into Adam (Gen. 2.7). In John's Gospel Jesus struggles against darkness, but it does not prevail against him (1.5). In our narrative he struggles against the power of death and raises Lazarus to life. The sign, however, remains proleptic of Jesus's final struggle against evil and death, since this conflict will not be resolved until his own death and resurrection.

John, moreover, associates Martha and Mary with a sign which reveals the glory of God (τῆς δόξης τοῦ θεοῦ, 11.4, 40). At the beginning of John 11 Jesus instructs his disciples that Lazarus's illness will not end in death. It is for the glory of God, so that

---

[44] M. M. Thompson, 'Lazarus: "Behold a Man Raised Up by Christ"', in *Character Studies in the Fourth Gospel*, edited by S. A. Hunt, D. F. Tolmie and R. Zimmermann, WUNT 314 (Tübingen: Mohr Siebeck, 2013), 460–72.
[45] Brown, *John*, 1:430.

the Son of God may be glorified by means of it (δοξασθῇ, 11.4). Jesus's reference to glory recalls the account of his first sign at the wedding at Cana which also revealed his glory (2.11). The mother of Jesus brought the lack of wine to Jesus's attention, and he transformed the water in the stone jars into abundant wine. In our passage Martha and Mary send word to Jesus to request his help, and he raises Lazarus to life. Jesus responds to the requests of the women by carrying out signs which reveal his glory. As Rudolf Bultmann notes, Jesus seeks the 'glory' of God (τὴν δόξαν, 7.18), and in turn he is 'glorified' (δοξάζων, 8.54), and in this way the term 'glory' expresses the unity of the Father and the Son.[46] The first and the last sign are connected with the revelation of glory (2.11; 11.4), and both signs foreshadow the glorification of God and Jesus at the crucifixion (ἐδοξάσθη, 13.31-32; δόξασόν, δοξάσῃ, 17.1-5).

Martha and Mary are witnesses to Jesus's power to raise the dead, and this sign is proleptic of the resurrection at the end of the age. John depicts the crucifixion as the time of Jesus's victory over evil when 'the ruler of the world' is cast out (12.31). Within John's Gospel 'the ruler of the world' is linked with the power of death since Jesus's enemies seek to end his mission by putting him to death. Jesus has come to bring humanity eternal life and to inaugurate the new creation. The request from the mother of Jesus initiated his first sign, and Jesus transformed water into wine. He revealed his glory, and his disciples believed in him (2.11). In our passage Martha and Mary are present at Jesus's final sign which is connected with the revelation of Jesus's glory. Women are thus associated with the first and final sign in which Jesus reveals his glory. In our passage John links the glory of Jesus with his power to restore Lazarus to life.

Martha and Mary of Bethany and the Johannine community

In John's Gospel Martha's confession of Jesus as the Messiah and Son of God is the highest Christological confession made by a human being during Jesus's lifetime (11.27). John places Martha's confession of faith in a prominent position shortly before the events of the Passion Narrative. As Sandra Schneiders observes, the key position of Martha's confession is difficult to understand unless women had leadership roles in the Johannine community.[47] Mary comes out to meet Jesus, and she falls at his feet, weeping. Her grief leads Jesus to express his own sorrow at the death of Lazarus. In this section we will assess the extent to which John's presentation of Martha and Mary points to the roles of women in John's community. Martha's confession of faith represents the faith of the Johannine tradition. Why has John linked this confession of faith with a woman? Does Martha's confession of faith indicate that women held leadership roles in the Johannine community?

[46] R. Bultmann, *The Gospel of John*, translated by G. R. Beasley-Murray (Oxford: Blackwell, 1971), 397–8.
[47] S. M. Schneiders, 'Women in the Fourth Gospel and the Role of Women in the Contemporary Church', *BTB* 12 (1982): 41.

John connects Martha's confession of faith to Jesus's final sign in which he raises Lazarus from death. Jesus reveals his identity with the statement, 'I am the resurrection and the life', and Martha responds with her confession of faith (11.25-27). Throughout the gospel Jesus is associated with gifts that reveal his identity. Jesus feeds a crowd of five thousand (6.1-14), and he identifies himself with the statement, 'I am the bread of life' (6.35). He identifies himself as the 'light of the world' (9.5), and he heals a blind man (9.1-7). In our passage Jesus's identity as the Messiah and Son of God is reflected in his raising of Lazarus. Jesus has come into the world to bring the gift of eternal life. At the end of the gospel belief in Jesus is linked to the gift of life. Those who believe that Jesus is the Messiah and Son of God receive life in his name (Jn 20.31).

In John's Gospel women not only confess their faith in Jesus, they are also characters who come to a recognition of Jesus's identity during their conversations with him. The conversation between Jesus and Martha culminates in Martha's confession of faith that Jesus is the Messiah and Son of God. John's portrayal of Martha is reminiscent of his account of the Samaritan woman (4.7-26). The Samaritan woman recognized Jesus as a prophet and wondered if Jesus could be the Messiah. John places the confession of faith of Martha in the midst of a conversation in which Jesus and Martha debate theological issues. Martha believes in the resurrection on the last day, and Jesus reveals his identity as 'the resurrection and the life'. Jesus and the Samaritan woman discuss the correct location of the Temple and the nature of true worship. John's association of women with confessions of faith and theological issues suggests that women's faith and beliefs are valued in John's community. John depicts women characters who participate in theological discussions and who act as role models for women and men in his community.

John situates the women's confessions of faith in accounts which take place in the settings of everyday life. Martha and Mary go out to meet Jesus when he arrives in Bethany, and Jesus meets the Samaritan woman at a well in Sychar. John does not depict extraordinary women who have high social status or who have received some theological education. John portrays ordinary women who live in the towns of Judea and Samaria. He develops the conversations between Jesus and these women to reflect the credal confessions of his tradition. Jesus questions the women, and they respond with confessions of faith. In our passage Jesus reveals that he is the resurrection and the life. He then directly asks Martha, 'Do you believe this?' (11.20), and Martha then confesses her faith. John employs a similar structure in the account of the healing of the blind man (9.35-41). Jesus asks the former blind man, 'Do you believe in the Son of Man?' Jesus reveals his identity as the Son of Man, and the man confesses his faith with the statement, 'Lord, I believe'. Martha and the blind man represent individuals who come to faith in Jesus. The form of these narratives suggests that these questions are addressed to individuals within John's community.

In our narrative Martha speaks directly to Jesus with her confession of faith, 'You are the Messiah, the Son of God, the one coming into the world' (11.27). Peter Dschulnigg notes that John includes another two personal confessions of faith in which individuals address Jesus directly with the statement, 'You are …'.[48] Nathanael says, 'Rabbi, you are

---

[48] P. Dschulnigg, *Jesus Begegnen: Personen und ihre Bedeutung im Johannesevangelium* (Münster: Lit Verlag, 2002), 200–1.

the Son of God! You are the King of Israel!' (1.49), and Peter confesses his faith in the 'Holy One of God' (6.69). Martha's confession of faith is the most extensive statement of belief in John's Gospel, and it reflects the faith of the Johannine community. John's association of this confession of faith with Martha raises the question of the role of gender in John's community. Dschulnigg rightly argues that the confession of Martha indicates that women are valued in a similar way to the male disciples in the Johannine community. John presentation of Martha indicates that women and men together form the community of faith who believe that Jesus is the Messiah.

The belief that Jesus is the Messiah, however, forms one of the key points of conflict between Jesus and the religious authorities. On several occasions John states that those who confess their faith in Jesus as the Messiah face exclusion from the synagogue (9.22; 12.42; 16.2). In John 9, the parents of the former blind man are afraid to answer the questions of the religious authorities because they do not want to be put out of the synagogue (ἀποσυνάγωγος γένηται, 9.22). J. L. Martyn argues that John's account of the healing of the blind man may be interpreted on two levels which reflect the time of Jesus and also the time of the Johannine community.[49] Martyn proposes that this passage alludes to a formal decision which has been made by an authoritative group to exclude those who believe in Jesus from the synagogue. There is no evidence of a formal synagogue ban during the lifetime of Jesus.[50] Martyn proposes that John has developed the account of the healing of the blind man to allude to the later experiences of members of the Johannine community.

Martyn's analysis raises the question of whether or not Martha and Mary experience opposition on account of their belief that Jesus is the Messiah. Adele Reinhartz argues that there are no indications of any conflicts between the sisters and their neighbours over their belief in Jesus.[51] In our narrative Reinhartz rightly notes that Martha and Mary have good relations with the people from Jerusalem who come to support them during their time of bereavement. Jesus's act of raising Lazarus, however, leads to a division within the mourners. Some witnesses go to the Pharisees and report what has happened. The chief priests and Pharisees call a meeting of the council and decide to arrest Jesus (11.45-54). In John's Gospel the final sign of Jesus is instrumental in leading to the death of Jesus. John does not depict the persecution of Martha and Mary on account of their faith. The women, however, are connected to the hostility of the authorities because their brother faces persecution. In John 12 the crowd wishes to see Lazarus because he has been raised from the dead (12.9-11). John states that the chief priests seek to put Lazarus to death because many people believe in Jesus on

---

[49] J. L. Martyn, *History and Theology in the Fourth Gospel*, 2nd edn (New York: Crossroad, 1995), 135.

[50] Scholars who reject Martyn's theory about a formal exclusion of Jewish Christians from the synagogue in the first century CE include R. Kimelman, 'Birkat Ha-Minim and the Lack of Evidence for an Anti-Christian Jewish Prayer in Late Antiquity', in *Jewish and Christian Self-Definition. Vol. 2: Aspects of Judaism in the Graeco-Roman Period*, edited by E. P. Sanders with A. I. Baumgarten and A. Mendelson (London: SCM, 1981), 231–3, and S. T. Katz, 'Issues in the Separation of Judaism and Christianity after 70 CE: A Reconsideration', *JBL* 103 (1984): 43–76. For counterarguments to the views of Kimelman and Katz, see J. Marcus, '*Birkat Ha-Minim* Revisited', *NTS* 55 (2009): 523–51.

[51] A. Reinhartz, 'Women in the Johannine Community: An Exercise in Historical Imagination', in *A Feminist Companion to John*, edited by A.-J. Levine with M. Blickenstaff; Vol. 2 (London: Sheffield Academic Press, 2003), 23–4.

account of Lazarus. It is possible that John has developed the narrative to reflect the later experience of disciples who experience persecution on account of their faith.

John's account of the confession of Martha illustrates the way in which he highlights characters who are not part of Jesus's group of twelve male disciples. In John's Gospel several characters show greater insight into Jesus's identity than the twelve disciples. The Samaritans recognize Jesus as 'the Saviour of the world' (4.42). The blind man confesses his faith in Jesus as the Son of Man (9.38). John links key confessions of faith with individuals who are not part of the first group of twelve male disciples. In John's Gospel other individuals come to a deeper recognition of the question of who Jesus is. John selects other characters beyond the twelve to reflect the faith of his community. John's confessions of faith indicate that his tradition has developed Christological insights into the identity of Jesus which deepen the meaning of the title 'the Messiah'. Martha identifies Jesus as 'the Messiah, the Son of God, the one coming into the world'. Martha's confession of faith connects the title 'the Messiah' to a belief in the incarnation. John's association of women with key Christological developments demonstrates that women are regarded as models of faith in his community. His choice of Martha indicates that she is an example of discipleship. She is linked to the final and greatest sign in the gospel. Martha's confession of faith takes place before Jesus raises Lazarus to life. Martha has the highest confession of faith which a human being makes during Jesus's lifetime.

Martha's confession is significant because she recognizes Jesus before his death and resurrection. John's association of the main confession of faith with a woman suggests that women have leadership roles in his community. John does not define discipleship roles in terms of gender. He shows little interest in developing narratives which are concerned with church order. Martha places her trust in Jesus at a time of loss and suffering, and she confesses her faith. John associates this confession of faith with a woman who is not part of Jesus's itinerant group of disciples. Martha is not engaged in a mission to other towns but she may act as an example of discipleship to women and men who live in a settled community. John's narratives indicate that the faith of individual women and men is regarded as important to John's community. John's prominent location of Martha's confession of faith suggests that Martha serves as a role model for members of John's community.

Conclusion

Martha and Mary are portrayed as followers of Jesus who place their trust in him when their brother is ill. The sisters are models of discipleship since they remain faithful even when Lazarus dies. Jesus reveals his identity to Martha with an 'I am' saying, 'I am the resurrection and the life' (11.25), and Martha confesses her faith in Jesus as 'the Messiah, the Son of God, the one coming into the world' (11.27). Martha's confession of faith is the key statement of faith of the Johannine community, and it illustrates the high Christology of the Johannine tradition. John associates the term 'Messiah' with Jesus's power to raise the dead, and he links this title to the divinity of Jesus. Martha's statement of belief takes the place of Peter's confession that Jesus is the Messiah in the synoptic tradition. John does not downplay the role of Peter since Peter recognizes Jesus as the 'Holy One of God' (6.69), and he remains a leading figure in Jesus's group of disciples.

John also depicts Mary in a discipleship role since she places her trust in Jesus. The grief of Mary and the distress of the mourners prompt Jesus to express his own sorrow at Lazarus's death, and we catch a glimpse of the cost to Jesus of his mission. John associates Martha and Mary with Jesus's final sign which points to his power to overcome death. Woman are linked with the first and last signs of Jesus which reveal his glory. The prominent role of Martha and Mary in our passage points to the discipleship roles of women in John's community. John's portrayal of Martha and Mary reflects his presentation of other faithful women such as the mother of Jesus and the Samaritan woman. These women demonstrate insight into Jesus's identity, and they receive revelation of the purpose of his mission.

5

Mary of Bethany (12.1-8)

Introduction

At the beginning of John 12 Jesus returns to Bethany to visit Mary, Martha and Lazarus, and they hold a dinner for him. Lazarus reclines at the table with Jesus, Martha serves the meal and Mary anoints Jesus's feet with expensive perfume. The scene acts as a confirmation of Jesus's act of raising Lazarus from death, and it forms the conclusion to John's account of the family at Bethany. In our passage there is an atmosphere of joy and festivity at the dinner which celebrates the return of Lazarus to life, and Mary's act of anointing Jesus expresses her gratitude to him for the restoration of her brother. At the same time there are indications of the growing opposition of Jesus's enemies. The chief priests and the Pharisees have already given orders that they wish to know the whereabouts of Jesus so that they can arrest him, and it is dangerous for him to return to Bethany (11.57). Judas, moreover, is identified as the disciple who objects to Mary's extravagant gift. His response indicates his failure to understand Jesus, and it points forward to his betrayal of Jesus.

In John 11 Martha is presented as the sister who confesses her faith in Jesus as the Messiah and Son of God (11.27). In our narrative Mary, however, has the central role on account of her action of anointing Jesus. In Mark's Gospel and in Mathew's Gospel an anonymous woman anoints Jesus's head, and her action points to his identity as the royal Messiah (Mk 14.3-9; Mt. 26.6-13). Raymond Brown proposes that John does not depict a royal anointing since Mary anoints Jesus's feet rather than his head, and he argues that Mary anoints Jesus in preparation for his burial.[1] The anointing of Jesus's feet, however, may point to his death and to his role as the royal Messiah. C. K. Barrett rightly observes that John locates Mary's act of anointing Jesus prior to his entry into Jerusalem when he is acclaimed as the King of Israel by the crowd (12.13).[2] The title 'King of the Jews', moreover, forms the basis of the accusations against Jesus at his trial before Pilate (18.33-40), and the charge against him at his crucifixion reads the 'King of the Jews' (19.19). In our narrative Mary expresses her devotion to Jesus, and she acts as a model of

---

[1] R. E. Brown, *The Gospel according to John*, 2 vols, AB 29-29A (Garden City, NY: Doubleday, 1966-70), 1:454.
[2] C. K. Barrett, *The Gospel according to St. John: An Introduction with Commentary and Notes on the Greek Text*, 2nd edn (London: SPCK, 1978), 409.

discipleship. Elisabeth Schüssler Fiorenza contrasts the faithfulness of Mary with the role of Judas as the betrayer of Jesus.[3] Judas objects to the cost of the perfume by pointing out that the perfume could have been sold and the money given to the poor. Jesus defends Mary's gift by stating that the disciples will always have the poor with them but they will not always have him (12.8).

In this chapter we will explore the ways in which Mary's act of anointing Jesus points to Jesus's identity as the Messiah. Mary's act of anointing and drying Jesus's feet with her hair also foreshadows Jesus's action of washing and drying the feet of his disciples (13.1-20). Jesus's action expresses the purpose of his mission through his willingness to give his life to serve others. We will therefore examine the relationship between Mary's action and Jesus's act of washing the feet of his disciples. John's account of the anointing of Jesus concludes with his description of the spread of the perfume through the house (12.3). This feature is reminiscent of Jesus's prophecy in Mark's gospel that the anointing of Jesus will be told in memory of the woman who anoints him wherever the gospel is proclaimed throughout the world (14.9). We will assess the extent to which Mary of Bethany has a prophetic role in John's Gospel, and we will examine the contribution of Mary's act of anointing Jesus to John's definition of discipleship and his understanding of the new creation. Finally, we will analyse the extent to which John's portrayal of Mary of Bethany may provide indications of the roles of women in the Johannine community.

The anointing of Jesus in the four gospels

The anointing of Jesus appears in all four gospels (Mt. 26.6-13; Mk 14.3-9; Lk. 7.36-50; Jn 12.1-8) but with different presentations of the woman who anoints Jesus. In Mark's Gospel and Matthew's Gospel an anonymous woman anoints Jesus's head during a meal in the house of Simon at Bethany. In Luke's Gospel the woman who anoints Jesus is described as a 'sinner in the city', and she anoints Jesus in the house of Simon the Pharisee in Galilee at an earlier stage of Jesus's mission. This woman weeps over Jesus's feet and dries them with her hair before anointing him. Her action leads Jesus to teach a parable about forgiveness which compares the devotion of the woman favourably to the welcome that he received from Simon the Pharisee (7.40-50). John follows Mark and Matthew by situating the anointing of Jesus in Bethany shortly before the arrest of Jesus but he identifies the woman who anoints Jesus as Mary. His account also includes features similar to Luke's Gospel since Mary anoints Jesus's feet and dries them with her hair.

The similarities between the accounts raise the question of whether John's narrative has been influenced by the synoptic accounts of the anointing of Jesus.[4] Firstly, there

---

[3] E. Schüssler Fiorenza, *In Memory of Her: A Feminist Theological Reconstruction of Christian Origins*, 2nd edn (New York: Crossroad, 1995), 330–1.

[4] For an analysis of the gospel accounts of the anointing of Jesus, see S. Miller, 'Anointing', in *Dictionary of Jesus and the Gospels*, edited by J. B. Green, J. K. Brown and N. Perrin (Leicester: InterVarsity, 2013), 17–18.

are a number of verbal similarities between John's account and Mark's narrative. Mark refers to the perfume as 'an alabaster jar of costly perfume of pure nard' (ἀλάβαστρον μύρου νάρδου πιστικῆς πολυτελοῦς, 14.3), and John describes the perfume as 'a pound of costly perfume of pure nard' (λίτραν μύρου νάρδου πιστικῆς πολυτίμου, 12.3). John, therefore, describes the perfume with four similar words in the same order. The adjective πιστικός is a rare word with an uncertain meaning which occurs only in these passages in the New Testament. This term may derive from the adjective πιστός (faithful) and may be translated as 'genuine, unadulterated' (Eus. *Dem. Ev.* 989) but on the other hand it may come from the Greek form of the Latin term spicatum (Galen XII 604 k.) or πιστάκια 'pistachio tree' or the East Indian piccata.[5] C. K. Barrett notes the difficulty in establishing the meaning of πιστικός, and he proposes that Mark has employed this adjective as a transliteration of the Aramaic term for the pistachio nut.[6] He suggests that John has misinterpreted Mark's use of this word as an adjective meaning 'genuine', and he has thus incorporated the term into his gospel. It is possible, however, that the description of the perfume has been preserved in the oral tradition. As Joel Marcus points out, the Johannine term for 'costly' (πολυτίμου, 12.3) is more unusual than the Markan form (πολυτελοῦς, 14.3) which suggests that John may preserve the earlier tradition.[7] In addition, Mark states that the perfume is worth 'more than three hundred denarii' (14.5), and John values the perfume at 'three hundred denarii' (12.5). This sum of money is not mentioned in Matthew or Luke, but it may have been part of the oral tradition.

The similarities between John's account of the anointing and Mark's account of the anointing consist of a small number of verbal correspondences. On the other hand the setting of the accounts, the identification of the woman and the descriptions of the act of anointing are different. Percival Gardner-Smith points out that the large number of differences in the accounts outweighs the significance of the small number of verbal correspondences.[8] He rightly proposes that the verbal correspondences, including the descriptions of the perfume, are the type of details which could have been preserved within the oral tradition.

It is difficult to assess the relationship between John's account of the anointing and Matthew's description of the anointing since Matthew follows Mark's account closely. Matthew includes Mark's account of the saying of Jesus, 'For you always have the poor with you … but you will not always have me' (πάντοτε γὰρ τοὺς πτωχοὺς ἔχετε μεθ' ἑαυτῶν καὶ ὅταν θέλητε δύνασθε αὐτοῖς εὖ ποιῆσαι, ἐμὲ δὲ οὐ πάντοτε ἔχετε, 14.7) but he omits the phrase 'and whenever you wish you can do good to them' (14.7). In John's Gospel Jesus similarly states, 'The poor you always have with you, but you will not always have me' (τοὺς πτωχοὺς γὰρ πάντοτε ἔχετε μεθ' ἑαυτῶν, ἐμὲ δὲ οὐ πάντοτε ἔχετε, 12.8). This similarity is also not strong enough evidence to demonstrate that John

---

[5] W. Arndt, *A Greek-English Lexicon of the New Testament and Other Early Christian Literature*, rev. and edited by F. W. Danker, 3rd edn (London: University of Chicago Press, 2000), 818.
[6] Barrett, *St. John*, 412.
[7] J. Marcus, *Mark 8-16: A New Translation with Introduction and Commentary*, AB27A (New Haven, CT: Yale University Press, 2009), 934.
[8] P. Gardner-Smith, *Saint John and the Synoptic Gospels* (Cambridge: Cambridge University Press, 1938), 47–9.

knew Matthew's Gospel since it is possible that John and Matthew both independently omitted this phrase.

There are some similarities between the description of the anointing of Jesus in John's Gospel and in Luke's Gospel, since the women anoint and dry Jesus's feet with their hair in both gospels. In Luke's Gospel the anonymous woman weeps over Jesus's feet and then dries her tears before anointing Jesus's feet. In John's Gospel, however, Mary anoints Jesus's feet and then dries them with her hair. Mary's action is unusual because she removes the perfume by drying Jesus's feet. Barrett proposes that John's account has been influenced by Luke's narrative in which the woman dries her tears from Jesus's feet.[9] In John's Gospel Mary's action of anointing and drying Jesus's feet with her hair foreshadows Jesus's act of washing and drying the feet of his disciples. John may intend to draw a comparison between the role of Mary in our passage and the role of Jesus in the account of the foot washing, and we will explore this issue in a later section of this chapter. John's description of the anointing of Jesus reflects his own theological interpretation of the significance of the service of Jesus in giving his life to bring life to others.

The complex relationships between the gospels make it difficult to assess the origins of the anointing of Jesus in John's Gospel. C. H. Dodd proposes that there is only one story of an anointing behind the gospel accounts.[10] On the other hand André Legault argues that Luke has combined Mark's account of the anointing of Jesus in Bethany with a story of a woman whose sins are forgiven by Jesus in Galilee.[11] Legault's theory is more convincing because Luke's account focuses on the repentance of the woman and Jesus's parable of forgiveness. Luke does not include an extended description of the perfume, and the anointing of Jesus is a demonstration of the woman's gratitude towards Jesus.

In the synoptic gospels the woman who anoints Jesus is anonymous whereas John names the woman as Mary of Bethany. Raymond Brown suggests that John may have had independent knowledge of the identity of this woman as Mary.[12] Winsome Munro, moreover, notes that Mark has a tendency to focus on anonymous female characters until he names Mary Magdalene, Mary of James and Salome at the crucifixion (15.40-41).[13] On the other hand the name of the woman who anoints Jesus may have been lost in the oral tradition. John may have identified Mary as the one who anoints Jesus in order to connect the account of the anointing of Jesus to the account of the raising of Lazarus at Bethany.

John's Gospel, moreover, is the only gospel which identifies Judas as the person who objects to the cost of the perfume. In Mark, unnamed witnesses criticize the woman (14.4), and in Matthew, the disciples object to the woman's actions (26.8). J. Ramsey

---

[9] Barrett, *St. John*, 343.
[10] C. H. Dodd, *Historical Tradition in the Fourth Gospel* (Cambridge: Cambridge University Press, 1963), 162–73.
[11] A. Legault, 'An Application of the Form-Critique Method to the Anointings in Galilee (Lk 7, 36-50) and Bethany (Mt 26, 6-13; Mk 14, 3-9; Jn 12, 1-8)', *CBQ* 16 (1954), 144–5.
[12] Brown, *John*, 1:453.
[13] W. Munro, 'The Anointing in Mark 14:3-9 and John 12:1-8', in *SBLSP 1*, edited by P. J. Achtemeier (Missoula, MT: Scholars Press, 1979), 129.

Michaels suggests that John correctly identifies Judas as the disciple who points out that the perfume could have been sold and the proceeds given to the poor.[14] He proposes that Mark and Matthew may wish to avoid drawing attention to Judas's concern for the poor because he was about to betray Jesus. This interpretation is unconvincing, since Jesus defends the cost of the woman's gift in both gospels (Mk 14.6-9; Mt. 26.10-13). John also has a tendency to focus on the portrayal of individuals rather than on anonymous groups. John's presentation associates the criticism of Jesus with a disciple who betrays Jesus. His narrative raises the question of Judas's motive in betraying Jesus. In Mark's Gospel the plot of Judas to betray Jesus (14.10-11) follows the account of the anointing of Jesus, and the literary structure suggests that the use of expensive perfume prompts Judas's decision to betray Jesus. The synoptic gospels also state that religious leaders offer Judas money to betray Jesus (Mt. 26.14-16; Mk 14.10-11; Lk. 22.5). John emphasizes the greed of Judas, and he contrasts the willingness of Mary to give the expensive perfume to Jesus with Judas's wish to keep the money for himself. Mary's gift is an indication of her devotion to Jesus whereas Judas's protests about the poor conceal his own wish to steal the money. Mary is silent throughout the account, and her faithfulness to Jesus is illustrated by her actions. Judas's words are recorded but his motives are hidden from the guests at the dinner.

In our narrative Jesus defends Mary, and he associates her generous gift with the day of his burial. In Mark's Gospel and Matthew's Gospel, however, Jesus links the woman's act of anointing him with the proclamation of the gospel throughout the world (Mk 14.9; Mt. 26.13), and the account of the woman's action will be told 'in memory of her' (εἰς μνημόσυνον αὐτῆς, Mk 14.9; Mt. 26.13). Elisabeth Schüssler Fiorenza points out that this prophecy is ironic because we are not told the name of the woman who is to be remembered.[15] John, however, does name the woman as Mary, and she is known for her act of anointing Jesus (cf. 11.2). John thus associates the anointing of Jesus with a named woman who is a disciple of Jesus. In our narrative Mary is a friend of Jesus who offers hospitality and support during his visit to Jerusalem. Mary of Bethany has knowledge of Jesus's identity, and her gift points to her faith in him. John's portrayal of Mary differs from the presentation of the woman who anoints Jesus in the synoptic tradition. In the synoptic gospels there is no indication of the woman's previous knowledge of Jesus, and she does not appear again in any gospel narrative. On the other hand Mary of Bethany is a friend of Jesus who recognizes him as the Messiah, and her act of anointing him reflects her commitment to him as one of his disciples.

The portrayal of Mary of Bethany

Martha and Mary send word to Jesus when their brother falls ill, and their request for his help leads to the final sign in the gospel, the raising of Lazarus from death. Mary's gift is an expression of her gratitude towards Jesus but it is also linked to his identity as the Messiah. In Mark's Gospel and Matthew's Gospel an anonymous woman anoints

---

[14] J. Ramsey Michaels, *The Gospel of John*, NICNT (Grand Rapids, MI: Eerdmans, 2010), 668.
[15] Schüssler Fiorenza, *In Memory*, xliii–xliv.

Jesus's head, and her action recalls the accounts of the anointing of kings (1 Sam. 9.15-10.1; 16.12-13; 1 Kgs 1.38-40) and of priests and prophets (Exod. 28.41; 1 Kgs 19.16). In the Old Testament the act of anointing was carried out by priests such as Zadok (1 Kgs 1.45) and prophets including Samuel (1 Sam. 10.1; 16.1). In Mark's Gospel and Matthew's Gospel the anonymous woman takes the role of a prophet or priest who anoints Jesus prior to the events of the Passion Narrative. Mark and Matthew, however, describe the woman's act of anointing Jesus's head at a dinner in Bethany whereas Luke and John describe the anointing of Jesus's feet. Mary's act of anointing Jesus's feet thus raises the question of whether she intends to anoint Jesus as the Messiah. There are only a few references to the anointing of the feet in classical writings, and they depict the anointing of the feet as an exceptional action. As André Legault points out, it is customary to anoint the head rather than the feet at meals (cf. Ps. 23.5; Eccl. 9.7).[16] The anointing of the feet of guests at Trimalchio's feast is viewed as an example of the extravagance of the dinner (Petronius, *Sat.* 69).[17] In Luke's Gospel, a woman weeps at Jesus's feet and then anoints them, and Luke emphasizes the woman's repentance and Jesus's act of forgiveness.

In Mark's Gospel the anonymous woman performs a prophetic action, however, since Jesus's identity as Messiah is revealed in the Passion Narrative. In John's Gospel Jesus has been recognized by his disciples as Messiah and Son of God from the beginning of his mission (1.41, 49; 2.11). The Samaritan woman asked if Jesus could be the Messiah, and she led others in her town to Jesus (4.39). Jesus's disciples recognize him as the Messiah but for others his identity remains hidden. In John 2 Jesus's act of transforming water into wine revealed his glory. The disciples believed in Jesus but the bridegroom, the steward and guests did not know about the source of the new wine. In John 11 Martha confessed her faith in Jesus as the Messiah and Son of God (11.27). John's account of Mary suggests that Mary is also aware of Jesus's identity as the Messiah. She has witnessed the raising of Lazarus which demonstrated Jesus's identity as the Messiah and Son of God. Martha's confession of faith occurs during a conversation with Jesus, and there are no other people present. In our passage, however, Mary makes a public demonstration of her faith in Jesus. She acknowledges Jesus's identity as the Messiah before all the guests at the meal, and her act of anointing draws attention to John's portrayal of Jesus as the hidden Messiah. Mary's act of anointing Jesus's feet reflects the humble nature of his mission. She anoints Jesus as the suffering Messiah, and her expensive gift foreshadows the cost of Jesus's mission which will result in his death.

Judas, however, criticizes Martha's act of anointing Jesus. He objects to the cost of the perfume by arguing that the perfume could have been sold and the money given to the poor. Judas values the perfume at three hundred denarii which is almost equivalent to a year's wages for a labourer (12.5; cf. Mt. 20.2). Judas's objection suggests that he expects Jesus and the other guests to agree with his view that the money should have been spent on the poor. Jesus, however, defends Mary by noting that she has kept the

---

[16] Legault, 'Application', 137–8.
[17] T. J. Hornsby, 'Anointing Traditions', in *The Historical Jesus in Context*, edited by A.-J. Levine, D. C. Allison and J. D. Crossan (Princeton, NJ: Princeton University Press, 2006), 339–42.

perfume for the day of his burial (12.7). Jesus is aware of the imminence of his death, and he points out that the disciples will always have the poor with them but they will not always have him. The phrase 'with you' (μεθ' ὑμῶν, 12.8) occurs in Jesus's prophecy that he will be with his disciples for only a short time (μεθ' ὑμῶν, 7.33-34), and it also acts as a refrain throughout his Farewell Discourse (μεθ' ὑμῶν, 13.33; 14.9; 16.4-5). The imminent absence of Jesus from his disciples is thus contrasted with the continual presence of the poor.

In our narrative Mary's expensive gift is justified by the imminence of Jesus's death. As David Daube notes, the burial of the dead takes precedence over charitable giving in rabbinic texts (*t. Pe'ah* 4.19; *b. Sukkah* 49b).[18] John denigrates Judas by describing him as a thief who had charge of the common purse and who helped himself to the funds (12.6). Nevertheless, the Johannine Jesus does not disregard the needs of the poor, since he alludes to the commandment which requires the care of the poor (Deut. 15.11). His response implies that the disciples have a continuing responsibility to care for the poor in the period following his death. Jesus's concern for the poor is a characteristic of his mission. In earlier narratives Jesus has shown concern for the poor by healing the man who waited at the pool of Bethesda for thirty-eight years (5.1-9) and by giving sight to a blind man who had to beg for his living (9.1-7).[19]

John presents Mary as a prophetic figure since her act of anointing prepares Jesus for his burial.[20] Jesus connects Mary's act of anointing him with his imminent death, since it was customary to anoint bodies before burial (2 Chron. 6.14; Josephus, *Ant.* 17.199; *m. Šabb.* 23.5). In our passage Mary breaks social conventions because respectable women were usually expected to wear their hair up. In Luke 7 the woman who anoints Jesus and dries his feet with her hair is described as 'a sinful woman from the city' (γυνὴ ἥτις ἦν ἐν τῇ πόλει ἁμαρτωλός, 7.37), and in 1 Corinthians Paul criticizes the Corinthian women who loosen their hair while they pray and prophesy during public worship (11.2-16). Mary's act of loosening her hair may be interpreted as a sign of her grief because women often loosen their hair at the time of mourning (cf. *Esth.* 4.17 LXX; *Jos. Asen.* 10.4). Charles Cosgrove, for example, discusses several passages which associate women's unbound hair with mourning (Plutarch, *Mor.* 267; Virgil, *Aen.* 3.65; Ovid, *Metam.* 583-99; Petronius, *Sat.* 111).[21] In our passage Mary's grief at Jesus's forthcoming death leads her to break social conventions.

John's portrayal of Mary's extravagant gift suggests that she performs a prophetic action, because the expensive perfume indicates the cost to Jesus of his mission that will shortly result in his arrest and execution. Jesus is willing to give up his life to bring life to others (10.15-18; 12.27-33). The description of the spread of the fragrance

---

[18] D. Daube, *The New Testament and Rabbinic Judaism* (London: Athlone Press, 1956), 315.

[19] R. J. Karris (*Jesus and the Marginalized in John's Gospel* (Collegeville, PA: Liturgical Press, 1990), 11–12) notes that Jesus's concern for the poor may be seen in his openness to those who are marginalized such as those who do not know the Law (7.49), the Samaritans (4.1-42) and those who suffer from chronic illnesses (9.1-41).

[20] For an analysis of John's portrayal of Mary as a prophetic figure, see S. Miller, 'Mary (of Bethany): The Anointer of the Suffering Messiah', in *Character Studies in the Fourth Gospel*, edited by S. A. Hunt, D. F. Tolmie and R. Zimmermann, WUNT 314 (Tübingen: Mohr Siebeck, 2013), 480–2.

[21] C. H. Cosgrove, 'A Woman's Unbound Hair in the Greco-Roman World, with Special Reference to the Story of the "Sinful Woman" in Luke 7:36-50', *JBL* 124 (2005): 682–3.

through the house (ἡ δὲ οἰκία ἐπληρώθη ἐκ τῆς ὀσμῆς τοῦ μύρου, 12.3) alludes to the abundant life that comes about through his death (10.10). In John's Gospel God is glorified through Jesus's sacrificial death (12.23-24; 17.1-5). In our passage the spread of scent is reminiscent of the scent which is linked with sacrifices in the Old Testament (cf. ὀσμὴ εὐωδίας, Gen. 8.21; Exod. 29.18; Lev. 2.2). John's portrayal of Jesus's death as a sacrifice reflects the setting of the account at Passover, since Jesus is identified as the 'lamb of God' (1.29, 36; 19.14-16, 36). John emphasizes the sacrificial nature of Jesus's death since Jesus is willing to lay down his life for others (10.11). He does not include the account of the struggle of Jesus to follow the will of God in Gethsemane (cf. Mk 14.32-42; Mt. 26.36-46). Instead, the Johannine Jesus has foreknowledge of the events of his Passion, and he willingly accepts his forthcoming hour (13.1, 3; 18.4; 19.28).

In our passage Mary's act of anointing Jesus anticipates the visit of Joseph of Arimathea and Nicodemus to Jesus's tomb to anoint Jesus at the time of his burial. They bring a mixture of myrrh and aloes which weigh about a hundred pounds (19.38-42). It was customary to use extravagant perfumes at the burial of kings, and the expensive perfume points to the royal identity of Jesus. In 2 Chronicles, King Asa is placed on a briar that has been filled with various kinds of spices (16.14). Brown notes that the royal associations of the use of spices at the time of a burial are also evident in Josephus's reference to five hundred servants who carry spices at the funeral of Herod the Great (*Ant.* 17.196-99).[22] Josephus emphasizes the royal nature of Herod's burial by describing his purple robes, gold crown and sceptre. In our passage John's presentation of Mary's expensive gift thus associates the kingship of Jesus with his death.

Mary anoints Jesus as the Messiah but his identity remains unrecognized by many. In John's Gospel the disciples recognize Jesus as the Messiah and Son of God but the crowds debate the question of Jesus's identity (5.10-13; 7.25-31). The religious leaders are concerned about Jesus's growing popularity, and they seek to arrest him (7.32, 48-49). Throughout the gospel Jesus's opponents reject his claims about his identity (7.48), and they accuse Jesus of making himself equal to God (5.18; 10.33). In the Passion Narrative the claims of Jesus's identity as King come to the fore in his trial before Pilate (18.33, 36-37, 39; 19.14-15, 19). The religious leaders, moreover, argue that Jesus should be put to death because he has made himself 'Son of God' (19.7). In the account of the feeding of the five thousand the members of the crowd wished to make Jesus their king but he withdrew from them (6.15). The Johannine Jesus did not wish to claim the title of 'king' at this stage of his mission. John associates the revelation of Jesus as king with the events of the last week of Jesus's life.

Mary, moreover, anoints Jesus as the royal Messiah in preparation for his entry into Jerusalem as king (12.12-19). The crowd goes out to meet Jesus because they have heard about the raising of Lazarus (12.9-11), and the people welcome Jesus as the 'King of Israel' (12.13). The crowd waves palm branches, and this action is associated with the welcome of a victorious ruler (1 Macc. 13.51; 2 Macc. 10.7; 14.4).[23] John, however, stresses the humble nature of Jesus's kingship, since he enters Jerusalem on a donkey rather than on a war horse (cf. Zech. 9.9). John does not depict Jesus as a military king

---

[22] Brown, *John*, 2:960.
[23] R. Schnackenburg, *The Gospel according to St. John*, 3 vols (London: Burns & Oates, 1968–82), 2:374.

who seeks to overthrow the Roman Empire by force. He contrasts the kingship of Jesus with the rule of Caesar since Caesar rules through military power and oppression (cf. 18.33-38). In the Passion Narrative the true nature of Jesus's kingship is revealed in his willingness to face death to bring life to humanity. In our narrative Mary anoints Jesus as the royal Messiah who will lay down his life to bring abundant life to others.

John presents Mary of Bethany in the role of a prophet since she anoints Jesus as the suffering Messiah. Mary anoints Jesus with expensive perfume to point to his identity as Messiah at the public occasion of a dinner. She carries out a prophetic action before all the guests because she anoints Jesus in preparation for his burial. Mary breaks social conventions by anointing Jesus's feet and drying them with her hair. Her act of anointing Jesus's feet represents the humble nature of his mission. Mary takes advantage of Jesus's presence at Bethany to anoint him before his death, and the expensive perfume reflects the cost of Jesus's mission. John's description of the spread of the perfume through the house is symbolic of the glorification of Jesus at the time of his death.

Discipleship and Mary of Bethany

In John's Gospel Mary of Bethany recognizes Jesus as the Messiah and Son of God, and her extravagant gift expresses the nature of his sacrificial death. In this section we will examine the relationship between John's portrayal of Mary's act of anointing and his understanding of discipleship. Mary's act of anointing and drying Jesus's feet (ἐξέμαξεν, 12.3) has links with discipleship since it foreshadows Jesus's action of washing and drying the feet of his disciples at the Last Supper (ἐκμάσσειν, 13.5). As Barnabas Lindars notes, Mary's action is similar to an act of washing Jesus's feet, since she dries the perfume from them.[24] There are also several similarities between the description of the anointing of Jesus and the account of the foot washing. The dinner at Bethany takes place 'six days before the Passover' (12.1), and the Last Supper is held 'before the feast of the Passover' (13.1). Mary disrupts the dinner at Bethany in order to anoint Jesus's feet, and Jesus waits until the meal has started before washing his disciples' feet, thus in a way disrupting the meal. It is possible that John has described the anointing of Jesus's feet rather than his head partly in order to highlight the ways in which Mary's action foreshadows Jesus's act of washing his disciples' feet. In John's Gospel Jesus demonstrates his role as a servant by washing the feet of his disciples. John portrays Mary as a model of discipleship because she anticipates Jesus's teaching about service.

Mary of Bethany and Jesus both carry out symbolic actions which are related to the purpose of Jesus's mission. John associates Mary's act of anointing with the sacrificial nature of Jesus's death. He also links the account of the foot washing with the willingness of Jesus to give his life to serve others. John's account of the foot washing expresses the salvation that Jesus brings humanity. This symbolic action foreshadows the willingness of Jesus to take on the humble role of giving his life on the cross. Jesus takes off his

---

[24] B. Lindars, *The Gospel of John*, NCBC (London: Marshall, Morgan & Scott, 1972), 415.

robe and wraps a towel around himself, and then removes the towel and puts his robe on again, resuming his place. Raymond Brown interprets this action as an allusion to Jesus's death and resurrection, since Jesus descends to earth, serves humanity and then returns to God.[25] As Brown notes, the verb τίθημι (lay down) refers to Jesus's action of taking off his robe and to the laying down of his life (10.11, 15, 17, 18). The verb λαμβάνω (take) is also used for the taking up both of his robe and of his life (13.12; cf. 10.17-18). Jesus's act of washing the feet of his disciples foreshadows his death. In our narrative Jesus interprets Mary's act of anointing Jesus in relation to his imminent death. In John 12 Jesus tells his disciples, 'You always have the poor with you (μεθ' ἑαυτῶν), but you will not always have me' (12.8). At the Last Supper Jesus teaches his disciples, 'I am with you only for a short time' (μεθ' ὑμῶν, 13.33).

In our passage, moreover, Mary breaks social conventions by appearing in public with her hair undone. In the account of the foot washing Jesus also breaks social conventions by removing his garments and girding himself with a towel. The change in his appearance indicates that he is taking on the role of a servant or a slave (cf. Lk. 12.37; 17.8). As John Thomas notes, those whose feet are washed are regarded as the social superiors of those who carry out this action (1 Sam. 25; *Jos. Asen.* 13.15; 20.15; Herodotus 6.19; Plutarch, *Pomp.* 73.6-7).[26] The task of washing someone's feet is also associated with the role of women. In the Old Testament Abigail wishes to wash the feet of the servants of David, and she is willing to take the role of a slave in order to demonstrate her devotion to David (1 Sam. 25). In *Joseph and Aseneth*, the devotion of Aseneth to Joseph is illustrated by her refusal to permit a servant to wash Joseph's feet because she wishes to wash them herself. Thomas points out that Jesus's action is unusual since he takes the role of a slave to wash the feet of people who have lower status than he has.[27] Jesus's action thus challenges the view that leaders should not wash the feet of their followers.

Mary's act of anointing Jesus's feet and drying them with her hair is an expression of her devotion to Jesus. Her action of service to Jesus foreshadows the service of Jesus to his disciples. Peter, however, objects to Jesus's act of washing his feet because he does not believe his lord should wash his feet. In response Jesus teaches that the foot washing is necessary for his disciples to have a 'share' (μέρος) with him (13.8). Brown notes that the term μέρος is used in the Septuagint to refer to the heritage given to the tribes of Israel who receive a 'share' in the promised land (Num. 18.20; Deut. 12.12; 14.27).[28] As Brown points out, this term is associated with the heavenly reward of eternal life in Revelation (20.6; 21.8; 22.19). The term 'share' (μέρος) also has eschatological associations in the New Testament (Mt. 24.51; Lk. 12.46; Acts 8.21). Jesus teaches his disciples that they will share his destiny. In John's account of the foot washing, the term 'share' points to the disciples' participation in Jesus's death and resurrection and looks forward to the gift of eternal life.

---

[25] Brown, *John*, 2:551.
[26] J. C. Thomas, *Footwashing in John 13 and the Johannine Community*, JSNTSup 61 (Sheffield: JSOT Press 1991), 42.
[27] Thomas, *Footwashing*, 42.
[28] Brown, *John*, 2:565–6.

Peter's objection, moreover, reflects the contemporary understanding of social hierarchies in which leaders and lords are not expected to serve others. Ernst Haenchen points out that Peter is portrayed as the spokesperson of the disciples, and his response represents the lack of understanding of the disciples.[29] Jesus does not deny his role as leader but he argues that leaders have the role of serving others. Although Jesus is the 'lord' of the disciples, his role is to serve them, and similarly, they are to serve one another (13.12-17). Jesus's teaching depicts a new form of relationship which challenges the hierarchical roles of masters and slaves that were taken for granted in the first century. As Sandra Schneiders notes, the context of Jesus's service to his disciples is one of friendship, and Jesus's love for his friends is illustrated by his willingness to die for them (13.34-35; 15.12-14).[30] The relationship between Jesus and his disciples stands in opposition to the power structures of the world. Jesus, the leader, takes the role of the one who has least status within the group, and he wishes to serve the whole group of disciples. Jesus also interprets his action as an example for his disciples to follow, and he teaches his disciples to serve one another (13.12-20). In John's Gospel service is defined in terms of the willingness of the disciples to die for one another. As D. Moody Smith rightly notes, John employs the metaphor of foot washing to express the significance of the salvation that comes about through Jesus's death.[31]

In John 13 Jesus's teaching is not only directed to Jesus's first disciples but is also presented as an example which all his future disciples, both women and men, are to follow. John, however, does not refer to the presence of women in his account of the foot washing at the Last Supper. Raymond Brown notes that all the named disciples in this narrative are members of the Twelve.[32] The Beloved Disciple is mentioned for the first time, and it is probable that he is not a member of the Twelve. John's reference to the Beloved Disciple suggests the presence of a wider group of disciples, perhaps including some women. The mother of Jesus, her sister, Mary the wife of Clopas and Mary Magdalene are witnesses of the crucifixion (19.25). They have accompanied Jesus and his disciples to Jerusalem, and it is unlikely that they would eat separately from the male disciples. Nevertheless, John does not directly refer to the presence of women, and his account centres on the male disciples. John's focus upon the male disciples may reflect his concern about the future leadership of the group of disciples. As Ernst Haenchen observes, Jesus's instructions to the disciples that they should wash one another's feet indicates that they are not to claim authority over one another.[33] Jesus's act of foot washing represents a reordering of hierarchical structures within the discipleship group.

In John's Gospel there is a contrast between Mary's silent act of anointing Jesus's feet and Peter's protests at Jesus's act of washing his feet. In our passage Mary takes the role of a servant and anoints Jesus's feet. Mary has therefore acted in the way that Jesus instructs his disciples to act. The disciples, moreover, have been present at the dinner

---

[29] E. Haenchen, *John 2* (Philadelphia, PA: Fortress, 1984), 107–8.
[30] S. M. Schneiders, 'The Foot Washing (John 13:1-20): An Experiment in Hermeneutics', *CBQ* 43 (1981): 76–92.
[31] D. M. Smith, *John* (Nashville, TN: Abingdon, 1999), 252–4.
[32] Brown, *John*, 2:551.
[33] Haenchen, *John 2*, 109.

at Bethany, and they have witnessed Mary's gift. Jesus vindicates Mary's action, and she is portrayed as a model of discipleship for all disciples. In the account of the foot washing Peter is the spokesperson of the twelve male disciples but he is unwilling to accept Jesus's role as a servant. In our passage Mary accepts the imminence of Jesus's death but Peter is unwilling to accept the necessity of Jesus's suffering and death. John's portrayal of Mary suggests that she has greater insight into the significance of Jesus's mission than Peter, the representative of the male disciples.

John's presentation of Mary recalls the favourable portrayal of the Samaritan woman in John 4. The Samaritan woman responded positively to Jesus's offer of 'living water' but the disciples were amazed to find Jesus talking to the Samaritan woman (4.27). John portrayed the Samaritan woman as a representative of the Samaritans who respond to Jesus but the male disciples did not understand the extent of Jesus's mission to the Samaritans. At times the male disciples are unable to understand Jesus's mission but they still wish to be faithful to Jesus. In John 11 Thomas assured Jesus that he was willing to face death with Jesus in Judea (11.16), and in John 13 Peter also states that he is willing to die for Jesus but Jesus predicts that Peter will deny him three times (13.36-38). Peter is unable to follow Jesus to death at this time but Jesus prophesies that Peter will follow him afterwards (13.36). The Johannine Jesus knows that the disciples will only understand the significance of his teaching after his death and resurrection.

In our narrative Mary of Bethany anoints and dries Jesus's feet, and her action looks forward to Jesus's act of washing and drying the feet of his disciples. Mary takes on the role of a servant, and she anticipates Jesus's act of service to his disciples. Mary breaks social conventions to anoint Jesus, and Jesus disregards social hierarchies in order to wash the feet of his disciples. John links Mary of Bethany with his understanding of discipleship since Jesus interprets her action as an anointing in preparation for the day of his burial. Mary is aligned with Jesus's identity as the suffering Messiah. John's portrayal of Mary, moreover, is reminiscent of the presentation of faithful women in earlier narratives. In several ways these women have greater insight into discipleship than the male disciples. The intervention of Jesus's mother at the wedding of Cana led the disciples to have faith in Jesus (2.11). The Samaritan woman asked if Jesus could be the Messiah whereas the male disciples were surprised to find Jesus speaking to the woman at the well (4.27). Martha's confession of faith takes the place of the confession of Peter in the synoptic tradition (11.27). In our narrative Mary of Bethany's act of anointing Jesus anticipates Jesus's own teaching on discipleship. Mary anoints Jesus as the Messiah, and her action prepares him for his royal entry into Jerusalem and the forthcoming events of the Passion Narrative.

Mary of Bethany and the new creation

In our passage Mary of Bethany anoints Jesus with expensive perfume which is valued at three hundred denarii. Jesus defends the cost of Mary's gift by stating that she has kept the perfume for the day of his burial (ἵνα εἰς τὴν ἡμέραν τοῦ ἐνταφιασμοῦ μου τηρήσῃ αὐτό, 12.7). This verse has an awkward grammatical construction and may be translated literally as 'in order that she may keep it for the day of my burial'. Jesus's explanation is puzzling because Mary does not keep the perfume for Jesus's burial, and she anoints Jesus ahead of time. Raymond Brown translates the phrase as 'the purpose was that she might keep', and he suggests that Mary has been unaware that she has been keeping the perfume until the present to anoint Jesus.[34] On the other hand Andrew Lincoln notes that the term ἐνταφιασμός and its cognate verb are associated with the preparation of bodies for burial (cf. 19.40; Gen. 50.2-3 LXX; Mt. 26.12). Lincoln argues that Mary has 'kept' the perfume to anoint Jesus as a preparation for his burial.[35] Mary's gift of expensive perfume and her act of anointing Jesus in the midst of the dinner indicate the extraordinary nature of her action. Jesus's statement that Mary has 'kept' the perfume suggests that she is aware of the imminent danger to his life, and she anoints Jesus ahead of time so that he will receive her gift while he is still alive.

Jesus's reference to Mary's act of 'having kept' the perfume, moreover, recalls the account of the wedding at Cana in which the host of the wedding feast noticed that the best wine had been 'kept' until the end of the feast (σὺ τετήρηκας τὸν καλὸν οἶνον ἕως ἄρτι, 2.10). The two accounts depict the reservation of the best goods until a decisive period of time has arrived. The transformation of the water into wine foreshadows the abundance of the new creation, and the setting of a wedding is often used to represent the new age. As Ernest Bammel points out, the new age is associated with abundance and the absence of poverty in the pseudepigrapha (*T. Jud.* 25.4; *4 Ezra* 14.13; *Sib. Or.* 3.378; 8.208) and in rabbinic writings (*b. Sabb.* 151b; *b. Pes.* 50a).[36] Jesus comes to bring abundant life to all human beings, and in the new creation social inequalities will no longer exist (10.10). In our passage Mary's act of anointing Jesus with expensive perfume looks forward to the abundance of the new creation.

Mary anoints Jesus with expensive perfume and as a result the fragrance spreads through the house. Rudolf Bultmann proposes that the description of the perfume filling the house represents the knowledge of Christ filling the world.[37] He notes the use of a similar metaphor in 2 Corinthians in which Paul writes of the fragrance of the knowledge of Christ which spreads through his followers everywhere (τὴν ὀσμὴν τῆς γνώσεως αὐτοῦ, 2.14). For some people this scent represents life, but for others it represents death. Nevertheless, John does not directly refer to knowledge in our passage. Raymond Brown compares the description of the perfume to Midrash Rabbah on Eccles. 7.1: 'The fragrance of a good perfume spreads from the bedroom to the dining room; so does a good name spread from one end of the world to the other.'[38] As Brown notes, if this tradition was known at the time of the composition of John's Gospel, it could suggest that John had developed Mark's account of the anointing of Jesus in which Jesus prophesies that wherever the gospel is proclaimed throughout the world what the woman has done will be told in memory of her (14.9). In John's Gospel, however, the spread of the perfume is more closely associated with the death of Jesus

---

[34] Brown, *John*, 1:449.
[35] A. T. Lincoln, *The Gospel according to Saint John*, BNTC (London: Continuum, 2005), 339.
[36] E. Bammel, 'πτωχός, πτωχεία, πτωχεύω', in *Theological Dictionary of the New Testament*, edited by G. Kittel and G. Friedrich, 10 vols, translated by G. W. Bromiley (Grand Rapids, MI: Eerdmans, 1964–1976), 4:895.
[37] R. Bultmann, *The Gospel of John*, translated by G. R. Beasley-Murray (Oxford: Blackwell, 1971), 415.
[38] Brown, *John*, 1:453.

than with the mission of the disciples. The scent lingers and fills the room, and in the same way Jesus will continue to have an influence after his death.

After Mary anoints Jesus, the perfume fills the house and the spread of the perfume symbolizes the invincible power and lasting effects of Jesus's death. Charles Giblin rightly proposes that Mary's act of anointing Jesus's feet and drying them with her hair symbolizes not only Jesus's death but also his resurrection.[39] The spread of the perfume may allude to the abundant life of the new creation which comes about through Jesus's death. This feature of John's Gospel may be seen in Jesus's description of his forthcoming death in terms of a seed that falls into the ground and bears an enormous amount of fruit (12.24). John's description of the scent filling the house recalls the account of the transformation of water into fine wine at the wedding at Cana (2.1-11) and the miraculous multiplication of the loaves to feed the hungry crowd (6.1-15). In these passages Jesus transformed a situation of scarcity into one of abundance. John's descriptions of abundant wine and bread look forward to the new creation which is characterized by fruitfulness and abundance (cf. Jer. 31.12; Hos. 2.21-22; Amos 9.13-14; Zech. 8.12). In our passage Jesus faces death but the spread of the perfume through the house foreshadows the abundant life of the new creation.

Mary's act of anointing Jesus not only serves Jesus but enables everyone present in the house to smell the fragrance. As Gail O'Day points out, the spread of the perfume suggests that all may participate in Mary's act of anointing.[40] Throughout John's Gospel the human ability to recognize the new creation is connected to the power of the senses. At the wedding at Cana the steward tasted the wine, and then recognized that the best wine had been reserved till last (2.9-10). His sense of taste enabled him to notice that a change had occurred in the material realm, and this transformation pointed to the abundance of the new creation. After the feeding of the five thousand the people are described as looking for Jesus not because they had seen signs but because they had eaten their fill of the bread (6.26). In John 11 Martha was afraid that there would be an odour when Lazarus's tomb was opened whereas in John 12 the scent of the perfume filling the house indicates the power of Jesus over death. The physical acts of eating and drinking bring human beings to an understanding of Jesus which goes beyond the effect of seeing signs. John chooses sensual images which express salvation in concrete and earthly terms. The act of inhaling the perfume enables those present to share in Mary's gift to Jesus, and this description expresses the participation of Jesus's followers in his gift of salvation.

In our passage Mary anoints Jesus as the Messiah since he is about to give his life to bring salvation to humanity. Jesus states that Mary has kept the perfume for 'the day of his burial' (12.7) but Mary will not be present at Jesus's burial. Mary's act of anointing Jesus foreshadows the burial of Jesus by Joseph of Arimathea and Nicodemus at the end of the gospel (19.38-42). Her gift of expensive perfume looks forward to the perfume which Nicodemus brings to the tomb of Jesus. Mary's gift is described as 'a pound of costly perfume of pure nard' (λίτραν μύρου νάρδου πιστικῆς πολυτίμου,

---

[39] C. H. Giblin, 'Mary's Anointing for Jesus' Burial-Resurrection (John 12, 1-8)', *Bib* 73 (1992): 560–4.
[40] G. R. O'Day, 'John', in *Women's Bible Commentary*, edited by C. A. Newsom and S. H. Ringe, exp. edn (Louisville, KY: Westminster John Knox, 1998), 387.

12.3), and Nicodemus brings an enormous amount of perfume, 'a mixture of myrrh and aloes about a hundred pounds in weight' (μίγμα σμύρνης καὶ ἀλόης ὡς λίτρας ἑκατόν, 19.39). Mary's extravagant gift of perfume is surpassed by the abundance of the perfume brought by Nicodemus. John associates the two acts of anointing with Jesus's death since Jesus states that Mary has kept the perfume for 'the day of my burial' (12.7). Mary anoints Jesus openly at a dinner in Bethany but Joseph of Arimathea and Nicodemus anoint Jesus away from the crowds. John portrays Joseph of Arimathea as a secret disciple 'for fear of the Jews' (19.38), and he introduces Nicodemus with a reference to his earlier visit to Jesus as one who 'first came to him at night' (ὁ ἐλθὼν πρὸς αὐτὸν νυκτὸς τὸ πρῶτον, 19.39). Nicodemus is an ambiguous figure who is attracted to Jesus but who does not openly confess his faith during the lifetime of Jesus.[41] John presents Nicodemus as a Pharisee who attempts to prevent the arrest of Jesus (7.45-52). At the end of the gospel Nicodemus aligns himself with a man who has been condemned by the High Priest and executed by the Roman authorities.

The account of the anointing of Jesus by Mary of Bethany and the account of the anointing of Jesus by Nicodemus surround the events of the Passion Narrative. Mary anoints Jesus as the suffering Messiah before he enters Jerusalem where he will be arrested by the religious leaders and executed by the Roman authorities. After his death Joseph of Arimathea, a member of the Council, and Nicodemus, a Pharisee and leader of his people, carry out the burial of Jesus. It is ironic that John's account of Nicodemus and Joseph of Arimathea may point forward to the future acceptance of Jesus by members of these groups. In our passage two representatives from the groups who have opposed Jesus during his lifetime take responsibility for his burial. Mary's extravagant gift of perfume foreshadows the enormous amount of perfume which is brought by Nicodemus. The precious gifts point to the royal identity of Jesus and look forward to the new creation that will come about through his death. Mary of Bethany, moreover, foreshadows Mary Magdalene and the other female disciples who are present at the crucifixion of Jesus. John's account highlights the faithfulness of the women who follow Jesus. At the end of the gospel Mary Magdalene goes to the tomb, and she is the first person to see the risen Jesus (20.1-18).

In our narrative Mary of Bethany anoints Jesus with expensive perfume, and the scent of the perfume spreads through the house. John's account of Mary's act of anointing alludes to the abundance of the new creation. John employs the account of Mary of Bethany to prepare his audience for the events of the Passion Narrative. Jesus is the one who interprets Mary's gift, and he connects her act of anointing with the day of his burial. Jesus's response indicates that he has foreknowledge of the events of the Passion Narrative. John's description of the spread of perfume through the house foreshadows the abundant life that comes about through Jesus's death. His account of the spread of the perfume is also proleptic of the new creation. In our passage the people in the house may inhale the perfume, and they experience the abundance of the new creation.

---

[41] For an analysis of the character of Nicodemus, see J. M. Bassler, 'Mixed Signals: Nicodemus in the Fourth Gospel', *JBL* 108 (1989): 635-46.

Martha and Mary of Bethany and the Johannine community

In our narrative Martha and Mary have prominent roles at the beginning of the last week of Jesus's life. The sisters' request for Jesus's help leads to the final sign in the gospel, the raising of Lazarus from death. Martha confesses her faith in Jesus as the Messiah and Son of God, and Mary anoints Jesus as the suffering Messiah. The prominent roles of both women suggest that John depicts them as examples of discipleship. John's positive portrayal of Martha and Mary raises the question of the extent to which the sisters reflect the roles of women in the Johannine community. Raymond Brown, for example, notes that John does not make any specific references to church offices in his gospel but he suggests that our passage may allude to the discipleship roles of women.[42] At the beginning of the passage Lazarus reclines with Jesus while Martha serves, and Mary anoints him. In our narrative Martha serves a meal, and she may be seen as taking a traditional female role within a household. Brown, however, suggests that the description of the service of Martha (διηκόνει, 12.2) may allude to the role of a deacon (διάκονος) in the early church (1 Cor. 3.5; 2 Cor. 3.6; 6.4; 11.23; Phil. 1.1; Rom. 16.1; Col. 4.7). The frequent references to deacons in the early church support the view that John's audience would be familiar with this position in the church. John's use of the verb διακονέω suggests that his audience may associate Martha's service with a discipleship role.

John's description of the service of Martha recalls the portrayal of a group of women in Mark's Gospel who are described as serving Jesus during his mission. In Mark's Gospel the women are mentioned for the first time at the crucifixion. These women have followed and 'served' Jesus in Galilee before accompanying him to Jerusalem (διηκόνουν αὐτῷ, 15.40-41). Mark does not define the nature of the women's service but the concrete meaning of the verb διακονέω is to 'wait at table' and serve food.[43] In Mark's Gospel the verb διακονέω (serve), however, is also discipleship term, since Jesus instructs the twelve male disciples that they should take the role of a servant (διάκονος, 9.35; 10.43). Jesus defines his mission in terms of service, and he states that he has come not 'to be served but to serve' and give his life a ransom for many (διακονηθῆναι ἀλλὰ διακονῆσαι, 10.45). In Mark's Gospel the male disciples are not described as serving Jesus but women do serve Jesus.[44] The language of service is also linked with discipleship in John's Gospel. In John 12 Jesus teaches that whoever 'serves' him (διακονῇ) must follow him, and he states that his servant (διάκονος) must be wherever he is (12.26). In our passage Martha serves a meal at Bethany but the associations of the verb διακονέω with discipleship in the New Testament suggest that John portrays her as a model of discipleship.

---

[42] R. E. Brown, *The Community of the Beloved Disciple: The Life, Loves, and Hates of an Individual Church in New Testament Times* (New York: Paulist Press, 1979), 183-98.
[43] H. Beyer, 'διακονέω, διακονία, κτλ', in *TDNT* 2:81-93.
[44] For an analysis of the service of the women disciples, see S. Miller, *Women in Mark's Gospel*, JSNTSup 259 (London: T&T Clark, 2004), 161-6.

John's portrayal of Mary of Bethany, moreover, may also provide indications of the roles of women in the Johannine community. In our narrative Mary of Bethany is depicted as a prophetic figure, since her act of anointing Jesus demonstrates her insight into Jesus's identity as the Messiah and Son of God. Mary takes a role which is associated with men, since male prophets and priests anoint kings. In the Passion Narrative traditional expectations of a powerful Messiah are reversed, and Jesus comes to Jerusalem to suffer and die. Mary recognizes that Jesus's death is imminent, and she anoints Jesus as King before he enters Jerusalem. Jesus defends Mary's expensive gift, and he interprets her action in relation to his death. John's portrayal of Mary is reminiscent of several other female characters who show insight into the identity of Jesus as Messiah and Son of God. The Samaritan woman asked if Jesus could be the Messiah (4.29), and Martha confessed her faith in Jesus as the Messiah and Son of God (11.27).

In our passage Mary expresses her understanding of Jesus's identity by her prophetic action. In the Old Testament prophets carried out symbolic actions to convey God's purposes. Jeremiah shattered a potter's jar to foreshadow the imminent disaster facing his people. Jesus also carried out prophetic actions such as his act of overturning the tables in the Temple (2.13-22), his entry into Jerusalem on a donkey (12.12-19) and his act of washing the feet of his disciples (13.1-20). Mary is thus aligned with the prophetic actions of Jesus since she seeks to communicate her faith through her act of anointing Jesus as the Messiah. She demonstrates her devotion to Jesus with her costly gift which anticipates Jesus's own service in giving his life for others. The spread of the scent through the house looks forward to the abundance of the new creation that comes about through the death and resurrection of Jesus. The presentation of Mary of Bethany and the other women suggests that the theological insights of women were respected by the Johannine community.

John's portrayal of Mary may reflect the prophetic roles of women in the early church. There are other accounts of female prophets in the New Testament such as the seven daughters of Philip who have the gift of prophecy (Acts 21.9), and a woman, Jezebel, is criticized as one 'who calls herself a prophet' (ἡ λέγουσα ἑαυτὴν προφῆτιν, Rev. 2.20). The prophecies of these women, however, are not recorded whereas we do have prophecies of men including Agabus who speaks of the forthcoming arrest of Paul in Jerusalem (Acts 21.10-11). The gift of prophecy was valued highly in the early church. Paul lists prophets after apostles (1 Cor. 12.29-30), and he mentions prophecy first in his list of the gifts that are given to the church (Rom. 12.6-8). In 1 Corinthians women pray and prophesy during the worship of the church (11.2-16). Paul describes the shared worship of the church in which the members come together with hymns, lessons, revelation and speaking in tongues (1 Cor. 14.26-32). Some prophesy and others interpret their speech, and Paul states that all can prophesy one by one (14.31). The association of women with prophecy has led Antoinette Wire to argue that women prophets held prominent roles in the Corinthian church.[45] Her theory is supported by Paul's concerns about women who prophesy with their heads uncovered in the church

---

[45] A. C. Wire, *The Corinthian Women Prophets: A Reconstruction through Paul's Rhetoric* (Minneapolis, MN: Fortress, 1990), 117–26.

(1 Cor. 11.2-16). Paul describes the shared role of women and men as prophets in the Corinthian church. Ute Eisen rightly argues that Paul's presentation of prophecy may be reinterpreted as a 'community phenomenon' since women and men prophesy.[46] Mary of Bethany does not speak in our narrative but her prophetic action may be interpreted as an example of the ways in which the prophetic insights of women were valued in some early Christian communities.

The positive portrayal of Martha and Mary may reflect the discipleship roles of women in the Johannine community. Martha has confessed her faith in Jesus as the Messiah and Son of God, and her service of a meal at Bethany recalls the discipleship of women in the early church. Mary carries out a prophetic action by anointing Jesus before his death. Her act of anointing Jesus's feet with expensive perfume and drying them with her hair is a prophetic action which looks forward to Jesus's act of washing the feet of his disciples. She interrupts the dinner at Bethany to anoint Jesus as the suffering Messiah. Mary carries out an action which Jesus will later teach his disciples to perform, and she is portrayed as a model of discipleship for the Johannine community.

Conclusion

In our narrative Mary of Bethany anoints Jesus at a dinner in Bethany while her sister Martha serves the meal and her brother reclines with Jesus. The anointing of Jesus demonstrates the gratitude of Mary for the raising of Lazarus but it also expresses his identity as the Messiah. Whereas the Samaritan woman and Martha engaged in conversation with Jesus and confessed their faith, Mary remains silent throughout the narrative. Mary breaks social conventions by loosening her hair and anointing Jesus's feet in the middle of a meal. She takes the role of a servant or slave in order to show her devotion to Jesus. Her prophetic action points forward to the role of Jesus as the suffering Messiah. The expensive perfume symbolizes the cost of Jesus's mission, and the spread of the perfume through the house anticipates the abundant life of the new creation.

Mary's act of anointing Jesus's feet foreshadows Jesus's act of washing the feet of his disciples (13.1-20). John's account of the foot washing is intended to prepare his audience for the events of the Passion Narrative. John has been anointed as the Messiah and King, and now he takes the role of a servant or slave in order to wash his disciples' feet. His humble nature will be seen in the Passion Narrative. John's description of the foot washing indicates Jesus's willingness to take on a lowly role to bring salvation. At the same time Jesus instructs his disciples to follow his example of service. Mary is a model of discipleship, since she takes the role of a servant to anoint Jesus's feet. Mary of Bethany's act of anointing Jesus concludes John's account of the family at Bethany. In the next chapter we will examine the role of the women who followed Jesus and who were the witnesses to his death.

---

[46] U. E. Eisen, *Women Officeholders in Early Christianity: Epigraphical and Literary Studies* (Collegeville, PA: Liturgical Press, 2000), 68.

6

The women at the cross (19.25-27)

Introduction

In all four gospels a group of women is described as being present at the crucifixion of Jesus. These women have come up to Jerusalem with Jesus, and they remain faithful to him at the time of his death. John identifies four women: the mother of Jesus, her sister, Mary of Clopas and Mary Magdalene (19.25). The women act as witnesses to Jesus's death, and one of the women, Mary Magdalene, will be the first person to meet the risen Jesus (20.1-18). John's list of women who witness the crucifixion differs from the lists of the women in the synoptic gospels. Mark names Mary Magdalene, Mary the mother of James and Joses, and Salome (15.40); and Matthew mentions Mary Magdalene, Mary the mother of James and Joseph, and the mother of the sons of Zebedee (27.55-56). Luke refers to the women who have travelled from Galilee to Jerusalem but he does not name them at this stage of his gospel (23.49). John's Gospel is the only gospel to refer to the presence of the mother of Jesus at the crucifixion. She was a witness to Jesus's first sign at the wedding at Cana (2.1-11), and she is also present at his death.

John lists women who are present at the cross but he does not give a detailed account of their roles. The women may have come up to Jerusalem for the celebration of Passover. It is possible, however, that John expects his audience to know that the women were part of Jesus's group of disciples. Luke refers to female disciples who travel with Jesus and the Twelve in Galilee in the course of Jesus's mission (8.1-3). Mark and Matthew also refer to the women who accompanied Jesus but they are not mentioned until the account of the crucifixion. Mark describes the women in terms of discipleship by stating that they have 'followed' and 'served' Jesus in Galilee (15.40-41). In Mark and Matthew, the male disciples flee at the arrest of Jesus (Mk 14.50; Mt. 26.56), and these women are thus the only followers of Jesus who witness the crucifixion. John also mentions the women for the first time at the crucifixion but he does not describe the role of the women within Jesus's mission, and he introduces the Beloved Disciple into his account.

In the Johannine crucifixion scene the mother of Jesus stands next to the Beloved Disciple, and Jesus addresses her, 'Woman, here is your son', and he says to the Beloved Disciple, 'Here is your mother' (19.26-27). The prominent position of this passage in the account of the crucifixion has led scholars to look for a symbolic interpretation of Jesus's words. Rudolf Bultmann proposes that the mother of Jesus represents

Jewish Christianity and the Beloved Disciple represents gentile Christianity.[1] On the other hand Raymond Brown suggests that the mother of Jesus represents the church, and the Beloved Disciple may be interpreted as an ideal disciple.[2] Rudolf Schnackenburg, moreover, argues that Mary is a representative of 'that part of Israel which is receptive to messianic salvation'.[3] In this chapter we will examine the theological significance of John's presentation of the mother of Jesus and the Beloved Disciple at the crucifixion. We will begin by assessing John's portrayal of the women who are present at the cross. We will then examine the role of these women in relation to John's understanding of discipleship. John associates the mother of Jesus with the beginning of Jesus's mission and with the time of Jesus's death. We will analyse the relationship between John's portrayal of the mother of Jesus and the theme of new creation. Finally, we will assess the extent to which John's portrayal of the mother of Jesus may provide an indication of the role of women within the Johannine community.

The portrayal of the women at the cross

John does not name the mother of Jesus in his account of the wedding at Cana (2.1-11), and she is also not named at the crucifixion. John's omission of Mary's name emphasizes her unique role as the mother of Jesus. In our narrative three of the women are called Mary, and the description 'the mother of Jesus' enables her to be distinguished from Mary of Clopas and Mary Magdalene. John, moreover, is the only evangelist who mentions the presence of the mother of Jesus at the crucifixion. Some scholars such as Robert Gundry, however, argue that Mark's reference to 'Mary, the mother of James and Joses' (15.40) may be identified with the mother of Jesus.[4] The names of this woman's sons recall the first two names of the sons of Mary who are listed in Mark's Gospel as James, Joses, Judas and Simon (6.3). Nevertheless, it is improbable that Mark would identify Mary by her relationship to Jesus's brothers rather than by her relationship to Jesus. Richard Bauckham proposes that the presence of the mother of Jesus at the crucifixion is historical, since Luke describes her with the first disciples and Jesus's brothers and sisters in the church in Jerusalem (Acts 1.14).[5] If Luke knew that Mary was a witness to the crucifixion, however, it is likely that he would have mentioned her in his Passion Narrative.

The second woman in John's list is anonymous, and she is identified as the sister of Jesus's mother. The third woman is called Mary of Clopas, and it is possible that her husband is the same man who is named as Cleopas in Luke's account of the

---

[1] R. Bultmann, *The Gospel of John*, translated by G. R. Beasley-Murray (Oxford: Blackwell, 1971), 673.
[2] R. E. Brown, *The Gospel according to John*, 2 vols, AB 29-29A (Garden City, NY: Doubleday, 1966–70), 2:922–7.
[3] R. Schnackenburg, *The Gospel according to St. John*, 3 vols (London: Burns & Oates, 1982), 3:278.
[4] R. H. Gundry, *Mark: A Commentary on His Apology for the Cross* (Grand Rapids, MI: Eerdmans, 1993), 977.
[5] R. Bauckham, 'Mary of Clopas (John 19:25)', in *Women in the Biblical Tradition*, edited by G. J. Brooke, Studies in Women and Religion 31 (Lewiston: Edwin Mellen Press, 1992), 252–3.

appearance of the risen Jesus on the road to Emmaus (24.13-32). Eusebius identifies Mary as the wife of Clopas and the mother of Simeon who became the leader of the Jerusalem church after the martyrdom of James (*Eccl. Hist.* 3.32.1-6; cf. 3.11.1; 4.22.4). Richard Bauckham, however, proposes that the sister of the mother of Jesus is the same person as Mary of Clopas.[6] Bauckham notes that Clopas is described as the brother of Joseph according to Hegesippus (*Eccl. Hist.* 3.11.1; 4.22.4), and he suggests that Mary of Clopas is the sister-in-law of Jesus's mother. Bauckham argues that the term for sister-in-law (γάλως) was not used frequently and that the term 'sister' ἀδελφή could refer to sister-in-law. It is not necessary, however, to interpret 'sister' in this way since John identifies Mary of Clopas by her husband's name. The mother of Jesus and Mary Magdalene, moreover, play a greater part in the Passion Narrative than Mary of Clopas, and there is no reason for John to provide an extended description of a woman who has a subsidiary role. Mary of Clopas may be mentioned because she was known in the Johannine tradition as a witness to the death of Jesus, and her son became a prominent leader of the Jerusalem church.

Mary Magdalene is named in all four gospels as a key witness to the death and resurrection of Jesus. In the synoptic gospels Mary Magdalene is named first in the list of women but in John's Gospel the mother of Jesus takes the most prominent place. John, however, will focus on Mary Magdalene in his account of the resurrection of Jesus (20.1-18). John's reference to Mary Magdalene in our passage prepares his audience for the prominent role of Mary Magdalene in the resurrection narrative. In our passage there is no introduction to Mary Magdalene or any description of her role in Jesus's mission. John does not need to provide any information about her because his audience would know that Mary Magdalene is one of the first witnesses to the resurrection, and her testimony is integral to the kerygma of the early church. She appears as a rival to Peter in the *Gospel of Thomas* (114), and she is described as a disciple in the *Gospel of Peter* (12.50). Mary also receives visions and special teaching from Jesus which the male disciples have not heard in the *Gospel of Mary*.

Mary Magdalene is not identified by the name of any male relative unlike the mother of Jesus and Mary of Clopas. The omission of a husband's name suggests that Mary Magdalene was not married, but it is possible that her husband has died or that she was divorced. In the first century most women married at a young age, and parents arranged marriages for their daughters.[7] Mary Magdalene is identified by her association with her hometown of Magdala, a fishing village in Galilee. Mary's identification by her hometown is similar to the way in which male characters such as Joseph of Arimathea are identified (19.38). The identification of Mary with Magdala indicates that she has become well-known among people outwith her hometown. She was recognized as a disciple of Jesus and a member of his itinerant group of disciples who had accompanied him from Galilee to Jerusalem.

John's reference to the four women raises the question of whether he knows the synoptic tradition of the presence of women at the crucifixion. There are variations in the lists of the women's names in the gospel accounts. In Mark's Gospel three

---

[6] Bauckham, 'Mary of Clopas', 238.
[7] T. Ilan, *Jewish Women in Greco-Roman Palestine* (Peabody, MA: Hendrickson, 1996), 65–9.

women are named: Mary Magdalene, Mary the mother of James the younger and Joses, and Salome (15.40), and in Matthew's Gospel two women are named: Mary Magdalene and Mary the mother of James and Joseph (27.56). Matthew does not include Salome but adds a reference to the mother of James and John. It is possible that the mother of James and John was called Salome. On the other hand Matthew may omit the reference to Salome because he has no information about her, and she is not known to his community. Salome's name appears in Gnostic literature but these texts may reflect the later tendency of Christians to develop traditions based on the named women in the gospels. Luke mentions the female disciples at an earlier stage of Jesus's mission naming Mary Magdalene, Joanna, the wife of Herod's steward Chuza, and Susanna (8.2-3). He also states that women from Galilee are witnesses to the death of Jesus but he does not name the women at the crucifixion (23.49).

John refers to three women who are not mentioned in the synoptic tradition, and with the exception of Mary Magdalene, he does not include the names of the women who are witnesses in the synoptic gospels. It is likely that John has an independent source which mentions the mother of Jesus, her sister, Mary of Clopas and Mary Magdalene. The sister of the mother of Jesus is anonymous, and it is probable that she was linked to the mother of Jesus in the Johannine tradition. Mary of Clopas could be identified with one of the women named Mary in the synoptic tradition but the reference to Clopas suggests that John has employed an independent source. The only woman who appears in all four accounts is Mary Magdalene. She is well known as a witness to the resurrection, and John's account of her meeting with the risen Jesus suggests that he has independent traditions concerning her role.

The inclusion of a number of women's names in the gospel traditions highlights the prominence of women among Jesus's disciples. Each evangelist records the presence of women as witnesses to Jesus's crucifixion but with the exception of Mary Magdalene they refer to different women. One of the difficulties in identifying the women arises from the small number of women's names used at this time. Tal Ilan notes that almost 50 per cent of all women were named either Mariamme or Salome in her study of the distribution of Jewish women's names in Palestine in the Second Temple and Mishnaic periods.[8] For this reason it would have been easy for the women's names in the gospel tradition to become confused. As Richard Bauckham rightly argues, the differences in the list of names indicate that each evangelist wishes to remain faithful to the names of the women in his own tradition.[9] Each gospel records a small number of women's names out of the larger group who followed Jesus. Some of the names recorded in the gospels, moreover, may be known to members of the gospel communities. Mark names the sons of Joseph of Arimathea as Alexander and Rufus (15.21) but Matthew and Luke both omit these names. It is possible that the members of Mark's community know Alexander and Rufus but Matthew and Luke have left out these names in their

---

[8] T. Ilan, 'Notes on the Distribution of Jewish Women's Names in Palestine in the Second Temple and Mishnaic Periods', *JJS* 40 (1989): 186–200.
[9] R. Bauckham, *Jesus and the Eyewitnesses: The Gospels as Eyewitness Testimony* (Grand Rapids, MI: Eerdmans, 2006), 49–51.

gospels because their audiences would not recognize these men.[10] In Mark's Gospel, Mary is described as 'the mother of James the younger and Joses', and her sons may be known to Mark's community (15.40). The women's names in each gospel may reflect the particular interests of each evangelist. John's Gospel is the only gospel which mentions the presence of the mother of Jesus at the crucifixion. It is possible that the veneration of Mary within the Johannine tradition has led to the inclusion of Mary and her sister in the list of women who are present at the crucifixion. If Mary of Clopas was married to the man named Cleopas who appears in Luke's Gospel, she may have been remembered in the Johannine tradition on account of their association with the church in Judea.[11]

John refers to the presence of four women at the cross whereas the other evangelists refer to the presence of a larger group of anonymous women (ἄλλαι πολλαὶ, Mk 15.41; γυναῖκες πολλαὶ, Mt. 27.55; ἕτεραι πολλαί, Lk. 8.3). John's focus on four women may downplay the significance of the larger group of women who support Jesus. Jesus enters Jerusalem with a crowd of supporters who disappear after he has been arrested. These people, however, form the basis of the mission of the early church after Jesus's death. Many ordinary women and men who supported Jesus formed Christian communities in their own villages and towns. John's narrative technique, however, tends to emphasize individual characters who have a representative function. The individual characters are mentioned in order to illustrate the deepening of each person's relationship with Jesus, and John's audience is encouraged to identify with each woman or man. In this account John focuses on the mother of Jesus and her relation to the Beloved Disciple, and in the resurrection narrative he will describe the visit of Mary Magdalene to the tomb of Jesus and her recognition of the risen Jesus.

John's reference to the mother of Jesus, her sister and Mary of Clopas reflects the distinctive Johannine tradition. No member of the Twelve, however, is present at the crucifixion, and Mary's sons, the brothers of Jesus, are also not described. On the other hand John mentions the Beloved Disciple who is the founder of the Johannine tradition. The Beloved Disciple appears as a witness to the events in the Passion Narrative but he is not named. He is defined by his relationship to Jesus, and he is portrayed as an ideal disciple. As Raymond Brown points out, the mother of Jesus and the Beloved Disciple are both defined in terms of their relation to Jesus, and they are both anonymous.[12] The presence of the Beloved Disciple at the crucifixion highlights his role as a witness since he is the only male disciple who remains faithful to Jesus at the time of his death. John associates the mother of Jesus with the disciple who is the founder of the Johannine tradition. John's description of the mother of Jesus and the Beloved Disciple at the crucifixion situates the origins of the Johannine tradition within the lifetime of Jesus.

---

[10] J. Marcus, *Mark 1-8: A New Translation with Introduction and Commentary*, AB 27 (Garden City, NY: Doubleday, 1999), 25.

[11] C. K. Barrett (*The Gospel according to St. John: An Introduction with Commentary and Notes on the Greek Text*, 2nd edn (London: SPCK, 1978), 21) examines the possibility that a Judean source was one of the sources for John's Gospel. Barrett notes that Jesus's mission is primarily conducted in Judea with the exception of chs 2, 4, 6 and 7.

[12] R. E. Brown, *The Death of the Messiah. From Gethsemane to the Grave: A Commentary on the Passion Narratives in the Four Gospels*, 2 vols, ABRL (Garden City, NY: Doubleday, 1994), 2:1021.

At the end of the gospel the narrator states that the Beloved Disciple bears witness about these things and has written these things (ὁ μαρτυρῶν περὶ τούτων καὶ ὁ γράψας ταῦτα, 21.24). The narrator speaks for the Johannine community in the statement, 'We know that his testimony is true' (21.24). John links the mother of Jesus with the Beloved Disciple to give authority to the Johannine tradition.

Discipleship and the women at the cross

In John's Gospel four women stand as witnesses to the crucifixion, and Jesus is aware of their presence. The women demonstrate courage since they are followers of a man who has been condemned to death by the Roman governor. John's portrayal of the women suggests that they are models of discipleship. In our passage the women stand near the cross but in the synoptic gospels the women stand at a distance from the crucifixion, and they are not mentioned until after the death of Jesus. The differences between John's Gospel and the synoptic gospels raise questions about which account is historical. Mark Goodacre suggests that the synoptic account of the women has been influenced by the Psalms of the Righteous Sufferer in which the friends of the sufferer stand at a distance.[13] It is possible that the phrase 'at a distance' (ἀπὸ μακρόθεν, Mk 15.40) has been added to Mark's Gospel as a scriptural allusion to the Psalms of the Righteous Sufferer (ἀπὸ μακρόθεν, Ps. 37.11; 87.8 LXX). Luke's account also shows the influence of the Psalms of the Righteous Sufferer in which the man's friends 'stand' at a distance (εἱστήκεισαν ... ἀπὸ μακρόθεν, 23.49; cf. Ps. 87.8 LXX). In the synoptic gospels the distance between Jesus and the women alludes to the portrayal of Jesus as the righteous sufferer who is separated from his friends.

All four gospels, however, describe people near the cross, and it is probable that the women may also have been able to approach Jesus. Mark refers to the distance of the women from Jesus to heighten Jesus's sense of abandonment (15.40). He wishes to emphasize that Jesus dies alone, suffering a bleak and cruel death. Jesus is mocked by the passers-by and the chief priests, and even those crucified with Jesus revile him (15.29-32). The distance of the women reflects Mark's distinctive portrayal of the isolation of Jesus, since Jesus does not know that the women are present. In John's Gospel Jesus has not been abandoned by his followers, and he is able to speak to his mother and the Beloved Disciple.

John's account of the presence of the women at the cross demonstrates their courage and loyalty to Jesus. Luise Schottroff points out that the families and friends of crucified men could also face persecution (Tacitus, *Ann.* 6.10, 19; Suetonius, *Tib.* 61; Philo, *Flacc.* 72; Josephus, *War* 2.253).[14] Jesus is condemned to death by the Roman governor, Pilate, and Roman soldiers guard the crucifixion scene. In Mark's Gospel members of the

---

[13] M. S. Goodacre, 'Scripturalization in Mark's Crucifixion Narrative', in *The Trial and Death of Jesus: Essays on the Passion Narrative in Mark*, edited by G. Van Oyen and T. Shepherd (Leuven: Peeters, 2006), 33–47.

[14] L. Schottroff, *Let the Oppressed Go Free: Feminist Perspectives on the New Testament* (Louisville, KY: Westminster John Knox, 1993), 171–2.

crowd mock Jesus, and they may also be hostile towards his followers (15.29). John does not include the hostile mockery of the crowd but he does refer to four soldiers who are in charge of the crucifixion. His reference to the soldiers emphasizes the strength of Roman military power and the role of crucifixion as a deterrent to anyone who dared to challenge the authority of the Roman Empire.

John describes the way in which the four soldiers divide Jesus's clothes into four parts with one part for each soldier (19.23). Edwyn Hoskyns rightly proposes that the four women are contrasted with four soldiers who are present at the crucifixion (19.24-25).[15] John refers to the actions of the four soldiers, and then he introduces the four women with the phrase μὲν ... δέ. The hostile actions of the four soldiers are thus contrasted with the faithful presence of four women. John's account of the four women highlights the positive response of human beings to Jesus. Jesus has been condemned to death by his enemies but John indicates that some of Jesus's followers remain faithful to him. In the synoptic gospels the Roman centurion recognizes Jesus (Mt. 27.54; Mk 15.39; Lk. 23.47) but in John's Gospel the mother of Jesus and the Beloved Disciple are the main witnesses to Jesus's death. The women are powerless to intervene to stop the crucifixion but their presence is a sign of their commitment to Jesus. John does not give any account of the women's emotions. The women stand together as a group, and they give support to one another as witnesses.

John does not refer to the presence of the twelve male disciples who followed Jesus. It is probable, however, that he knows the tradition of the flight of the disciples at the arrest of Jesus (cf. Mt. 26.56; Mk 14.50). The flight of the male disciples points to the dangers which disciples faced on account of their association with Jesus. John seeks to avoid the portrayal of the weakness of the male disciples by stating that Jesus commands his captors to let his disciples go free when he is arrested (18.8). In John's Gospel Jesus is crucified as a rebel, and the charge against him reads the 'King of the Jews' (19.19). If his disciples are recognized as his followers, they may also be viewed as rebels and arrested. In the Johannine account of the trial of Jesus, the High Priest questions Jesus about his disciples (18.19), and John thus emphasizes the danger that disciples of Jesus face. Peter is specifically asked if he is a disciple of Jesus (18.17, 25-27), and his fear of arrest leads him to deny Jesus three times (18.15-18, 25-27). After the death of Jesus the disciples are described behind locked doors because they are afraid of the religious authorities (διὰ τὸν φόβον τῶν Ἰουδαίων, 20.19).

John not only refers to four women, he also adds a reference to the Beloved Disciple. Mark and Matthew depict a contrast between the presence of the women and the absence of the male disciples. John's reference to the Beloved Disciple reflects his more positive attitude towards the male disciples. In Mark and Matthew, the women are not described until after the death of Jesus, and there is no indication that Jesus is aware of their presence. In John's Gospel Jesus knows that his mother and the Beloved Disciple are present, and he is able to speak to them. John portrays the four women as examples of faith and discipleship, since they may risk arrest by their presence at the crucifixion. John's account focuses on Jesus's speech to his mother and the Beloved Disciple, and

---

[15] E. C. Hoskyns, *The Fourth Gospel*, edited by F. N. Davey, 2 vols (London: Faber, 1940), 631.

he mentions Mary Magdalene because she is the first person to see the risen Jesus. Mary is able to bring continuity to the kerygma of the early church because she is a witness to the death and resurrection of Jesus. It is important for John to identify Mary Magdalene, since her testimony gives authority to the proclamation of the church.

The mother of Jesus and the Beloved Disciple

The mother of Jesus appears at the beginning of Jesus's mission at the wedding at Cana (2.1-12) and at the crucifixion of Jesus (19.25-27). These two narratives which feature Mary form a frame around Jesus's mission. They also have several features in common, since both describe Mary as the 'mother of Jesus' (2.1; 19.25) and both refer to the 'hour' (2.4; 19.27). In the account of the wedding at Cana, Jesus was reluctant to intervene because his 'hour' had not yet come (2.4). As Margaret Beirne notes, the 'hour' has now come (13.1), and she points out that the Beloved Disciple first appeared at the Last Supper at the time of Jesus's hour (13.23).[16] Mary is present at the first sign in which Jesus reveals his glory (2.1), and she is described as standing near Jesus's cross at the hour of his glorification (12.23; 13.1; 17.1-5). The mother of Jesus and the Beloved Disciple have key roles as witnesses to the revelation of Jesus.

In our passage Jesus announces that his mother is now the mother of the Beloved Disciple and that the Beloved Disciple is her son (19.26-27). Several symbolic interpretations of the role of the mother of Jesus and the Beloved Disciple have been proposed. Rudolf Bultmann suggests that Mary is intended to represent Jewish Christianity and the Beloved Disciple to represent gentile Christianity.[17] The Beloved Disciple, however, is Jewish, and he is not associated with gentiles in any gospel narrative. On the other hand Raymond Brown argues that the mother of Jesus represents 'the church', and the Beloved Disciple represents the 'Christian disciple'.[18] Brown associates the mother of Jesus with the church which produces children who are 'modelled after Jesus'. It is probable that the Beloved Disciple represents the group of disciples but John does not give any indication that Mary is to be interpreted as the 'church'. The Greek term 'church' (ἐκκλησία) does not appear in John's Gospel, and John does not show any interest in church order (cf. Matthew 18). John's portrayal of Mary as 'mother' suggests that she holds the honorific role of 'mother' in relation to the disciples. The Johannine community may venerate Mary as the mother of Jesus and regard her as their 'mother'. Mary is present at the beginning of Jesus's mission, and she remains faithful at the time of Jesus's death. The disciples may view Mary as a 'mother' who will remain present with them in the midst of their suffering.

In this section we will examine John's portrayal of the mother of Jesus and the Beloved Disciple. There has been no indication that Mary knows the Beloved Disciple in the earlier narratives. Why does John link these two figures for the first time in the

---

[16] M. M. Beirne, *Women and Men in the Fourth Gospel: A Genuine Discipleship of Equals*, JSNTSup 242 (Sheffield: Sheffield Academic Press, 2003), 174–5.
[17] Bultmann, *John*, 673.
[18] Brown, *John*, 2:926.

account of the crucifixion? The Beloved Disciple is identified as the disciple whom Jesus loves (19.26) but he is not mentioned in the synoptic gospels. He does not appear in the opening chapters of John's Gospel, and he is not depicted as one of the twelve male disciples chosen by Jesus (13.23). The Beloved Disciple comes to the fore in the Passion Narrative, and he shows special insight into Jesus's mission. At the Last Supper he is the disciple who asks Jesus about the identity of the disciple who will betray him (13.25). He is present at the crucifixion, and he will go with Peter to the empty tomb. It is possible that the Beloved Disciple was from Jerusalem and had not been one of Jesus's followers in Galilee.[19] He is often identified as the 'other disciple' who accompanies Peter to the court of the high priest (ἄλλος μαθητής, 18.15). This theory would explain why the disciple is known to the high priest, and it would provide an explanation for his ability to gain access for Peter into the courtyard (18.15). In the resurrection account, moreover, the Beloved Disciple is identified as 'the other disciple whom Jesus loved' (τὸν ἄλλον μαθητὴν ὃν ἐφίλει ὁ Ἰησοῦς, 20.2) and as the 'other disciple' (ὁ ἄλλος μαθητής, 20.8). The Beloved Disciple is unnamed and described in terms of Jesus's love for him. John depicts the Beloved Disciple as an ideal disciple who demonstrates insight into Jesus's mission. James Resseguie points out that the Beloved Disciple demonstrates greater understanding of Jesus's mission than the other disciples.[20] As Resseguie observes, John employs the Beloved Disciple as a representative of 'the ideal point of view of the narrative' since this disciple 'sees and judges' events correctly (cf. 7.24). The Beloved Disciple is an exemplary disciple but he is also a representative of the group of disciples, since Jesus instructs his disciples to love one another as he loved them (13.34-35; 15.17). Jesus loves all his disciples, and each disciple is a 'Beloved Disciple'.

John's portrayal of the Beloved Disciple as 'an ideal disciple' leads some scholars, such as Rudolf Bultmann, to propose that the Beloved Disciple is not a historical figure.[21] Andrew Lincoln notes that the character of the Beloved Disciple in some ways serves as a literary device since he does not change the course of events in any of the scenes in which he appears but he does have a significant role as a witness.[22] At the end of the gospel, however, the disciple has died, and his death appears to be unexpected because the community believed that Jesus had prophesied that he would return while this disciple was still alive (21.20-23). The community's concern over the unexpected death of the Beloved Disciple suggests that he is a historical figure who is associated with the foundation of the Johannine community. The Beloved Disciple is anonymous in the gospel but his identity is known to John's community. John's omission of the disciple's name enables the Beloved Disciple to act as a model of discipleship for John's audience to follow.

---

[19] D. M. Smith, *John* (Nashville, TN: Abingdon, 1999), 334–5.
[20] J. L. Resseguie, 'The Beloved Disciple: The Ideal Point of View', in *Character Studies in the Fourth Gospel*, edited by S. A. Hunt, D. F. Tolmie and R. Zimmermann, WUNT 314 (Tübingen: Mohr Siebeck, 2013), 537–49.
[21] Bultmann, *John*, 483–5.
[22] A. T. Lincoln, 'The Beloved Disciple as Eyewitness and the Fourth Gospel as Witness', *JSNT* 85 (2002): 3–26.

In our passage Jesus addresses his mother first, 'Woman, here is your son' (γύναι, ἴδε ὁ υἱός σου, 19.26), and he then speaks to the Beloved Disciple, 'Here is your mother' (ἴδε ἡ μήτηρ σου, 19.27). Jesus speaks to his mother with the address 'woman' which he also used at the wedding at Cana (2.4). In John 2 this address had a distancing effect, since Jesus was reluctant to intervene at the wedding at Cana. In our passage Jesus is facing death, and the address also has a distancing effect because he is about to leave his mother. Jesus's speech shows concern for the future welfare of his mother, and the Beloved Disciple will now take Jesus's place as her son. Jesus's speech, moreover, is reminiscent of the language of adoption rites. As C. K. Barrett points out, the adoption terminology suggests the formation of a new relationship between the mother of Jesus and the Beloved Disciple.[23] In the Graeco-Roman world it was common to adopt adults as heirs because many children died at a young age. It was usual for adoption rites to be expressed as a direct address, 'You are ...' as in Ps. 2.7; 1 Sam. 18.21 and Tob. 7.12.[24] George Beasley-Murray cites the example of the address to Tobit, 'From now on you are her brother, behold she is your sister' (Tob. 7.12).[25] In John's Gospel, however, there is a difference to the usual pattern of parents adopting children, since Jesus is a son who arranges the adoption of another son for his mother.

Mary becomes the symbolic mother of the Beloved Disciple, and he takes the place of Jesus as her son. Mary's role as 'mother' thus continues after the death of Jesus. The Beloved Disciple also represents the future discipleship community, and the mother of Jesus becomes the 'mother' to all the disciples. John's account links the origins of the new discipleship community to the death of Jesus. Jesus's last action before his death is to form a new relationship between his mother and the Beloved Disciple. John's account of the last words of Jesus to his mother and the Beloved Disciple emphasizes the lasting relationship of the mother of Jesus and the Beloved Disciple. The relationship of mother and son will continue beyond Jesus's death and will form the basis of the relationships between disciples in the new discipleship community. The mother of Jesus and the Beloved Disciple have significant roles in the new community because they are present at the death of Jesus. Colleen Conway observes that the mother of Jesus and the Beloved Disciple are both necessary for the future of the mission of Jesus.[26] As Conway notes, Mary's role as mother contributes to the formation of the new people of God who will continue Jesus's mission.

Jesus shows concern for his mother, and he wishes the Beloved Disciple to take care of her. From that 'hour' the Beloved Disciple takes her into his house, and she becomes part of his household (ἀπ' ἐκείνης τῆς ὥρας, 19.27). John's reference to the 'hour' recalls Jesus's reference to his 'hour' in his response to Mary at the wedding at Cana. Initially, he was reluctant to assist the wedding party because his 'hour' had not yet come (ἡ ὥρα μου, 2.4). In the account of the wedding at Cana, Jesus alluded to the

---

[23] Barrett, *St. John*, 552.
[24] R. E. Brown, K. P. Donfried, J. A Fitzmyer and J. Reumann (eds), *Mary in the New Testament: A Collaborative Assessment by Protestant and Roman Catholic Scholars* (London: Geoffrey Chapman, 1978), 213.
[25] G. R. Beasley-Murray, *John*, WBC 36, 2nd edn (Nashville, TN: Thomas Nelson, 1987), 349.
[26] C. M. Conway, *Men and Women in the Fourth Gospel: Gender and Johannine Characterization*, SBLDS 167 (Atlanta, GA: Society of Biblical Literature, 1999), 83.

'hour' of his Passion. In our passage the mother of Jesus is also associated with the 'hour' of Jesus. Mary now has a role as mother of the Beloved Disciple who represents the disciples. The 'hour' acts as a turning point in the account of the crucifixion because from that time the Beloved Disciple takes Mary into his household (19.27). John brings the characters of the mother of Jesus and the Beloved Disciple together for the first time at the death of Jesus since the 'hour' of Jesus's death is the critical time for understanding the nature of Jesus's identity and mission.

Our analysis of the role of Mary at the wedding at Cana has highlighted her prominent role as the one who initiated Jesus's first sign which led to the faith of his disciples (2.11). In our narrative Jesus has accomplished his mission, and John introduces members of the future discipleship community in his account of the crucifixion. Jesus prepares his mother and the Beloved Disciple to continue his mission after his death. John's reference to the 'hour' indicates that the time has come for the formation of the new discipleship community. The Beloved Disciple takes Mary into his household, and his household will become the home of the new discipleship community. The future relationship between disciples will reflect their identity as sisters and brothers of Jesus.

The mother of Jesus is present at the first sign and at the death of Jesus. We have noted several correspondences between John's account of the wedding at Cana and his account of the crucifixion. In the wedding at Cana, Jesus's 'hour' is linked to the transformation of water into abundant wine (2.1-11). John also refers to wine at his account of the crucifixion. Jesus is thirsty, and he is offered a sponge of wine (19.28-30). At the beginning of the Passion Narrative Jesus states, 'Am I not to drink the cup that the Father has given me' (18.11). In our narrative Jesus's last drink of wine indicates his acceptance of death, and it points to the completion of his mission. John states that Jesus completes his mission by handing over the Spirit (παρέδωκεν τὸ πνεῦμα, 19.30). John employs the verb παραδίδωμι which has the meaning 'to hand over' but he does not include an object for this verb. Barnabas Lindars proposes that Jesus hands his spirit over to God.[27] John, however, does not specifically refer to 'his' spirit but 'the' spirit which suggests that he may allude to the Holy Spirit.[28] As Brown rightly argues, the presence of the mother of Jesus and the Beloved Disciple at the foot of the cross implies that Jesus hands the Spirit over to them.[29] John's association of the gift of the Spirit with the death of Jesus is established in an earlier passage. Jesus has prophesied that the Spirit will be given when he is glorified, and the crucifixion is the time of his glorification (cf. 7.39).

Jesus's last act of handing over the Spirit is depicted briefly but it raises theological questions concerning the future role of the Spirit within the group of disciples. In his Farewell Discourse Jesus promised that 'the Paraclete' will be given to the disciples after his death (16.7). Jesus's prophecy about the gift of the Spirit is placed in the context of his preparation of the disciples for his departure from the world. The term 'Paraclete' (παράκλητος) is from the Greek verb παρακαλέω which has the literal meaning 'to call

---

[27] B. Lindars, *The Gospel of John*, NCBC (London: Marshall, Morgan & Scott, 1972), 582–3.
[28] A. T. Lincoln, *The Gospel according to Saint John*, BNTC (London: Continuum, 2005), 478.
[29] Brown, *John*, 2:931.

alongside', and it may be translated as 'to encourage' or 'to comfort'.[30] Some scholars such as Barrett argue that John does not refer to the Holy Spirit in our passage because John includes a later account in which the risen Jesus gives the Holy Spirit to the disciples (λάβετε πνεῦμα ἅγιον, 20.22).[31] It is possible, however, to interpret Jesus's action of handing over the Spirit in our passage as an act that foreshadows his gift of the Spirit to the disciples in the resurrection narrative. At the crucifixion the mother of Jesus and the Beloved Disciple represent the group of disciples who will receive the Spirit.

The mother of Jesus and the Beloved Disciple are present at the 'hour' of Jesus's glorification when his divine identity is revealed. In the Passion Narrative Jesus announces that the mother of Jesus is now the mother of the Beloved Disciple and that he is her son. Mary becomes the 'mother' of all the disciples since the Beloved Disciple represents the group of disciples. Jesus hands over the Spirit to his mother and the Beloved Disciple, and they form the basis of the new discipleship community that is formed at the cross. The mother of Jesus is present at the first sign that reveals Jesus's glory (2.11), and his death is depicted as the time of glorification (12.23; 13.1; 17.1-5). At the wedding at Cana, Mary brought the lack of wine to Jesus's attention and initiated his first sign which led to the belief of the disciples, and in this account she stands together with the Beloved Disciple at the beginning of the new discipleship community.

The mother of Jesus and the new creation

In this section we will assess John's portrayal of the mother of Jesus in relation to the theme of new creation. In our analysis of the mother of Jesus at the wedding at Cana, we noted that John associated Mary with the figure of Eve. Jesus addressed his mother as 'woman' (γύναι, 2.4), and Eve is identified as the 'woman' in the creation account of Genesis (2.15-17; 3.8, 15). In John 2 Jesus distanced himself from his mother's request for assistance because his 'hour' had not yet come. In our passage Jesus's 'hour' has arrived, and he addresses his mother again as 'woman' (γύναι, 19.26). Jesus announces that Mary is now the mother of the Beloved Disciple, and the Beloved Disciple is her son. John presents a change of identity for both the mother of Jesus and the Beloved Disciple. Mary has a new identity as 'mother' to the Beloved Disciple, and he has a new identity as her 'son'. John depicts the Beloved Disciple as a representative of all Jesus's disciples. He thus suggests that Mary has a new identity as 'mother' to all the disciples of Jesus.

John presents Jesus's announcement to his mother and the Beloved Disciple as an act of new creation. Jesus creates a new relationship between his mother and the Beloved Disciple, and this relationship forms the foundation of the new community of

---

[30] For an assessment of the role of the Paraclete in John's Gospel, see R. E. Brown, 'The Paraclete in the Fourth Gospel', *NTS* 13 (1967): 126–8 and C. K. Barrett, 'The Holy Spirit in the Fourth Gospel', *JTS* 1 (1950): 1–15.

[31] Barrett, *St. John*, 554.

disciples. The role of Mary as 'mother' of the new community echoes the description of Eve as the 'mother of all who live' (Gen. 3.20), and in *1 Enoch* the Son of Man is described as the 'son of the mother of all that live' (62.7). In our passage Mary becomes the 'mother' of all who follow Jesus. John depicts a change of identity in the character of Mary since she now becomes the 'mother' of the new community of disciples. John's association of Mary with Eve reflects John's belief that those who believe in Jesus are 'reborn'. In the prologue John states that those who believe in Jesus are born 'not of bloods nor the will of flesh nor the will of man but of God' (1.13). In John 3, Jesus told Nicodemus that anyone who wishes to see the kingdom of God must be 'born again' or 'born from above' (ἄνωθεν, 3.3). In John's apocalyptic world view there is a contrast between those who are born in the present world and those who are born of God. In our passage John's use of the imagery of motherhood associates the rebirth of the disciples with the time of Jesus's death. Jesus's announcement is an act of new creation which forms a new relationship between his mother and the Beloved Disciple. Those who believe in Jesus receive a new 'mother', and they become sisters and brothers of Jesus.

John's association of Mary with the role of Eve alludes to the Johannine theme of the new creation which is inaugurated by Jesus's death and resurrection. In Genesis, Eve is present at the beginning of creation, and in our passage John presents Mary as the new Eve who is present at the beginning of the new creation. John depicts the crucifixion of Jesus as the 'hour' of his glorification. In John's apocalyptic world view Jesus casts out the 'ruler of the world', and the new age begins (cf. 12.31; 16.11). In Genesis, Adam's disobedience to God brought death into the world but in John's Gospel Jesus has come to bring humanity eternal life. Jesus's last words, 'It is finished' (τετέλεσται, 19.30), indicate that he has completed his creative work. John uses the verb τελειόω (complete) to emphasize that Jesus has accomplished his mission. Barrett rightly notes that the Johannine Jesus is concerned to complete the work that God has given him (τελειώσω αὐτοῦ τὸ ἔργον, 4.34; ἐγώ σε ἐδόξασα ἐπὶ τῆς γῆς τὸ ἔργον τελειώσας ὃ δέδωκάς μοι ἵνα ποιήσω, 17.4).[32] John's account suggests that Jesus's mission is brought to completion at the time of his death on the cross. Jeannine Brown, moreover, rightly points out that John uses the term 'work' to refer to Jesus's mission (αὐτοῦ τὸ ἔργον, 4.34; αὐτὰ τὰ ἔργα, 5.36) and in Genesis God's acts of creation are described as 'works' (τὰ ἔργα, Gen. 2.2 LXX).[33] John's account of the crucifixion indicates that Jesus has been sent into the world to complete God's 'work' of creation.

John's portrayal of the motherhood of Mary, moreover, has eschatological associations. Raymond Brown proposes that John's reference to 'mother' in our passage recalls the Old Testament image of Zion as 'mother' in Isaiah (49.14-22; 54.1-3; 66.7-13).[34] In Isaiah, 'mother Zion' is promised numerous children who will prosper in the land. Brown argues that Mary is portrayed as 'mother Zion' who suffers birth pangs before she produces a new people. He interprets the role of the mother of Jesus in

---

[32] Barrett, *St. John*, 553–4.
[33] J. K. Brown, 'Creation's Renewal in the Gospel of John', *CBQ* 72 (2010): 284–6.
[34] Brown, *John*, 2:925–6.

relation to Jesus's parable about a woman who suffers labour pains but who forgets her suffering once she has given birth (16.21). The metaphor of birth pangs occurs frequently in prophecies of the new age (Isa. 26.17; *1 En.* 62.4; *4 Ezra* 4.42; Mt. 24.8; Mk 13.8). In these passages a period of fear and suffering precedes the joy and peace of the new age. Brown notes that the Old Testament imagery of a woman with birth pangs forms the background to the Johannine Jesus's parable (16.21).[35] Jesus compares the sorrow of the disciples at his death to the suffering of a pregnant woman. John gives an eschatological interpretation of the parable since the joy of the woman at the birth of her child is compared to the joy of the disciples at the resurrection of Jesus. John's portrayal of Mary as 'mother Zion' may be compared to other New Testament texts in which the imagery of motherhood is applied to the city of Jerusalem. Paul links the heavenly Jerusalem to the motherhood of Sarah in Galatians. Sarah is the mother of the Christians who do not obey the Law, whereas the earthly Jerusalem is associated with Hagar, who is the mother of the law-observant Jewish-Christian community in Jerusalem (4.21–5.1).

John's portrayal of the motherhood of Mary links Mary with the eschatological hopes of Israel. Donald Senior rightly observes that John's association of the mother of Jesus and the Beloved Disciple indicates that the new discipleship community has 'its roots in the faith of Israel'.[36] Mary is the mother of Jesus, and she is the 'mother' of all the disciples who become his brothers and sisters. In the Old Testament 'mother Zion' is associated with the hopes and expectations of the new age. The term 'mother Zion' is linked to the communal restoration of the people of Israel, and in John's Gospel the mother of Jesus is associated with the formation of the community of disciples. John's portrayal of Mary recalls Jesus's statement to the Samaritan woman that salvation comes from the Jewish people (4.22). In our narrative the mother of Jesus becomes the 'mother' of the Beloved Disciple who is a representative of Jesus's disciples. Mary is a figure of unity within the Johannine tradition, since the disciples all share the same mother, regardless of their racial background.

John's presentation of Mary and the Beloved Disciple contains additional allusions to the theme of new creation. At the crucifixion Jesus hands over the Spirit to Mary and the Beloved Disciple. The Spirit is the eschatological gift of the new creation (cf. Ezek. 36.26-27; Joel 2.28-29). Edwyn Hoskyns points out that the Spirit is the 'means of re-creation' just as the Spirit is the means of creation in the account of creation in Gen. 1.2.[37] Jesus passes on the creative power of God to the new discipleship community which is formed at the cross. John's description of the piercing of Jesus's side also alludes to the gift of life (19.34-37). The soldier pierces Jesus's side with the result that blood and water pour from Jesus's wound. John emphasizes the life-giving nature of Jesus's death by describing the blood and water which come out of Jesus's side. On the one hand John's references to blood and water confirm that Jesus is dead but blood and water also have symbolic associations with salvation.

---

[35] Brown, *John*, 2:731.
[36] D. Senior, *The Passion of Jesus in the Gospel of John* (Leominster: Gracewing/Fowler Wright Books, 1991), 114.
[37] E. C. Hoskyns, 'Genesis I-III and St John's Gospel', *JTS* 21 (1920): 211.

In our passage the description of the water recalls Jesus's prophecy of the Spirit as 'living water' which is linked to Jesus's death (ὕδατος ζῶντος, 7.37-39). The significance of water is emphasized in an earlier passage in which Jesus told Nicodemus that he must be born of 'water and spirit' to enter the kingdom of God (ἐξ ὕδατος καὶ πνεύματος, 3.5). John's description of the blood, moreover, is reminiscent of John 6 in which Jesus states, 'Unless you eat the flesh of the Son of Man and drink his blood, you have no life in you; the one who eats my flesh and drinks my blood has eternal life' (6.53-54). Ernst Haenchen argues that our passage alludes to the sacraments of Baptism and the Eucharist.[38] As Haenchen proposes, John's account indicates that the life-giving power of the sacraments comes through the death of Jesus. The blood and water that flow from Jesus's side are thus signs of the abundant life which Jesus brings humanity.

In our narrative John's portrayal of Mary as a new Eve alludes to the theme of new creation. Eve is the first mother, and Mary becomes the 'mother' of the discipleship community which is formed at the cross. Jesus's announcement to Mary and the Beloved Disciple is an act of new creation. Their new relationship of mother and son forms the basis of the new community of disciples. Jesus completes his mission, and he hands over the Spirit which is the creative power of the new age. John's portrayal of Mary also recalls 'mother Zion' who gives birth to the people of Israel. John associates Mary with the heritage of Israel, and Mary links the disciples to the Jewish origins of Jesus. Mary is the 'mother' of all disciples, and she connects the disciples to Jesus because the disciples are all brothers and sisters of Jesus. The mother of Jesus links the disciples to the beginning of Jesus's mission. After the death and resurrection of Jesus, the disciples are connected to the time of Jesus's earthly mission through their relationship with her.

The mother of Jesus and the Johannine community

In John's Gospel Jesus prepares his disciples to continue his mission after his death. He announces to his mother that she is now the mother of the Beloved Disciple and that the Beloved Disciple is her son. The formation of the discipleship community indicates that the work of Jesus has now been accomplished. Jesus is concerned about the future welfare of his mother, and he entrusts the Beloved Disciple with her care. John's account of the new relationship between the mother of Jesus and the Beloved Disciple, however, is unusual since Jesus's brothers are still living, and they would be expected to care for their mother.[39] Jesus's brothers travelled with Jesus, his mother and the disciples after the wedding at Cana but they are not depicted as disciples (2.12). At the Feast of Tabernacles they urged Jesus to go up to Jerusalem to show himself to the crowd since they did not believe in him (7.5). When Jesus set off for Jerusalem, he did not let his brothers know. There is a contrast between John's positive portrayal of Mary and his negative presentation of Jesus's brothers.

---

[38] E. Haenchen, *John 2* (Philadelphia, PA: Fortress, 1984), 201.
[39] Barrett, *St. John*, 552.

John's presentation of Jesus's brothers is unexpected since Jesus's brother, James, became leader of the Jerusalem church. In the New Testament James is frequently associated with law observance (cf. Acts 12.17; 15.13-21; 21.8; Gal. 2.11-14). On the other hand John links Mary with Jesus's first sign in which Jesus transforms the water reserved for the purity regulations into abundant wine. John's presentation of this sign suggests that his community no longer observes the purity regulations. It is possible that John wishes to distance Jesus and Mary from the law-observant leadership of James. John depicts the mother of Jesus as mother of all his disciples, and James no longer has a special place as one of Jesus's birth brothers. At the crucifixion Jesus gives the Spirit to his mother and the Beloved Disciple who represent the new discipleship community (19.30). John links the mother of Jesus with the Beloved Disciple in order to give authority to the tradition of his community.

John's positive portrayal of Mary raises the question of the nature of her role within the discipleship group. Our analysis of Jn 2.1-12 suggested that John has given her a different role from that of the disciples. She had faith in Jesus before the beginning of his mission. She prompted Jesus to carry out his first sign, and this sign led to the faith of the disciples (2.11). In our passage Mary becomes the symbolic mother of the Beloved Disciple, and the Beloved Disciple is a representative of all Jesus's disciples. As Gail O'Day suggests, the mother of Jesus is present at the beginning of Jesus's mission, and she brings continuity to Jesus's mission whereas the Beloved Disciple represents the Johannine community.[40] The relationship between the mother of Jesus and the Beloved Disciple thus expresses the link between Jesus's ministry and the Johannine tradition.

John's presentation of Mary at the beginning of Jesus's mission and at his death indicates that Mary has an honoured place in the Johannine tradition. It is possible that John's understanding of the role of 'mother' has been influenced by the honorific references to women as 'mothers' within Jewish texts. Sidnie White Crawford argues that the term 'mothers' refers to an authoritative group of women in the Qumran text 4QD^{e}7 I, 13-15.[41]

> Whoever murmu[r]s against the Fathers [shall be expelled] from the congregation and shall not return; [but if] against the Mothers, then he shall be punished te[n] days, because the Mo[th]ers do not have 'authority' in the midst of [the congregation].

Crawford argues that the terms 'mothers' and 'fathers' are employed as parallel references, and she proposes that the 'mothers' and 'fathers' have positions of leadership in the community. This text, however, implies that the fathers have a greater leadership role than the mothers since women do not have authority in the

---

[40] G. R. O'Day, 'John', in *Women's Bible Commentary*, edited by C. A. Newsom and S. H. Ringe, exp. edn (Louisville, KY: Westminster John Knox, 1998), 388.

[41] S. White Crawford, 'Mothers, Sisters, and Elders: Titles for Women in Second Temple Jewish and Early Christian Communities', in *The Dead Sea Scrolls as Background to Post Biblical Judaism and Early Christianity*, edited by J. R. Davila (Leiden: Brill, 2003), 177-91.

congregation. There are some indications that women had the role of 'mothers' in early Christian communities. In Mark's Gospel, Jesus refers to the new group of disciples as his 'brother and sister and mother' (ἀδελφός μου καὶ ἀδελφὴ καὶ μήτηρ, 3.35), and he tells his disciples that those who lose their birth families will receive 'brothers and sisters, mothers and children' (ἀδελφοὺς καὶ ἀδελφὰς καὶ μητέρας καὶ τέκνα, 10.30). Mark's references to 'mothers' suggests that some women had the role of 'mothers' to the disciples in the synoptic tradition. Mark refers to 'brothers', 'sisters' and 'mothers', and similarly, the term 'sisters' is employed to refer to members of the community (1 Cor. 7.15; Rom. 16.1; Jas 2.15).[42]

There are, moreover, references to the term 'mother' in some synagogue inscriptions. Bernadette Brooten has analysed a range of inscriptions which relate to women, and she notes three references to women as 'mother of the synagogue' in Italy.[43] Brooten identifies a Latin inscription 'mater synagogarum Campi et Columni' (CII 523), and a reconstructed Greek inscription as [μή] τηρ συνα[γωγῆς] (CII 496) from Rome. She reconstructs an additional inscription as [μήτηρ συ] ναγωγῆς (CII 166) but this example lacks the word 'mother'. In addition, Brooten notes a Latin inscription 'matri synagogue' (CII 639; CIL V 411) from Venetia in Brescia, and another Latin inscription with the term μήτηρ used as a title from Venosa in Apulia. The use of the term 'mother' in honorific inscriptions may have influenced the portrayal of Jesus's mother in John's Gospel. In these inscriptions women are honoured as the 'mothers' of the synagogue, and in John's Gospel Mary is portrayed as the 'mother' of the new discipleship community. John's identification of Mary as the 'mother of Jesus' may suggest that she has an honorific role in the Johannine tradition.

In several New Testament texts the term 'mother' may refer to women who hold positions of leadership within the early Christian communities. In Romans, Paul sends a greeting to Rufus and his mother who is described as 'his mother and mine' (τὴν μητέρα αὐτοῦ καὶ ἐμοῦ, 16.13). The mother of John Mark is an example of women who provided a house for the Christians to meet (Acts 12.2). The author of 2 John addresses his letter to 'the elect lady and her children' (2 Jn 1). Mary D'Angelo proposes that the author of this epistle refers to a woman who is the leader of a Christian community.[44] D'Angelo points out that the author of Revelation refers to a woman leader of a Christian community as 'Jezebel' and identifies her followers as her 'children' (Rev. 2.20, 23). D'Angelo's interpretation of the address in 2 John is supported by the reference at the end of the letter to the 'children of your elect sister' (2 Jn 13). Adele Reinhartz, moreover, argues that the mother of Jesus in John's Gospel represents 'elder female leadership at the core of the community'.[45] Reinhartz proposes that the anonymity of

---

[42] White Crawford, 'Mothers', 177–91.
[43] B. J. Brooten, *Women Leaders in the Ancient Synagogue: Inscriptional Evidence and Background Issues*, BSJ 36 (Chico, CA: Scholars Press, 1982), 57–72.
[44] M. R. D'Angelo, '(Re)Presentations of Women in the Gospels: John and Mark', in *Women and Christians Origins*, edited by R. S. Kraemer and M. R. D'Angelo (Oxford: Oxford University Press, 1999), 132.
[45] A. Reinhartz, 'Women in the Johannine Community: An Exercise in Historical Imagination', in *A Feminist Companion to John Volume II*, vol. 2, edited by A.-J. Levine with M. Blickenstaff(London: Sheffield Academic Press, 2003), 18–21.

Mary in John's Gospel supports the theory that she is a representative of women in the community.

Our analysis of John's portrayal of Mary, however, indicates that she holds a unique role in the Johannine tradition as the mother of Jesus. John's location of passages that feature Mary at the beginning of Jesus's mission and at the crucifixion points to her distinctive role in the gospel. Mary's request for Jesus's assistance leads to a sign that deepens the faith of the disciples. The mother of Jesus and the Beloved Disciple form the basis of the new discipleship community. Although there is evidence that some women were known as 'mothers' within the early church, John does not use the term 'mothers' in this way (cf. Mk 10.30). John's presentation of the mother of Jesus suggests that she is honoured within the Johannine community on account of her unique role as the mother of Jesus. At the cross she becomes 'mother' to all disciples of Jesus, and there are no indications that her role is shared by others.

John's portrayal of Mary as the 'mother' of all disciples, moreover, may bring comfort to some members of John's community. In the Farewell Discourse Jesus refers to the future conflicts between the disciples and the religious authorities (15.18-25; 16.1-4, 33). In the early church some disciples may experience conflicts with their birth families, and these people may find a new symbolic mother in Mary. The community becomes a source of relationships which supports disciples in the midst of their suffering and enables them to give support to others. Mary is portrayed as an ideal figure since she embraces others who are not part of her family. John's portrayal of Mary recalls the account of the mother of Jesus at the beginning of the gospel in which she interceded with Jesus on behalf of the hosts and guests when the wine ran out at the wedding at Cana. The presentation of joy and festivity in the opening scene emphasizes the power of Jesus to transform the world. At the beginning of the gospel John placed a narrative which alludes to the abundant joy that will come about through Jesus's death and resurrection. The glory glimpsed throughout Jesus's mission enables John's audience to recognize the abundant life that comes through Jesus's death.

Conclusion

The mother of Jesus, her sister, Mary of Clopas and Mary Magdalene are all described as witnesses to the crucifixion of Jesus. These women are representatives of the women disciples of Jesus, and they show courage by remaining with him at the time of his death. John associates the mother of Jesus with the Beloved Disciple because he is the source of the Johannine tradition. Jesus entrusts his mother to the care of the Beloved Disciple. This passage also has theological significance since the mother of Jesus becomes the symbolic mother of the Beloved Disciple, and he becomes her son. Jesus's address 'woman' associates the portrayal of Mary with the figure of Eve in Genesis. Eve is the first mother of humanity, and Mary is the 'mother' of the disciples. John depicts the Beloved Disciple as a representative of her children, and Mary is the symbolic mother of all who believe in Jesus.

John's presentation of Mary may also have been influenced by the honorific use of the term 'mother' which may be seen in Jewish writings such as the Dead Sea Scrolls and synagogue inscriptions. In John's Gospel the mother of Jesus has a unique role as 'mother' to Jesus, and this role continues after the death of Jesus. John links the characters of the mother of Jesus and the Beloved Disciple for the first time at the cross. The mother of Jesus and the Beloved Disciple are the chosen successors of Jesus. Jesus gives his mother and the Beloved Disciple a new identity as 'mother and son'. John depicts their new relationship as an act of new creation. This relationship forms the basis of the new community of disciples which is created at the cross. At his death Jesus hands over the Spirit to his mother and the Beloved Disciple, and they are given the power to continue the mission of Jesus.

7

Mary Magdalene (20.1-18)

Introduction

The final narrative in John's Gospel which features a woman character describes the visit of Mary Magdalene to the tomb of Jesus. In John 19, Mary Magdalene was among the group of women who witnessed the crucifixion of Jesus, and she is now portrayed as the first person to meet the risen Jesus. John's account of the conversation between Mary and Jesus is reminiscent of earlier conversations between the Samaritan woman and Jesus (4.1-26) and between Martha and Jesus (11.1-27). At first the Samaritan woman and Martha did not understand Jesus but they gradually recognized his identity in the course of their conversations with him. In our narrative Mary initially believes Jesus is the gardener but she recognizes him when he calls her by her name. John portrays Mary as a model of discipleship, since she passes on the news of the resurrection (20.18). Her testimony 'I have seen the Lord' is the foundational belief of the early church because she bears witness to the resurrection of Jesus.

The gospels all give an account of the visit of women to the empty tomb but their narratives differ in several ways. In John's Gospel Mary Magdalene goes to the tomb alone, and she is the first person to meet the risen Jesus. In Mark's Gospel, however, Mary Magdalene, Mary and Salome go to the tomb but they run away terrified to pass on the news of the resurrection (16.1-8). Matthew describes the visit of Mary Magdalene and another woman named Mary, and these two women meet the risen Jesus (28.9-10). In Luke's Gospel, Mary Magdalene, Joanna, Mary the mother of James and some other women visit the tomb and meet two angels but they do not see Jesus (24.1-10). John's Gospel is distinctive on account of its detailed description of the reunion of Mary Magdalene and Jesus. It also differs from the synoptic gospels since it includes an account of the visit of Peter and the Beloved Disciple to Jesus's tomb. Mary tells the male disciples that Jesus's body is missing, and they run to the tomb. Peter is the first disciple to go into the tomb but the Beloved Disciple then enters the tomb, and he 'saw and believed' (20.8). Peter and the Beloved Disciple go back home but Mary remains at the tomb weeping. Jesus then appears to Mary, and he asks her to tell the disciples that he is ascending to God.

In each gospel women are the central characters who discover that Jesus has been raised from death but John is the only evangelist to describe the visit of male disciples to the tomb before a resurrection appearance to Mary Magdalene. In Matthew's Gospel the male disciples are the recipients of the women's message and they do not go to the tomb (28.9-10). In Luke's Gospel the male disciples initially doubt the women's testimony but Peter goes to the tomb to find out if their report is true (24.12). John, however, has introduced the figure of the Beloved Disciple into an earlier stage of his resurrection narrative. The Beloved Disciple has greater insight than Peter because he is the first disciple to realize that the resurrection has taken place. John's situation of the visit of Peter and the Beloved Disciple to the tomb draws attention to the leading roles of the male disciples within the gospel. In this chapter we will examine the question of whether or not John's account of the male disciples downplays the discipleship role of Mary Magdalene.

The variations in the resurrection accounts, moreover, raise questions about the sources which John has employed for his resurrection account. It is probable that John has knowledge of three traditions concerning the resurrection: the visit of women to the empty tomb (cf. Mk 16.1-8), the meeting of Mary Magdalene with the risen Jesus (cf. Mt. 28.9-10) and the visit of disciples to the tomb (cf. Lk. 24.12, 24). There are some tensions, however, in the way that John has blended the accounts together. Mary goes to Peter and the Beloved Disciple to inform the disciples about the empty tomb. After the disciples enter the tomb, the Beloved Disciple 'saw and believed' (20.8) but there is no indication that he tells Mary about the resurrection. Mary remains weeping at the tomb, and she still believes that Jesus's body has been removed from the tomb. The Beloved Disciple is the first disciple to understand that the resurrection has taken place. John, however, does not develop the character of the Beloved Disciple as a witness to the resurrection. Instead, he gives an extended account of the meeting between Jesus and Mary Magdalene, and he focuses on Mary's recognition of Jesus.

In this chapter we will analyse the distinctive features of John's portrayal of Mary Magdalene. We will assess the ways in which John develops Mary Magdalene's recognition of the risen Jesus and the extent to which John depicts Mary as a model of discipleship. In the course of their conversation Jesus addresses Mary as 'woman' (γύναι, 20.15). This address recalls the earlier accounts in which Jesus addressed his mother and the Samaritan woman as 'woman' (γύναι, 2.4; 4.21; 19.26). In the account of the wedding at Cana, John links the address 'woman' with the character of Eve in the creation account of Genesis. We will examine the relationship between Mary Magdalene and the character of Eve, and we will assess the role of Mary Magdalene in relation to the Johannine theme of new creation. In our narrative Jesus sends Mary Magdalene to tell the disciples that he has been raised. Mary's testimony to the resurrection is foundational for the mission of the early church. We will analyse the extent to which John's portrayal of Mary Magdalene may provide any indication of the roles of women in the Johannine community.

The portrayal of Mary Magdalene

John presents Mary as a figure of courage since she goes alone to the tomb without any friend for support. In the synoptic gospels several women go to the tomb at dawn whereas in our passage Mary visits the tomb while it is still dark. Jesus has been executed as a rebel, and Mary risks arrest if she is identified as one of his followers. The Johannine account of the visit of the women to the tomb focuses on Mary Magdalene, and no other women are described. John's account differs from the resurrection narratives in the synoptic gospels. Mark refers to Mary Magdalene, Mary the mother of James and Salome (16.1); and Matthew names Mary Magdalene and the other Mary (28.1). On the other hand Luke mentions a large number of women: Mary Magdalene, Joanna, Mary the mother of James and other anonymous women (καὶ αἱ λοιπαὶ σὺν αὐταῖς, 24.10). The multiple attestation to the group of women suggests that the account of the large number of female disciples in the synoptic gospels is historical but the evangelists have remained faithful to the names of the women within their own traditions. Mary Magdalene is mentioned in each list of women which indicates her importance as a disciple of Jesus and as a witness to his death and resurrection.

The different accounts of the number of women who visit the tomb raise the question of whether the synoptic gospels have increased the number of women to strengthen their testimony or whether John has restricted the number of women to focus on Mary Magdalene. It is probable that John is aware of the tradition of the visit of a group of women because Mary employs a first-person plural verb in her speech to the disciples, 'We do not know where they have placed him' (οὐκ οἴδαμεν ποῦ ἔθηκαν αὐτόν, 20.2). Although John's audience may know the synoptic tradition of the visit of more than one woman to the tomb, it is characteristic of John's literary technique to focus on the conversation between Jesus and one character as in the account of the meeting of Jesus with Nicodemus (3.1-21) and his meeting with the Samaritan woman (4.1-26). This literary technique enables John to develop a detailed interchange between Jesus and each individual. John wishes to develop the personal relationship of each individual with Jesus and to explore the significance of each person's faith in Jesus.

In John's Gospel an individual's relationship with Jesus frequently has a representative function. Nicodemus acts as the representative of the Pharisees who have witnessed Jesus's signs (3.2), and the Samaritan woman speaks for the Samaritans in her conversation with Jesus (4.9, 12, 20). Mary Magdalene has travelled with Jesus from Galilee to Jerusalem, and she is known as a disciple of Jesus. John's narrative depicts a change in Mary's understanding of the identity of Jesus. Initially, Mary does not recognize Jesus because she does not expect the resurrection to have taken place. The meeting between Mary Magdalene and Jesus illustrates the change in Mary's character from her lack of understanding to her recognition of Jesus as the risen Lord. The growth in Mary's understanding of Jesus may reflect the experience of the members of John's audience who have just heard the account of Jesus's trial and execution and who now share Mary's joy. Mary Magdalene is thus a representative of all disciples who move from emotions of fear and despair at the death of Jesus to trust and belief in the risen Jesus.

In all four gospels the women are law-observant, and they wait until the Sabbath is over before going to the tomb. The evangelists, however, give different accounts of the purpose of the women's visits. Mark states that Mary Magdalene and the other women buy spices and go to the tomb to anoint Jesus (16.1), whereas Matthew says that the women go to see the tomb (28.1). In Luke's Gospel the women prepare spices and take them to the tomb (24.1). In John's Gospel, however, Joseph of Arimathea and Nicodemus anointed Jesus at the time of his death, and there is no need for Mary Magdalene to bring anointing oils (19.38-42). John gives no explanation for Mary's journey but his narrative may imply that she goes to the tomb to mourn Jesus. The custom of visiting the tomb of a loved one is mentioned in the earlier description of the mourners from Jerusalem who believed that Mary of Bethany had gone to the tomb of her brother Lazarus to mourn his death (11.31).[1]

John presents Mary as the last remaining follower of Jesus, and her visit to the tomb demonstrates her devotion to Jesus. Mary Magdalene is the first person to go to the tomb but she does not enter the tomb. She believes that some people have taken Jesus's body from the tomb. Mary leads Peter and the Beloved Disciple to the tomb, and the Beloved Disciple 'saw and believed' (εἶδεν καὶ ἐπίστευσεν, 20.8). Colleen Conway points out that the disciples return home, whereas Mary remains at the tomb weeping.[2] Conway argues that the disciples' response implies that they have not fully understood that the resurrection has taken place. John's statement that the Beloved Disciple 'saw and believed', however, implies that this disciple does believe that Jesus has been raised. Throughout John's Gospel verbs of sight have theological significance, and they are particularly associated with belief. At the beginning of the gospel Philip expressed his faith that Jesus is the one prophesized in the scriptures, and he invited Nathanael to 'come and see' (ἔρχου καὶ ἴδε, 1.46). The Samaritan woman told Jesus, 'I see you are a prophet' (κύριε, θεωρῶ ὅτι προφήτης εἶ σύ, 4.19). John's use of the language of sight and belief indicates that the Beloved Disciple has the correct understanding of Jesus.

John's portrayal of the faith of the Beloved Disciple raises the question of whether John downplays the discipleship role of Mary Magdalene. In our passage the Beloved Disciple is the first person to believe in the resurrection whereas Mary stands weeping outside the tomb. Andrew Lincoln suggests that the introduction of the Beloved Disciple and Peter into the narrative may reflect John's desire to highlight the presence of two male disciples as witnesses to the empty tomb because the testimony of women may be doubted (cf. Deut. 19.15).[3] This interpretation is supported by the portrayal of the male disciples in Luke's Gospel since they doubt the women's report about their meeting with the two angels at the tomb and their news of the resurrection (24.11). There is little contemporary evidence, however, concerning the authority of the testimony of women in Jewish texts. The Dead Sea Scrolls contain a reference to the authority of the testimony of a wife concerning her husband's obedience to the Law (1QSa 1.11) but the context of this testimony is not clear.[4] Josephus, moreover, does not accept

---

[1] K. E. Corley (*Maranatha Women's Funerary Rituals and Christian Origins* (Minneapolis, MN: Fortress, 2010)) notes that women in the Graeco-Roman world are traditionally associated with carrying out funerary rites on the third day after a bereavement.

[2] C. M. Conway, *Men and Women in the Fourth Gospel: Gender and Johannine Characterization*, SBLDS 167 (Atlanta, GA: Society of Biblical Literature, 1999), 188–92.

[3] A. T. Lincoln, *The Gospel according to Saint John*, BNTC (London: Continuum, 2005), 490.

[4] J. M. Baumgarten ('On the Testimony of Women in 1Qsa', *JBL* 76 (1957): 266–9) proposes that the feminine pronoun in this passage is a textual error. He argues that this text does not refer to the testimony of women since it is concerned with the initiation of a young man into the community at the age of around twenty, and it is unlikely that the testimony of his wife, who would be an adolescent woman, would be regarded as authoritative. The lack of sources, however, makes it difficult to discern the extent to which the testimony of women was accepted in the first century.

the validity of the testimony of women (*Ant.* 4.219). Tal Ilan examines the attitudes towards the testimony of women in some later rabbinic texts. She observes that the testimony of women was not permitted in court as a 'general principle' but if no male witnesses were available it was possible to call upon a woman to give testimony (*b. Ket.* 74b).[5] A woman could testify to the death of another woman's husband to enable her to remarry (*m. Yeb.* 16.5; *b. Bekh.* 46b). Ilan observes that Herod's sister, Salome, was a judge in the trial of Herod and Mariamme's two sons (*War* 1.538), and she gave testimony against Antipater (*Ant.* 17.93). She rightly points out, however, that the rules concerning the testimony of women are not applicable to the question of the validity of testimony of women to the resurrection because these women were not asked to testify in a formal court.

In our narrative John depicts Mary Magdalene as a witness to the resurrection since she is instructed by Jesus himself to pass on the news of the resurrection. John also presents other women characters as witnesses to Jesus. The Samaritan woman convinced the people of her town to come to see Jesus (4.39), and Martha is linked with the main Christological confession of faith within John's Gospel (11.27). It is probable that John wishes to highlight the faith of the Beloved Disciple because he is associated with the foundation of the Johannine tradition. John depicts the Beloved Disciple as someone who believes without seeing the risen Jesus. The Beloved Disciple has deeper insight into the role of Jesus than the other disciples. John thus presents the Beloved Disciple as an example of faith for later Christians who do not see the risen Jesus. John's concern for later disciples may be seen at the end of the gospel when the Johannine Jesus blesses the disciples who will believe without seeing (20.29). John, however, develops the role of Mary Magdalene as the first person who meets the risen Jesus. Mary is portrayed as independent and courageous since she goes alone to the tomb of a crucified man while it is still dark. She remains faithful to Jesus at the time of his death, and she is a witness to the resurrection. The Beloved Disciple is depicted as an ideal disciple because he believes in the resurrection without seeing the risen Jesus. On the other hand John does not downplay the discipleship role of Mary Magdalene since he develops an extended conversation between Mary Magdalene and Jesus in which she recognizes Jesus. In the next section we will examine the way in which Mary Magdalene comes to recognize the risen Jesus in the course of her meeting with Jesus.

The conversation between Mary Magdalene and Jesus

Several features of the conversation between Mary Magdalene and Jesus recall earlier conversations between Jesus and women such as his meeting with the Samaritan woman (4.1-26) and his meeting with Martha (11.1-27). In each narrative the women initially do not understand Jesus but then come to a recognition of Jesus's identity. These narratives portray women as those who have knowledge of Jesus's identity and who confess their faith in him. The Samaritan woman wondered if Jesus could be

---

[5] T. Ilan, *Jewish Women in Greco-Roman Palestine* (Peabody, MA: Hendrickson, 1996), 163–6.

the Messiah (4.29), and Martha confessed her faith in Jesus as the 'Messiah, the Son of God, the one coming into the world' (11.27). In our narrative Mary Magdalene recognizes Jesus as her 'Teacher' (20.16) and 'Lord' (20.18). Mary's recognition of Jesus, however, differs from that of the other women since she recognizes Jesus after his death and resurrection. John depicts a recognition scene in which Mary recognizes Jesus as the teacher of the past but she also comes to a new understanding of Jesus as the risen Lord.

Our narrative consists of two scenes in which John presents the meeting between Mary and the two angels (20.11-13) and then the meeting between Mary and Jesus (20.14-17). The presence of the angels indicates that a miraculous event has taken place, and the angels mark the place where Jesus's body had lain. In apocalyptic writings angels are depicted as messengers who reveal the mysteries of the end-time (cf. *1 Enoch*; *4 Ezra*), and in John's Gospel two angels are waiting to pass on the news of the resurrection. They ask Mary why she is weeping, and she replies that she is crying because they have taken Jesus away (20.13). Mary does not show any awareness that she is speaking to angels even though the angels have mysteriously appeared in the tomb. John describes the angels as dressed in white (ἐν λευκοῖς, 20.12), and white clothes are frequently associated with the heavenly realm (cf. Mk 9.3; 16.5; Rev. 7.9, 13-14). Mary does not grasp the spiritual implications of the empty tomb, and she focuses on the material question of the location of Jesus's missing body. Mary believes that some people have taken Jesus's body from the tomb. The possibility that Jesus's enemies have moved his body is raised in Matthew's account of the resurrection. In Matthew's Gospel guards are placed at Jesus's tomb in case the disciples attempt to steal his body (27.62-66). In our passage Mary's response to the angel's question may be intended by John to counter a similar charge that Jesus's body has been removed from the tomb by his disciples.

In the synoptic gospels the angels instruct the women to pass on the news of the resurrection but in our narrative Jesus himself appears at the tomb and speaks to Mary. At first Mary does not recognize Jesus but her lack of recognition is a characteristic feature of other gospel accounts of the resurrection. In Matthew's Gospel the risen Jesus meets the eleven remaining disciples on a mountain in Galilee, and they worship him but some of the disciples doubt (28.16-18). In Luke's Gospel two disciples meet Jesus on the road to Emmaus but do not recognize him until he breaks bread and gives it to them (24.13-35). In John's Gospel, the disciples do not recognize Jesus when he appears on the shore of the Sea of Tiberias (21.4). The failure of human beings to recognize Jesus highlights the difference between the earthly Jesus and the risen Jesus. The risen Jesus transcends the constraints of earthly life, since he appears and disappears suddenly (Lk. 24.31), and he is able to move through closed doors (Jn 20.19, 26).

John's narrative focuses on the way in which Mary comes to recognize Jesus. At first the angels address Mary as 'woman' (γύναι), and they ask her why she is weeping (20.13). Jesus then addresses Mary as 'woman' (γύναι, 20.15) which recalls the similar address to his mother (2.4; 19.26) and the Samaritan woman (4.21). This address forms a connection between the narratives that feature women, and it draws attention to the gender of the women. The address highlights Jesus's initiative in seeking a response from the women. Jesus asks Mary questions which are designed to lead her to a recognition of his identity. He repeats the words of the angels, 'Woman, why are weeping?' and he then asks Mary, 'Whom do you seek?' (τίνα ζητεῖς, 20.15). John Painter rightly observes that Jesus's question focuses Mary's attention on her search for Jesus.[6] Mary initially seeks the body of Jesus because she does not realize that Jesus has risen from the dead.

Mary's search for the body of Jesus leads to her failure to recognize the risen Jesus. Mary believes that Jesus is the gardener, and she assumes that he is responsible for the removal of Jesus's body (20.15). As Sandra Schneiders observes, Mary speaks to Jesus without recognizing his voice but she does recognize him when he calls her by her name (20.16).[7] John draws attention to Jesus's knowledge of the identity of each individual, and he emphasizes Jesus's desire to seek a relationship with each person. In our narrative there is a progression between Jesus's first address 'woman' and his later use of Mary's name. John employs the address 'woman' in his presentation of Mary's gradual recognition of Jesus. A stranger could address Mary as 'woman' but Jesus knows her name. This passage is the only example of an occasion in which Jesus calls a woman by her name. Jesus's use of Mary's name reveals his knowledge of her and recalls their prior relationship as teacher and disciple.

John's recognition scene is reminiscent of Jesus's earlier account of the good shepherd who calls his own sheep by name (10.1-6). The sheep follow the shepherd because they recognize his voice, and he protects the sheep leading them in and out of the sheepfold.[8] The good shepherd's knowledge of the names of all his sheep emphasizes Jesus's care of each individual and his willingness to lay down his life for his sheep. John's concept of discipleship is concerned with the personal relationship of Jesus with each one of his followers. In our narrative the relationship between Mary and Jesus is restored since she responds to Jesus by addressing him as her 'teacher' (ραββουνι, 20.16). Mary's address implies that she has known Jesus for some time as her 'teacher', and she is portrayed as one of his disciples. This address re-establishes the relationship between Jesus and Mary as teacher and disciple. John's account of the reunion between Jesus and Mary indicates that this relationship continues beyond death.

John depicts the reunion of Jesus and Mary but he also indicates that Jesus's identity has changed. When Mary recognizes Jesus, she clasps hold of him but he gives an unexpected response, 'Do not hold me' (μή μου ἅπτου, 20.17). Jesus's response is surprising since Mary has just recognized Jesus, and it is customary for people to embrace on the occasion of a reunion. Franz Neirynck argues that John has been influenced by Matthew's account of the meeting of Jesus with Mary Magdalene and the other woman named Mary (28.9-10).[9] In Matthew's gospel the women embrace Jesus,

---

[6] J. Painter, *The Quest for the Messiah: The History, Literature and Theology of the Johannine Community*, 2nd edn (Edinburgh: T&T Clark, 1993), 379.
[7] S. M. Schneiders, 'John 20:11-18: The Encounter of the Easter Jesus with Mary Magdalene – A Transformative Feminist Reading', in *What Is John? Vol. 1*, edited by F. F. Segovia (Atlanta, GA: SBL Symposium Series, 1996), 162–4.
[8] R. E. Brown, *The Gospel according to John*, 2 vols, AB29-29A (Garden City, NY: Doubleday, 1966–70), 2:1008–10.
[9] F. Neirynck, 'John and the Synoptics: The Empty Tomb Stories', *NTS* 30 (1984): 166–71.

and he instructs them to pass on the news of the resurrection. Neirynck suggests that the Johannine Jesus's instruction, 'Do not hold me' (μή μου ἅπτου, 20.17), corresponds to the Matthean Jesus's statement, 'Do not be afraid' (μὴ φοβεῖσθε, 28.10). In Matthew's Gospel, however, the women seize Jesus's feet (ἐκράτησαν αὐτοῦ τοὺς πόδας, 28.9), whereas in John's Gospel Mary is instructed to stop holding Jesus. Matthew uses the strong verb κρατέω (hold, hold fast, seize) but John employs the verb ἅπτομαι (take hold of, touch). The differences between John's narrative and Matthew's narrative suggest that John has not employed Matthew's Gospel as a source.

John's use of the verb ἅπτομαι, however, is unusual since it suggests that Jesus does not wish Mary to touch him. Mary D'Angelo argues that the verb ἅπτου in our passage implies that it is dangerous for Mary to touch Jesus.[10] She compares Jesus's instruction to Mary with the speech of Adam to Eve in the *Life of Adam and Eve* 'when I die, leave me alone and let no one touch me (μηδείς μου ἅψηται) until the angel of the Lord shall say something about me'.[11] D'Angelo proposes that the two passages have a similar function. She argues that Eve's act of touching Adam's body and Mary's act of touching Jesus are both considered to be dangerous. In the *Life of Adam and Eve*, however, Adam does not want Eve to touch his body after his death whereas in our account Jesus has returned to life. Nevertheless, D'Angelo's comparison of the texts points to the otherworldly nature of the risen Jesus. Jesus has not returned to his previous life. He is now returning to the heavenly realm, and the constraints of the earthly realm have no power over him.

In our passage, moreover, the verb ἅπτου is a present imperative which indicates continuous action. It is probable that Mary embraces Jesus when she recognizes him and she continues to hold him. Mary's action reflects her love for Jesus and her wish to keep Jesus with her. The Johannine Jesus, however, does not want Mary to hold him because he must ascend to God (οὔπω γὰρ ἀναβέβηκα πρὸς τὸν πατέρα, 20.17). Jesus's reply indicates that there is now a change in his relationship with Mary, and he is not returning to his previous life with his disciples. Nevertheless, Jesus's statement is puzzling since John does not include an account of the ascension (cf. Acts 2.33-35; 5.31; 7.55-56; 1 Pet. 3.22). John associates the language of ascending and descending with Jesus throughout the gospel (ἀναβαίνω, καταβαίνω, cf. 1.51; 3.13; 6.41-51, 60-65).[12] He depicts Jesus as one who ascends from God to conduct his mission and who ascends to God through his death and resurrection.

In a later resurrection appearance, however, Jesus invites Thomas to place his hands in his wounds (20.24-29). D. Moody Smith suggests that Jesus's instruction to Mary contrasts with his invitation to Thomas to place his hands in his wounds.[13] Thomas is not present when Jesus first appears to the disciples, and he refuses to believe that Jesus has been raised until he has touched his wounds (20.19-25). A week later Jesus appears again to his disciples, and he asks Thomas to put his hands in his wounds (20.27).

---

[10] M. R. D'Angelo, 'A Critical Note: John 20:17 and Apocalypse of Moses 31', *JTS* 41 (1990): 529–36.

[11] M. D. Johnson, 'Life of Adam and Eve', in *The Old Testament Pseudepigrapha*, edited by J. H. Charlesworth (Garden City, NY: Doubleday, 1985), 2:287.

[12] For an analysis of John's portrayal of Jesus as the one who descends and ascends to God, see W. A. Meeks, 'The Man from Heaven in Johannine Sectarianism', *JBL* 91 (1972): 44–72.

[13] D. M. Smith, *John* (Nashville, TN: Abingdon, 1999), 377–8.

Smith argues that Jesus has not yet ascended when he meets Mary whereas Thomas is asked to touch Jesus's wounds after the ascension. Jesus has told his disciples that he must ascend before he gives the Spirit to them (7.39; 16.7), and Jesus gives the Spirit to his disciples (20.22). There is no indication, however, that the ascension has taken place between the meeting of Jesus with Mary and his appearance to the disciples. In our passage Mary wishes to keep Jesus with her in the earthly realm whereas Jesus must return to God. On the other hand the conversation between Thomas and Jesus focuses on the act of touching the wounds of Jesus. It is more likely that John develops the conversation between Thomas and Jesus to demonstrate that the risen Jesus is the same person who was crucified.

In our narrative Jesus speaks of the ascension as a return to his 'Father' in the statement, 'I am ascending to my Father and your Father, to my God and your God' (20.17). Jesus's speech recalls the language of the covenant which occurs in Ruth's speech to Naomi, 'Your people shall be my people, and your God my God' (Ruth 1.16) and in the description of the new covenant in Jeremiah, 'I will be their God, and they shall be my people' (Jer. 31.31-34).[14] Jesus will no longer be present on earth but his followers will share in his own relationship with God.

John, moreover, employs family terminology to describe Jesus's relationship with God and his disciples. Throughout the gospel Jesus addresses God as 'Father' (cf. 5.17-18, 25-47; 6.37, 40; 8.18-20; 10.30). Jesus is the Son of God, and his disciples are incorporated into the relationship between God and Jesus as Father and Son. In the prologue human beings who receive Jesus and believe in his name are given the power to become the 'children of God' (1.12-13). Andrew Byers rightly points out that John's Christology is closely connected to his ecclesiology since those who believe in Jesus become part of a new community.[15] In the prologue John employs birth imagery to indicate the formation of a new community of faith. Birth imagery is also prominent in the account of the meeting between Jesus and Nicodemus in ch. 3. Jesus taught Nicodemus that it is necessary to be born 'from above' or 'again' to enter the kingdom of God (3.5).

The Johannine Jesus gives Mary Magdalene instructions to pass on the news of his resurrection to his 'brothers and sisters' (τοὺς ἀδελφούς μου, 20.17). The term ἀδελφούς, however, may be translated as 'brothers' or 'brothers and sisters'. Sandra Schneiders argues that John employs this term as a collective noun which refers to women and men as sisters and brothers of Jesus.[16] John's use of covenant terminology suggests that he does include Jesus's female followers in this message because women and men participate in the covenants between God and the people of Israel in the Old Testament. In Mark's Gospel Jesus refers to those who do the will of God as his 'brother', 'sister' and 'mother' (3.35). The terms 'brother' and 'sister' are also used of the members of the Pauline churches (Rom. 16.1, 17, 23; 1 Cor. 1.10, 11, 26), and they are prominent in the Johannine Epistles (1 Jn 2.10-11; 3.10, 13-17; 4.20-21; 5.16; 3 Jn

---

[14] Brown, *John*, 2:1016–17.
[15] A. J. Byers, *Ecclesiology and Theosis in the Gospel of John* (Cambridge: Cambridge University Press, 2017), 27–48.
[16] Schneiders, 'John 20:11-18', 166.

3, 5, 10). John suggests that a new relationship has now been formed between God, Jesus and the disciples. In our passage Jesus refers to his followers for the first time as 'brothers and sisters'. His speech recalls his announcement that his mother is now the mother to the Beloved Disciple and the Beloved Disciple is her son (19.26-27). The fictive kinship terminology suggests that a new relationship between God and humanity has become possible through the death and resurrection of Jesus.

John presents Mary's gradual recognition of the risen Jesus in the course of her conversation with Jesus. Mary does not expect the resurrection to take place, and she initially believes that Jesus is the gardener. She is portrayed as a disciple who recognizes Jesus as her teacher and as the risen Lord. Jesus gives Mary a commission to pass on the news of the resurrection to his disciples. Jesus's reference to 'my Father and your Father, my God and your God' alludes to the new covenant which has been inaugurated through his death. Mary is sent to the disciples with a message which reconstitutes the group of disciples on the basis of their belief in the resurrection. John employs family terminology to indicate that a new community of women and men has been created. Mary Magdalene is the first witness to the risen Jesus, and her testimony, 'I have seen the Lord', forms the basis of the proclamation of the Johannine community.

Discipleship and Mary Magdalene

In our passage Jesus appears to Mary Magdalene, and he asks Mary whom she is seeking (τίνα ζητεῖς, 20.15). Mary's search for Jesus recalls earlier instances of disciples who 'seek' Jesus. In the discipleship accounts at the beginning of the gospel Jesus asks the first two disciples, 'What do you seek?' (τί ζητεῖτε, 1.38). Gail O'Day rightly notes that the questions which are concerned with 'seeking' create continuity between the first disciples and the portrayal of Mary in our narrative.[17] John is concerned with the human search for life, and he demonstrates that life is found by believing in Jesus's name (20.30-31). The Johannine Jesus's questions about 'seeking' are designed to lead human beings to express their deepest wishes and motivations. Once they recognize their longing for life, they are able to come to faith in Jesus as the source of life. Jesus is identified with the deepest desires of human beings for life because he comes to bring human beings abundant life (10.10). The 'I am' sayings: 'I am the bread of life' (6.35), 'I am the light of the world' (8.12) and 'I am the way, and the truth, and the life' (14.6) indicate that human beings discover that their deepest desires are fulfilled in a relationship with Jesus.

At first Mary does not recognize Jesus because she believes that he is the gardener. The turning point in the conversation occurs when Jesus calls Mary by her name. John presents Mary as a disciple who recognizes Jesus when he calls her by her name (cf. 10.1-6). In the first century the name of a person was often believed to contain the identity of that person. The Johannine Jesus has supernatural knowledge of the motives of human beings because he comes from the heavenly realm. John's Gospel

---

[17] G. R. O'Day, 'John', in *Women's Bible Commentary*, edited by C. A. Newsom and S. H. Ringe, exp. edn (Louisville, KY: Westminster John Knox, 1998), 389.

depicts several other examples of Jesus's supernatural knowledge. John states that Jesus did not entrust himself to the crowd at Passover in Jerusalem because he had knowledge of the content of their hearts (2.23-25). In the account of the meeting between Jesus and the Samaritan woman, the turning point in the narrative occurs when Jesus reveals his knowledge of the woman's past and present relationships (4.16-19). In John's Gospel Jesus has greater knowledge of human beings than they have of themselves.

Our passage, moreover, concludes with John's portrayal of Mary in a discipleship role. At the beginning of the account Mary is a mourner but at the end of the account she takes on the task of passing on the news of the resurrection. The meeting between Mary Magdalene and Jesus is the first in a series of Johannine resurrection narratives. The structure of the resurrection narratives raises the question of whether the resurrection appearance to Mary Magdalene functions as a transitional account which connects the account of the empty tomb to the commissioning of the male disciples. In Matthew's Gospel, for example, the meeting of Mary Magdalene and the other Mary with the risen Jesus prepares for the meeting of Mary with the eleven remaining male disciples in Galilee (28.16-20). Pheme Perkins argues that the visit of women to the empty tomb serves as a transitional account between the crucifixion of Jesus and the reformation of the disciples.[18] Jesus, however, does not give Mary specific instructions about the place where he will meet the disciples. In Mark's Gospel and Matthew's Gospel, the women are asked to tell the disciples that they will see Jesus in Galilee (Mk 16.1-8; Mt. 28.1-10). In John's Gospel the appearance of Jesus to the disciples in Jerusalem is unexpected and is not connected to an instruction from Jesus to Mary (20.19-23). The content of Mary's testimony is a proclamation of the gospel since she testifies to her own meeting with the risen Jesus. Her testimony is not simply a message to tell the male disciples where to meet Jesus. Mary's testimony bears witness to the ascension of Jesus and the new relationship between God and humanity.

Mary's message 'I have seen the Lord' (20.18) is a personal testimony, and it depicts Mary in the discipleship role of bearing witness to Jesus. As Colleen Conway points out, the term κύριε may be translated as 'sir' but it also has Christological significance since it could be translated as 'Lord'.[19] The title 'Lord' (κύριος) is used of God in the Septuagint, and it associates Jesus with God. 'Jesus is Lord' is the testimony of the early church (cf. Κύριος Ἰησοῦς, 1 Cor. 12.3; Rom. 10.9; Phil. 2.11). This confession places Jesus above any human lord who seeks to rule on earth. The high Christology of the title 'Lord' may be seen in John's account of the healing of the blind man. At the end of this account, the former blind man recognized Jesus and addressed him, 'Lord, I believe' (Πιστεύω, κύριε), and 'worshiped' him (9.38).

Mary's testimony recalls John's association of women with confessions of faith in earlier chapters of the gospel. The Samaritan woman recognized Jesus as a prophet, and asked, 'Could this man be the Messiah?' (4.29), and Martha confessed her faith in Jesus as the 'Messiah, the Son of God, the one who is coming into the world' (11.27).

---

[18] P. Perkins, '"I Have Seen the Lord" (John 20.18). Women Witnesses to the Resurrection', *Int* 46 (1992): 38.
[19] Conway, *Men and Women*, 187.

John's presentation of the confessions of faith of women depicts women in the role of disciples. In John's Gospel disciples have the role of continuing Jesus's mission and of confessing their faith. The community is founded on the members' shared belief in the death and resurrection of Jesus. The disciples' experiences of resurrection appearances form the foundation of the early Christian beliefs. As Adele Reinhartz points out, Mary's testimony 'I have seen the Lord' gives authority to Mary as the first person who has seen the risen Jesus.[20] In our narrative we see the initiative of Jesus in seeking out Mary, since he asks her 'whom she seeks' while he is seeking her. Mary is the first to see the risen Jesus, and her testimony forms the basis of the mission of the Johannine community.

John depicts Mary Magdalene as a disciple since she recognizes the risen Jesus as her 'teacher' and 'Lord'. Mary's recognition of Jesus when he calls her by her name indicates that she is one of his group of disciples. Jesus's act of calling Mary by her name restores his relationship with her, and it reflects the personal relationship between Jesus and each one of his followers. Mary wishes Jesus to remain on earth but he is ascending to God. Jesus's response refers to the new relationship that he has with his disciples as his brothers and sisters. The Samaritan woman recognized Jesus as the Messiah, and the people of her town came to recognize him as the 'Saviour of the World' (4.42). The meeting between Martha and Jesus concluded with the confession of Martha that Jesus is the Messiah and Son of God (11.27). In our passage the risen Jesus appears to Mary, and she recognizes him as 'Lord' (20.18). In each narrative women receive revelation of Jesus's identity, and they confess their faith in him.

Mary Magdalene and the new creation

Mary Magdalene goes to the tomb on the first day of the week, and she discovers that Jesus has been raised from the dead. The timing of Mary Magdalene's visit to the tomb recalls the account of the creation of the world in Genesis. In Genesis, God creates the world in six days, and then rests on the Sabbath (Gen. 1–2.3). In John's Gospel Jesus is raised to life on the first day of a new week, which marks the first week of the new creation. Jeannine Brown observes that the phrase 'the first day of the week' (τῇ δὲ μιᾷ τῶν σαββάτων, 20.1) also occurs in the account of the appearance of Jesus to the disciples (τῇ ἡμέρᾳ ἐκείνῃ τῇ μιᾷ σαββάτων, 20.19).[21] As Brown points out, John's use of this phrase suggests that he associates the resurrection with a new week of creation. In John's Gospel the events of the last week of Jesus's life are described in the Passion Narrative. Jesus dies, and he is buried on the day before the Sabbath. Mary Magdalene observes the Sabbath, and she does not go to the tomb until the Sabbath has passed. John's reference to the first day of the week may be compared with similar references to the eighth day in other early Christian texts. Mary Coloe points out that the eighth day

---

[20] A. Reinhartz, 'Women in the Johannine Community: An Exercise in Historical Imagination', in *A Feminist Companion to John*, vol. 2, edited by A.-J. Levine with M. Blickenstaff (London: Sheffield Academic Press, 2003), 29.

[21] J. K. Brown, 'Creation's Renewal in the Gospel of John', *CBQ* 72 (2010): 283–4.

is regarded as the first day of the eschatological age in the *Epistle of Barnabas*.²² In this text the eighth day is associated with the theme of new creation since it is described as 'the dawn of another world' (*Barn.* 15.8-9).

In our passage Jesus's speech to Mary begins with the address, 'woman' (γύναι, 20.15). Jesus addressed his mother as 'woman' in the account of the wedding at Cana (2.4) and in the account of the crucifixion (19.25-26). John employs this address to portray the mother of Jesus as a new Eve at the beginning of Jesus's mission and at the beginning of the new discipleship community. Sandra Schneiders argues that the address 'woman' in our passage is reminiscent of the portrayal of Eve as the 'woman' in the creation account of Genesis (2.15-17; 3.8, 15).²³ It is possible that John also associates Mary Magdalene with the character of Eve because several features of the account recall the account of creation in Genesis. John's Gospel, for example, is the only gospel which states that Jesus's tomb was located in a garden (19.41). Edwyn Hoskyns proposes that John's reference to the setting of a garden recalls the account of the garden of Eden in Genesis (Gen. 2.8).²⁴ Hoskyns notes that John also situates the betrayal of Jesus in a garden (18.1), and he points out that the crucifixion takes place near a garden (19.41). On the other hand Carlos Siliezar argues that John's reference to the garden in our passage does not allude to the garden of Eden because John employs the term κῆπος (garden) whereas the term παράδεισος (garden) appears in Genesis 2 and 3 LXX.²⁵ Hoskyns, however, notes that κῆπος is used as a synonym for παράδεισος in the Septuagint (ἐποίησά μοι κήπους καὶ παραδείσους, Eccl. 2.15; ὡς ὑδραγωγὸς ἐξῆλθον εἰς παράδεισον εἶπα Ποτιῶ μου τὸν κῆπον, Sir. 24.23-34). He also observes that Aquila's Greek translation of the Old Testament employs the term κῆπος in Gen. 2.8 and 3.2. Hoskyn's research indicates that John may employ the term κῆπος to refer to the garden of Eden in Genesis.

John's allusions to Genesis may also be seen in Mary's initial belief that Jesus is a gardener (ἐκείνη δοκοῦσα ὅτι ὁ κηπουρός ἐστιν, 20.15). Mary's response is an indication of her failure to recognize the risen Jesus. Hoskyns, however, rightly notes that characters often make statements which may appear to be incorrect but at a deeper level are true.²⁶ He points out, for example, that the Samaritan woman believes that Jesus refers to 'running water' rather than the spiritual gift of 'living water' (τὸ ὕδωρ τὸ ζῶν, 4.11-12). In our narrative Hoskyns proposes that John portrays Jesus as the 'Lord of the Garden', and he suggests that John alludes to the description of the Lord who walks in the garden in Genesis (cf. Gen. 3.8). In Genesis, however, God is not directly identified as a gardener. On the other hand Adam is portrayed as a gardener since he is given the role of tilling the garden of Eden (Gen. 2.15). Jeannine Brown rightly proposes that John aims to link Jesus with Adam who was the first gardener.²⁷ In

---

[22] M. L. Coloe, 'Theological Reflections on Creation in the Gospel of John', *Pacifica* 24 (2011): 7. Coloe also cites *2 Enoch* which states, 'And I appointed the eighth day also, that the eighth day should be the first-created after my work' (33.1).
[23] Schneiders, 'John 20:11-18', 161.
[24] E. C. Hoskyns, 'Genesis I-III and John's Gospel', *JTS* (1920): 214–15.
[25] C. R. S. Siliezar, *Creation Imagery in the Gospel of John*, LNTS 546 (London: Bloomsbury, 2015), 23.
[26] Hoskyns, 'Genesis I-III', 214–15.
[27] Brown, 'Creation's Renewal', 281–2. See also N. Wyatt, ' "Supposing Him to Be the Gardener" (John 20, 15). A Study of the Paradise Motif in John', *ZNW* 81 (1990): 36–8.

Genesis, Adam disobeyed God, and death entered the world (3.22-24). In John's Gospel Jesus follows the will of God, and his resurrection signifies that he has overcome death to bring humanity eternal life (cf. 3.16; 10.10; 20.31).

John associates Jesus and Mary Magdalene with the figures of Adam and Eve in the garden of Eden. In Genesis, God 'drives out' Adam from the garden of Eden, and Adam is unable to reach the tree of life (ἐξέβαλε τὸν Ἀδάμ, 3.25). In John's Gospel Jesus 'drives out' the ruler of the world through his death on the cross (νῦν ὁ ἄρχων τοῦ κόσμου τούτου ἐκβληθήσεται ἔξω, 12.31). John's narrative indicates that a cosmological conflict between God and the power of evil is taking place in the events of the Passion Narrative. His allusions to Genesis demonstrate that the death and resurrection of Jesus have inaugurated the new creation.

Our narrative focuses on the meeting between Mary Magdalene and the risen Jesus in a garden. The Johannine Jesus's address 'woman' suggests that Mary is portrayed as a new Eve. Mary's belief that Jesus is the gardener alludes to the role of Adam as the first gardener. John's allusions to Genesis demonstrate that the resurrection of Jesus marks a new beginning for humanity. John depicts Jesus as the new Adam who brings the gift of eternal life. His reference to the first day of the week indicates that the first week of the new creation has begun. Jesus is the Son of God who brings God's work of creation to completion. Mary's testimony to the resurrection reveals that the power of death has been broken. In our passage John's association of Mary with Eve alludes to the new world that is emerging after the death and resurrection of Jesus.

Mary Magdalene and the Johannine community

Mary Magdalene has a prominent role in John's Gospel as the first witness to the resurrection. Mary meets the risen Jesus, and she is commissioned to pass on the news of the resurrection. John associates Mary Magdalene with the proclamation of the gospel message and the beginning of the mission of the church. John's portrayal of Mary suggests that women may hold the role of teachers and missionaries in the Johannine community. Raymond Brown observes that John presents Mary Magdalene in the role of an apostle.[28] As Brown points out, apostles are defined as those who have seen the risen Jesus and who have been sent to proclaim Jesus (cf. 1 Cor. 9.1-12; 15.8-11; Gal. 1.11-16). Sandra Schneiders argues that John's portrayal of Mary Magdalene provides insights into the role of women in the early church.[29] Schneiders rightly proposes that John's portrayal of Mary demonstrates that a woman was regarded as 'the primary witness' to the resurrection in at least one of the early Christian communities.

In some early Christian texts there is evidence of tensions between Mary Magdalene and the male disciples. In the apocryphal gospels Mary Magdalene has a leading role as an apostle and recipient of Jesus's revelation. Ernst Haenchen notes that there is

---

[28] R. E. Brown, *The Community of the Beloved Disciple: The Life, Loves, and Hates of an Individual Church in New Testament Times* (New York: Paulist, 1979), 189.

[29] S. M. Schneiders, 'Women in the Fourth Gospel and the Role of Women in the Contemporary Church', *BTB* 12 (1982): 44.

evidence of opposition to Mary in some texts including the *Gospel of Thomas* which presents Mary as a rival to Peter (114).[30] In the *Gospel of Mary*, Mary Magdalene receives visions from Jesus but Peter is critical of her role as a disciple. Karen King argues that the portrayal of Mary Magdalene suggests that she had a prominent role in early Christianity, and the dispute between Mary Magdalene and Peter reflects the debates in the early church over the leadership of women.[31] King rightly notes that there are tensions over the role of women in the apocryphal gospels but there is no suggestion of rivalry between the leadership of Mary Magdalene and that of the male disciples in John's Gospel. Mary Rose D'Angelo, moreover, observes that resurrection appearances may be employed to give authority to disciples in the Johannine community and in other early Christian communities.[32] D'Angelo points out that Peter becomes an authoritative figure in 'orthodox' communities, and she proposes that the Beloved Disciple and Mary Magdalene may have influential positions within the Johannine community.[33]

In our passage John gives no indication of any tensions between Mary and the two male disciples. Peter and the Beloved Disciple respond immediately to Mary's message by running to the tomb. John's presentation of the attitude of the disciples towards Mary thus differs from Luke's account in which the disciples initially doubt the women's message (24.11). In our narrative Peter and the Beloved Disciple discover the empty tomb but they do not see Jesus. The Beloved Disciple is the first disciple to realize that the resurrection has taken place but John highlights the role of Mary Magdalene since she is the first disciple whom Jesus meets after his death. John's development of the meeting between Mary Magdalene and Jesus presents Mary as a model of discipleship.

At the end of the gospel, however, John describes a resurrection appearance of Jesus to his disciples in Galilee (21.1-14), and he refers to this account as the 'third' appearance of Jesus to his 'disciples' (μαθηταῖς, 21.14). Jesus has appeared twice to the disciples in the room in Jerusalem (20.19-23, 26-29). The meeting of Mary Magdalene and Jesus is therefore not included in this list of resurrection appearances to the disciples. This omission has led C. K. Barrett to suggest that John does not regard Mary Magdalene as a disciple.[34] Mary D'Angelo, moreover, proposes that the omission of Mary Magdalene from the group of disciples may reflect the situation in which women had fewer opportunities for leadership roles in the community.[35]

---

[30] E. Haenchen, *John 2* (Philadelphia, PA: Fortress, 1984), 226.
[31] K. L. King, 'The Gospel of Mary Magdalene', in *Searching the Scriptures*, vol. 2, edited by E. Schüssler Fiorenza (New York: Crossroad, 1994), 620–4.
[32] M. R. D'Angelo, 'Reconstructing "Real" Women from Gospel Literature. The Case of Mary Magdalene', in *Women and Christian Origins*, edited by R. S. Kraemer and M. R. D'Angelo (Oxford: Oxford University Press, 1999), 112.
[33] For an analysis of the traditions concerning Mary Magdalene, Peter, Thomas and the mother of Jesus, see J. Hartenstein, *Charakterisierung im Dialog. Maria Magdalene, Petrus, Thomas und die Mutter Jesus im Johannesevangelium*, NTOA 64 (Göttingen: Vandenhoeck & Ruprecht, 2007).
[34] C. K. Barrett, *The Gospel according to St. John: An Introduction with Commentary and Notes on the Greek Text*, 2nd edn (London: SPCK, 1978), 582–3.
[35] M. R. D'Angelo, '(Re)Presentations of Women in the Gospels: John and Mark', in *Women and Christian Origins*, edited by R. S. Kraemer and M. R. D'Angelo (Oxford: Oxford University Press, 1999), 137.

It is probable that the concluding chapter was not part of the original gospel and may have been added by a redactor. The final verses of ch. 20 appear to be the original ending of the gospel since they express the purpose of the gospel which is to bring people to faith in Jesus as the Messiah and Son of God (20.30-31). Several features of the final account of the resurrection appearance of Jesus to his disciples suggest that it has been added to the gospel. As Andrew Lincoln points out, it seems strange that the disciples return to Galilee after Jesus has given them the Holy Spirit and commissioned them.[36] In this passage seven disciples are mentioned: Peter, Thomas, Nathanael, the sons of Zebedee and two others (21.2), and the Beloved Disciple is one of the unnamed disciples (21.7). Peter questions Jesus about the future of the Beloved Disciple. By the time this passage was written the Beloved Disciple has died but there has been a tradition that he would not die before Jesus returned (21.20-23). The author of the final chapter, moreover, may have differentiated between the appearance of the risen Jesus to Mary and the later appearances of Jesus to his group of disciples. Jesus meets Mary alone in our narrative whereas he meets the group of disciples in the later resurrection accounts.

In the course of the gospel, John's portrayal of Mary Magdalene implies that he does regard her as a disciple, and he demonstrates knowledge of her leading role within the group of women who followed Jesus. John, however, does not directly refer to a woman as a 'disciple' (μαθητής). Adele Reinhartz argues that the term 'disciples' sometimes refers to a wide group of the followers of Jesus which would include women (6.60; 7.3; 9.27).[37] She notes that John sometimes uses the term 'disciples' to refer to the members of the itinerant group who accompany Jesus (cf. 1.35-51), and she suggests that John employs the term 'disciples' to refer to the group of male disciples who are present at Jesus's final meal. It is probable that John primarily employs the term 'disciples' as a technical term to refer to the male disciples who accompany Jesus on his mission. In the account of the meeting between Jesus and the Samaritan woman the 'disciples' are amazed to find Jesus talking to a woman (4.27). In this passage the term 'disciples' appears to refer to male disciples, and John thus contrasts the faith of the Samaritan woman with the lack of understanding of the male disciples.

In our passage John portrays Mary Magdalene as a disciple since she addresses Jesus as her 'teacher' (ῥαββουνι, 20.16). This address indicates that Mary Magdalene has listened to the teaching of Jesus over a period of time. There is a similar portrayal of Martha and Mary of Bethany in the account of the raising of Lazarus. In this passage Martha told Mary that 'the teacher' is calling her (ὁ διδάσκαλος, 11.28). John, moreover, focuses on characters who are not part of the itinerant group of disciples including Nicodemus and the blind man. The mother of Jesus prompts Jesus to perform his first sign which deepens the faith of the disciples. Individual women such as the mother of Jesus, the Samaritan woman, Martha and Mary are depicted as model disciples throughout the gospel. John's presentation of these women suggests that women are regarded as disciples within the Johannine community.

---

[36] Lincoln, *Saint John*, 508–9.
[37] Reinhartz, 'Women', 26–30.

Mary Magdalene is central to the Johannine tradition because she is the first person to meet the risen Jesus. If John wished to restrict the discipleship of women, it is unlikely that he would have developed an extended account of the meeting between Mary Magdalene and Jesus which does not appear in the other gospels. Mary's testimony 'I have seen the Lord' is the confessional statement of the Johannine community (20.18). Her statement is repeated in the words of the disciples to Thomas, 'We have seen the Lord' (20.25). In the account of the fishing trip on the Sea of Tiberias the Beloved Disciple recognizes Jesus on the shore, and announces, 'It is the Lord' (21.7). In each narrative the risen Jesus is associated with the title 'Lord' (κύριος), and this title points to Jesus's lordship over humanity and creation. Mary's testimony is thus foundational for John's presentation of the resurrection. John's account of the resurrection appearances to the male disciples reinforces Mary's role as the first witness to the risen Jesus. Jesus ascends to God, and others come to faith through the testimony of witnesses to the risen Jesus. Mary is the first witness to Jesus, and John's description of her meeting with Jesus illustrates the ways in which individuals recognize Jesus. John's account of the meeting between Jesus and Mary Magdalene emphasizes the importance of the relationship of each person to Jesus. In John's Gospel Jesus has knowledge of each individual, and he seeks out each disciple.

Conclusion

Mary Magdalene is portrayed as the first person to visit the empty tomb, and she is the first witness to the resurrection. John develops an extended conversation between Mary and Jesus in which Mary recognizes Jesus when he calls her by her name. Mary is presented as a disciple since she addresses Jesus as her 'teacher'. John depicts Mary's transformation from a lack of understanding to a recognition of the risen Jesus. Her meeting with Jesus also acts as a paradigm for the way in which the future followers of Jesus come to faith in him. John emphasizes that Jesus seeks a relationship with each one of his followers, and he knows each one by name.

Mary Magdalene goes to the tomb on the first day of a new week, and she meets Jesus in a garden. Jesus's address 'woman' associates Mary Magdalene with the figure of Eve. John employs allusions to Genesis to indicate that the death and resurrection of Jesus inaugurate the new creation. In Genesis, Adam disobeyed God, and death entered the world. In John's Gospel, Jesus is presented as the new Adam who comes to bring humanity eternal life. John portrays Mary Magdalene as the first person to meet the risen Jesus. Mary's testimony 'I have seen the Lord' is the confession of faith of the Johannine community, and it expresses the foundational belief of the early church. Jesus sends Mary to pass on the news of the resurrection to his disciples. John's portrayal of Mary Magdalene suggests that women have the role of witnesses to Jesus in the Johannine community.

8

Conclusion

The portrayal of women

John presents detailed portraits of several women in his Gospel including the mother of Jesus, the Samaritan woman, Martha and Mary of Bethany, and Mary Magdalene. The mother of Jesus prompts Jesus to carry out his first sign, and he transforms water into wine at the wedding at Cana (2.1-11). Jesus meets the Samaritan woman at a well near Sychar, and she wonders if he could be the Messiah (4.1-42). Martha and Mary send a request for help to Jesus when their brother, Lazarus, falls ill. Martha confesses her faith in Jesus as 'the Messiah, the Son of God, the one coming into the world' (11.1-44), and Mary anoints him as the suffering Messiah (12.1-8). The mother of Jesus, her sister, Mary of Clopas and Mary Magdalene show faith and courage by their presence at his crucifixion, and the mother of Jesus and the Beloved Disciple form the basis of the new community of disciples (19.25-27). Mary Magdalene remains faithful to Jesus despite the apparent failure of his mission, and she is the first person to meet the risen Jesus (20.1-18).

John highlights the presence of women in Jesus's mission but he does not portray them in traditional ways. In the gospels women, such as Mary the mother of James and Joseph; the mother of the sons of Zebedee (Mt. 27.56); Joanna, the wife of Herod's steward Chuza (Lk. 8.3); and Mary, the wife of Clopas (Jn 19.25), are identified by references to their male relatives. John, however, does not usually present women in the passages which we have examined by referring to their male relatives. The Samaritan woman is identified by her race rather than by her husband, and she is not married to her current partner (4.1-42). Martha and Mary of Bethany do not appear to be married, and they form a household with their brother (11.1-44). There is no mention of any male relative of Mary Magdalene, and she is identified by her hometown of Magdala in Galilee (20.1-18). Although the mother of Jesus is defined in terms of her relation to Jesus, there is no reference to her husband, Joseph, who may have died before the start of Jesus's mission (2.1-11).

The women in John's Gospel, moreover, appear vulnerable in the context of first-century patriarchal society. It is strange that the Samaritan woman visits the well at midday when the weather is hot. This woman appears to be an outsider in her community because she visits the well alone whereas women usually go to the well together at the cooler times of day. The Samaritan woman lacks the security of marriage since she has been married five times, and her present partner is not her husband. Martha and Mary have lost their brother, who would have been regarded as the male head of their household. In the patriarchal society of first-century Graeco-Roman Palestine women did not have the same opportunities as men to work and support a household, and there is no indication that the sisters have any other male relatives. Martha leaves her home, and she goes out alone to meet Jesus on the road to Bethany. In this narrative John does not refer to the disciples who have accompanied Jesus on his mission. John also does not refer to any family members of Mary Magdalene. Her closest relationships are with the members of Jesus's itinerant group, and the existence of this group has been threatened by the death of Jesus. At the end of the gospel Mary Magdalene goes to the tomb alone, and she meets the risen Jesus in a deserted burial ground.

John includes several narratives in which women characters engage in conversations with Jesus. John's presentation of the conversations between Jesus and women is unusual, since the synoptic gospels contain short conversations of women with Jesus. In Mathew's Gospel and Mark's Gospel a gentile woman convinces Jesus to heal her daughter (Mt. 15.21-28; Mk 7.24-30). In Luke's Gospel Martha complains to Jesus about her sister Mary who is listening to his teaching (10.38-42). On the other hand John includes extended conversations in which women grow in their understanding of Jesus, and he reveals his identity to them. At this time it was not customary for women to engage in conversations with men whom they did not know.[1] As Tal Ilan observes, in rabbinic writings rabbis are instructed to avoid conversations with women who may distract them from their studies (*m. Abot* 1.5; *b. Ned.* 20a; *b. Ber.* 43b; *b. Erub.* 53b).[2] In the Graeco-Roman world women were also expected to be careful about their speech in public places. Plutarch states that the speech of a virtuous woman should not be heard in public since her speech reveals her 'feelings, character, and disposition' (*Mor.* 142CD). John's portrayal of women challenges the social expectations that women should not engage in conversations with men who are not members of their family.

The speech of the women characters, moreover, demonstrates their faith and theological insights. In the course of their conversations with Jesus, women reveal their recognition of his identity as the Messiah and the Son of God. The mother of Jesus trusts in Jesus's power to intervene at the wedding celebration at Cana before he has carried out any signs. The Samaritan woman recognizes Jesus as a prophet, and she asks if he could be the Messiah (4.29). Martha confesses her faith in Jesus as 'the Messiah, the Son of God, the one coming into the world' (11.27). Mary Magdalene recognizes Jesus when he calls her by her name, and her testimony 'I have seen the Lord' is the foundational proclamation of the church because she announces the resurrection (20.18).

In these conversations the Johannine Jesus frequently employs the address 'woman' (γύναι, 2.4; 4.21; 19.26; 20.15). John employs this address to draw attention to the

---

[1] For a study of attitudes towards the speech of women in the Graeco-Roman world, see S. E. Hylen, *Women in the New Testament World* (Oxford: Oxford University Press, 2019), 131–59.
[2] T. Ilan, *Jewish Women in Greco-Roman Palestine* (Peabody, MA: Hendrickson, 1996), 126–7.

gender of the women characters, and his use of the address suggests that he is aware of the issue of gender. In the account of the wedding at Cana, Jesus addresses his mother as 'woman' (γύναι, 2.4). Jesus's speech is unusual because sons were not expected to address their mothers in this way. In this narrative Jesus's use of the address 'woman' implies that he is distancing himself from his mother's claims upon him. Mary has brought the lack of wine at the wedding at Cana to Jesus's attention but he is reluctant to intervene. The address 'woman', however, also indicates that Mary has a role in the gospel which goes beyond that of the traditional role of mother. Mary's authority is demonstrated by her instructions to the servants to do whatever Jesus tells them (2.5). At the crucifixion Jesus also addresses his mother as 'woman' (Γύναι, ἴδε ὁ υἱός σου, 19.26). In this passage Jesus is about to leave his mother, and she takes on the new role of 'mother' to the disciples.

The Johannine Jesus addresses the Samaritan woman as 'woman' during their conversation at the well near Sychar (Πίστευέ μοι, γύναι, 4.21). In this passage Jesus's address 'woman' highlights the differences between Jesus and the woman in terms of their gender. The Samaritan woman is anonymous, and the address 'woman' indicates that she is a stranger. In the course of their conversation, however, Jesus reveals that he knows about her marriages and her current partner (4.17-18). At the end of the gospel the risen Jesus meets Mary Magdalene outside his tomb, and he addresses her as 'woman' (Γύναι, 20.15). In this narrative the address points to the isolation of Mary because she has gone to the tomb alone. The address enables Jesus to question Mary as a stranger by asking her why she is crying and who she is seeking (20.15). The turning point in the passage occurs when Jesus replaces the address 'woman' with Mary's name (20.16). Then Mary recognizes Jesus as her teacher, and she realizes that he has been raised from death.

In several narratives women act independently, and they break social conventions. The mother of Jesus notices that the hosts have run out of wine at the wedding at Cana, and she brings the situation to Jesus's attention (2.3). She instructs the servants in a household that is not her own even though the bridegroom and steward are present. The Samaritan woman disregards social and religious boundaries to speak to a stranger of a different gender and race. Mary of Bethany breaks social conventions by interrupting a meal in order to anoint Jesus's feet with expensive perfume and dries his feet with her hair ahead of the day of his burial. She demonstrates her faith by carrying out a prophetic action which points to Jesus's identity as the Messiah. The mother of Jesus, her sister, Mary of Clopas and Mary Magdalene remain faithful to Jesus after his arrest, and they are witnesses to his crucifixion. These women align themselves with Jesus who is executed in a public place as a rebel against the Roman Empire. At the end of the gospel Mary Magdalene demonstrates her courage by visiting the tomb of a man who has been crucified.

The unconventional portraits of women in John's Gospel raise the questions of whether women in John's community held traditional roles and whether they lacked traditional family relationships. John does not depict the marriages of the male disciples. Jesus is also not married, and his brothers do not understand his mission (7.1-9). The portraits of women in John's Gospel are countercultural. John's portrayal of women may reflect the ways in which women in early Christianity resisted the pressure to conform to the social values of the surrounding society. These women had to be willing to risk the condemnation of their family and friends in order to commit themselves to a new community who worshipped a man who had been crucified.

John emphasizes the independence of the women who appear in the gospel, and he depicts them in unconventional ways. The independence and autonomy of the women in John's Gospel contrast with other New Testament texts in which the authors urge wives to be subject to their husbands (Eph. 5.22-24; Tit. 2.3-5; 1 Tim. 5.9-14; 1 Pet. 3.1-6). John's omission of references to the women's male relatives reflects his characteristic emphasis on the significance of an individual's response to Jesus. Each woman and man must come to her or his own decision about Jesus. John's focus on individual women enables his audience to identify with these characters. He is able to develop more detailed characterizations than those in the synoptic gospels on account of his use of extended narratives which present the conversations between Jesus and women. John's account of the women's family relationships and their social circumstances is not incidental to the gospel. The Samaritan woman's past life forms an integral part of the gospel narrative, and John's presentation of the friendship of Martha, Mary and Lazarus with Jesus creates the discipleship background to the account of the raising of Lazarus from death. John's development of the account of the meeting of Jesus and Mary Magdalene encourages the audience to participate in the transformation of Mary Magdalene's sorrow into joy when she realizes that Jesus has risen from the dead.

The discipleship of women

One of the distinctive features of John's Gospel is the number of conversations between women and Jesus in which women grow in their understanding of Jesus and recognize his identity. The Samaritan woman recognizes Jesus as a prophet, and Jesus reveals that he is the Messiah (4.29). Martha confesses her faith in Jesus as 'the Messiah, the Son of God, the one coming into the world' (11.27). Martha's use of the title 'the one coming into the world' alludes to the incarnation. Jesus comes from God into the world to bring eternal life and to inaugurate the new creation. Mary Magdalene bears witness to Jesus with the testimony, 'I have seen the Lord' (20.18). Mary's testimony may be compared to one of the earliest confessions of the church that 'Jesus is Lord' (cf. 1 Cor. 12.3; Rom. 10.9; Phil. 2.11). John's portrayal of women characters points to the importance of individual confessions of faith within the Johannine community.

The women's confessions of faith, moreover, are frequently expressed as personal statements of belief using first-person singular pronouns. The Samaritan woman recognizes Jesus, 'I see you are a prophet', and she wonders if he could be the Messiah (4.29). Martha confesses her faith, 'Yes, Lord, I believe that you are the Messiah, the Son of God, the one coming into the world' (11.27). Mary Magdalene's testimony, 'I have seen the Lord' (20.18), is the foundational statement of faith of the early church. John's association of women with the main confessions of faith in his tradition indicates that he regards women as examples of discipleship for his community.

The conversations between women and Jesus focus on John's identity as the hidden Messiah whose heavenly origins are concealed from the world. John's portrayal of Jesus has probably been influenced by apocalyptic traditions concerning the hidden Messiah (cf. *1 En.* 48.6; *4 Ezra* 7.26-28).[3] The Messiah is concealed until the time has arrived for God to intervene at the climax of history. In John's Gospel Jesus's identity as the Messiah is revealed at the time of his glorification on the cross (13.31-32; 17.1-5). Jesus casts out the ruler of the world, and he inaugurates the new creation through his death on the cross. John depicts Jesus as the divine revealer who brings knowledge of God's imminent intervention in the world. In apocalyptic writings the mysteries of heaven are inaccessible to human beings, and God reveals the events of the end-time through a representative of the supernatural world.[4] John presents conversations between women and Jesus which lead to the revelation of Jesus's identity and the purpose of his mission.

The Johannine Jesus comes from heaven to reveal God's purposes, and he speaks in figurative language to reveal the events of the end-time. In the conversations between women and Jesus, women respond positively to Jesus's figurative language.[5] Jesus is initially reluctant to intervene when the wine runs out at the wedding at Cana, and he replies to his mother's request for help with the response, 'Woman, what has this to do with you and me? My hour has not yet come' (2.1-11). Jesus alludes to the forthcoming 'hour' of his Passion (7.20; 8.20; 12.23, 27-28; 13.1; 16.32; 17.1). Nevertheless, Mary continues to believe that Jesus will assist the wedding party, and she shows her faith in him by instructing the servants to follow his commands. Jesus's transformation of water into abundant wine is proleptic of the fruitfulness of the new creation that is inaugurated at the 'hour' of his death.

The Samaritan woman also responds positively to Jesus's figurative language. At first the Samaritan woman questions Jesus's ability to give her 'living water' but she progresses from a literal interpretation of 'living water' as running water to a recognition of her spiritual need for the 'living water' that wells up to eternal life (4.15). John employs the term 'living water' to refer to the Spirit, the eschatological gift of the new creation (7.38-39). Jesus's use of figurative speech also plays a role in the account of the conversation between Jesus and Martha. When Jesus tells Martha that her brother will rise again, Martha believes that Jesus refers to the resurrection of the dead at the end of the age whereas Jesus alludes to his ability to raise Lazarus in the present (11.23).

Throughout John's Gospel women are portrayed as models of discipleship who respond positively to his figurative language. Martha and Mary of Bethany have a continuous relationship with Jesus, and they regard him as 'the teacher' (11.28). Mary Magdalene also addresses Jesus as her 'teacher' (20.16). These references imply that women are among the disciples who learn from Jesus and follow him. John, however,

---

[3] M. De Jonge, 'Jewish Expectations about the "Messiah" according to the Fourth Gospel', *NTS* 19 (1973): 246–70.
[4] J. J. Collins, *The Apocalyptic Imagination: An Introduction to the Jewish Matrix of Christianity* (New York: Crossroad, 1984), 1–11.
[5] For an analysis of the ways in which John's metaphorical language is associated with the gift of life to those who accept Jesus' revelation, see J. Ashton, 'Riddles and Mysteries: The Way, the Truth, and the Life', in *Jesus in Johannine Tradition*, edited by R. T. Fortna and T. Thatcher (Louisville, KY: Westminster John Knox, 2001), 333–42.

does not describe a woman as a 'disciple' (μαθητής). He characteristically applies the term 'disciples' to the group of male disciples who accompany Jesus on his itinerant mission. Nevertheless, John does not develop the role of the twelve male disciples, and there are only a few references to the Twelve as a group (cf. 6.66-71; 20.24). John's Gospel includes extended accounts of the meetings of Jesus with individuals who are not members of the Twelve such as Nicodemus, the Samaritan woman, the blind man and Martha. As Ernst Käsemann points out, new characters come to the forefront of the gospel narrative and widen the group of disciples.[6] Käsemann rightly notes that the inclusion of women and men in the group of disciples weakens the theological significance of the group of twelve disciples. John's focus on these women and men, moreover, points beyond the time of the gospel to the mission of the early church. In these narratives John focuses on the ways in which women and men come to faith in Jesus. John portrays women and men who are representatives of a wide range of people who are attracted to early Christianity. John's account of the faith of the Samaritan woman looks forward to the Samaritans who join the Johannine community. Martha and Mary represent disciples of Jesus who live in a settled community.

In John's Gospel women are portrayed as representative figures of those who respond positively to Jesus's revelation of his identity. John encourages his audience to identify with the women characters who come to faith in Jesus. The Johannine Jesus engages in conversation with the Samaritan woman by asking her for a drink of water (4.7). He responds to the message of Martha and Mary, and he appears to Mary Magdalene as she stands weeping outside his tomb. Jesus offers the Samaritan woman 'living water', and he raises Lazarus to life. In apocalyptic texts the recipients of revelation are usually the male leaders of Israel such as Enoch, Ezra and Baruch. In John's Gospel Jesus speaks to ordinary women in the midst of their daily lives. He is the hidden Messiah who is sent into the world with the gift of eternal life. Jesus reveals his identity to women with 'I am' sayings. He admits that he is the Messiah to the Samaritan woman (ἐγώ εἰμι, ὁ λαλῶν σοι, 4.26), and he tells Martha that he is 'the resurrection and the life' (ἐγώ εἰμι ἡ ἀνάστασις καὶ ἡ ζωή, 11.25). At the end of the gospel Mary Magdalene represents disciples who come to a recognition of the risen Jesus and who are commanded to pass on the news of the resurrection. John depicts the women's search for life which is shared by his audience, and in the course of these narratives John demonstrates Jesus's ability to bring abundant life to humanity.

Women and the new creation

John's Gospel includes several narratives in which women meet Jesus and confess their faith in him. John links the identity of Jesus as the Messiah and Son of God with the gifts which Jesus brings humanity. Jesus offers the Samaritan woman 'living water' (ὕδωρ ζῶν) that wells up within an individual and leads to eternal life (4.14). John associates 'living water' with the Spirit which will appear after Jesus has been glorified

---

[6] E. Käsemann, *The Testament of Jesus: A Study of the Gospel of John in the Light of Chapter 17* (London: SCM, 1968), 29.

(7.38-39). Martha and Mary seek the help of Jesus when their brother falls ill, and Jesus raises Lazarus to life. In this passage Jesus identifies himself as 'the resurrection and the life' (11.25). In these accounts women receive the gift of life which looks forward to the abundant life of the new creation.

John associates women with the first and last signs of Jesus which point to his identity as the Messiah and Son of God who inaugurates the new creation. The mother of Jesus prompts Jesus to carry out his first sign in which the transformation of water into wine looks forward to the fruitfulness of the new creation. Martha and Mary initiate Jesus's final sign by sending word to Jesus for help, and he raises Lazarus from the dead. In the Old Testament God has the power to raise the dead, and in John's Gospel Jesus has a similar power. These signs also associate women with the revelation of Jesus's glory. Jesus's mother prompts Jesus to intervene in the wedding at Cana, and Jesus's act of transforming water into wine reveals his glory (ἐφανέρωσεν τὴν δόξαν αὐτοῦ, 2.11). Martha and Mary's request leads Jesus to raise Lazarus from death, and this sign is also linked to the revelation of Jesus's glory since Jesus tells Martha that she will see his glory (ὄψῃ τὴν δόξαν τοῦ θεοῦ, 11.40). These signs are proleptic of the glorification of Jesus and God at the cross.

In several narratives, moreover, John links women characters with the 'hour' of Jesus's Passion. At the wedding at Cana Jesus initially tells his mother that his 'hour' has not yet come (οὔπω ἥκει ἡ ὥρα μου, 2.4) but he later proceeds to transform the water into wine. Jesus prophesies that the 'hour' is coming and is now present when worshippers will no longer worship on Mount Gerizim or in Jerusalem since they will worship in spirit and in truth (ἔρχεται ὥρα καὶ νῦν ἐστιν, 4.23-24). The mother of Jesus, her sister, Mary of Clopas and Mary Magdalene are present at the crucifixion which John presents as the 'hour' in which God and Jesus are glorified (cf. ὥρα, 12.23; 13.31-32; 17.1-5). Jesus declares that his mother is the mother of the Beloved Disciple, and he is her son, and John adds that 'from that hour' the Beloved Disciple took her into his home (ἀπ' ἐκείνης τῆς ὥρας, 19.27). John links Jesus's gift of life with the 'hour' of Jesus's death (13.31-32; 17.1-5). John's association of women with the 'hour' of Jesus aligns women with Jesus's death and glorification.

John employs the term the 'hour' to allude to the apocalyptic concept of the decisive time in which Jesus confronts the forces of evil. In John's Gospel women are linked with Jesus's hour which marks the time when he overcomes the power of evil and inaugurates the new creation. In John's apocalyptic world view the world had been usurped by 'the ruler of the world' (12.31; 14.30; 16.11).[7] Jesus is engaged in a cosmic battle against evil, and he liberates humanity from the clutches of the 'ruler of the world'. Women are present at the crucifixion of Jesus, and Mary Magdalene's willingness to go to Jesus's tomb leads her to be the first witness to the resurrection.

We have noted that John draws attention to the gender of women by the frequent use of the address 'woman' (2.4; 4.21; 19.26; 20.13, 15). John employs this address to link women characters with the theme of new creation. The address 'woman' alludes to the figure of Eve who is identified as the 'woman' in Genesis (γυνή, 2.15-17; 3.8, 15). The

---

[7] J. L. Kovacs, '"Now Shall the Ruler of This World Be Driven Out": Jesus' Death as Cosmic Battle in John 12:20-36', *JBL* 114 (1995): 227–47.

mother of Jesus is the woman who is most closely associated with the character of Eve. Mary is not named in the gospel, and she is identified as 'the mother of Jesus' (2.1-12; 19.25-27). John's portrayal of Mary recalls the description of Eve as 'the mother of all who live' in Genesis 3.20. The mother of Jesus has a key role at the wedding at Cana. Her request leads Jesus to perform his first sign which marks the beginning of his mission. Jesus's act of transforming water into wine reveals his glory and his disciples believe in him. At the crucifixion Jesus announces that Mary is now the mother of the Beloved Disciple, and he is her son (Γύναι, ἴδε ὁ υἱός σου, 19.26). John presents the Beloved Disciple as a representative of the disciples, and he portrays Mary as the 'mother' of all the disciples. He associates Mary with the beginning of the church, and Mary's role as 'mother' continues after the death of Jesus. John depicts Jesus's announcement as an act of new creation. His account indicates that the new community of disciples has its origins at the death of Jesus.

John's presentation of Mary Magdalene in the resurrection narrative is also reminiscent of the presentation of Eve in Genesis. The setting of the meeting between Jesus and Mary in a garden recalls the account of Adam and Eve in the garden of Eden. Initially, Mary does not recognize Jesus, and she believes that Jesus is a gardener. John's account alludes to the portrayal of Adam as a gardener. In Genesis, God gives Adam the task of tending and tilling the garden of Eden (2.15). John presents Jesus as the 'divine gardener' since he tends the new creation, and he carries out the creative work of God. In Genesis, Adam disobeyed God, and death entered the world. In John's Gospel Jesus is portrayed as the second Adam who comes to bring humanity eternal life. Jesus's resurrection indicates that he has conquered the power of death. John's allusions to Genesis indicate that a new world has emerged through the death and resurrection of Jesus.

John's use of the address 'woman' associates women characters with the figure of Eve in Genesis. John, however, does not link women with the disobedience of Eve. In John's Gospel women respond positively to Jesus, and they confess their faith in him. In Genesis, Eve disobeys the commandment of God by giving Adam the fruit which God has prohibited them from eating (3.1-7). In John's Gospel the interventions of women lead Jesus to carry out signs which foreshadow the abundance of the new creation. The mother of Jesus leads Jesus to perform his first sign, and he transforms water in six stone jars into abundant wine. Martha and Mary's request for assistance prompts Jesus to carry out his final sign, and he raises Lazarus from death. The final sign looks forward to Jesus's own death and resurrection in which he overcomes the power of death.

John's portrayal of women as Eve evokes the presence of Adam and Eve in the garden of Eden before evil entered the world. God's creative power brought the world into being, and Jesus employs the same creative power in his inauguration of the new creation. In our narrative John presents Jesus as the agent of the new creation. Throughout the gospel Jesus carries out 'works' (ἔργα) which may be compared to God's 'work' of creation (ἔργα, Gen. 2.2 LXX; 5.20, 36; 9.3-4; 14.10; 17.4). Jesus's final words, 'It is finished' (19.30), indicate that he has brought God's creative work to completion on the cross. The theme of new creation demonstrates that Jesus not only brings salvation to humanity but also inaugurates the new creation of the world.

John's Gospel includes several narratives in which women are closely related to the theme of new creation. In these passages women recognize Jesus as the Messiah and Son of God who brings humanity the gift of eternal life. John portrays Jesus as a second Adam who overcomes the power of death and inaugurates the new creation. The mother of Jesus is portrayed as the 'new Eve' who becomes 'mother' of all who follow Jesus. The Samaritan woman responds positively to Jesus's gift of 'living water' which represents the eschatological gift of the Spirit. Martha and Mary's request leads Jesus to raise their brother, and he demonstrates his power over death. John associates women with the 'hour' of Jesus, and women are aligned with Jesus's suffering and glorification. The account of the visit of Mary Magdalene to the tomb of Jesus also highlights the theme of new creation. At the end of the gospel Mary Magdalene is the first person to recognize the risen Jesus. Jesus's resurrection indicates that the power of death has been conquered, and the new creation has begun.

Women and the Johannine community

John presents the mother of Jesus, the Samaritan woman, Martha and Mary, and Mary Magdalene as models of faith and discipleship. These women grow in their understanding of Jesus, and they confess their faith in him. The prominence of women in John's Gospel leads Raymond Brown[8] and Sandra Schneiders[9] to argue that women had the role of teachers and missionaries in the Johannine community. Adele Reinhartz proposes that John's presentation of women as examples of discipleship suggests that they held similar roles in the community as 'teachers, spiritual leaders, prophets, apostles, and theologians'.[10] To be sure, there are difficulties in reconstructing the roles of women in the Johannine community from an analysis of the gospel which primarily aims to give an account of the life of Jesus. John, however, has probably shaped his material in order to respond to the concerns of his audience. Many accounts such as the stories of the Samaritan woman (4.1-42) and of the blind man (9.41) may be read on two levels: the level of the time of Jesus and the level of the time of the Johannine community.[11] The conversations between women and Jesus provide some indications of the roles of women within the Johannine community. In their meetings with Jesus, women frequently show insight into his identity and the scope of his mission. John's presentation of the faith of women in these conversations thus raises questions about their roles in the Johannine community.

---

[8] R. E. Brown, *The Community of the Beloved Disciple: The Life, Loves, and Hates of an Individual Church in New Testament Times* (New York: Paulist Press, 1979), 183–98.
[9] S. M. Schneiders, 'Women in the Fourth Gospel and the Role of Women in the Contemporary Church', *BTB* 12 (1982): 35–45.
[10] A. Reinhartz, 'Women in the Johannine Community: An Exercise in Historical Imagination', in *A Feminist Companion to Jesus*, vol. 2, edited by A.-J. Levine with M. Blickenstaff (London: Sheffield Academic Press, 2003), 26–30.
[11] J. L. Martyn, *History and Theology in the Fourth Gospel*, 2nd edn (Nashville, TN: Abingdon, 1995), 24–62.

John portrays independent women who recognize Jesus's identity and demonstrate faith in Jesus. The Samaritan woman and Jesus discuss the location of the Temple and the gift of the Spirit. Martha talks to Jesus about the resurrection of the dead, and he interprets Mary's act of anointing him in terms of his imminent death (12.7-8). John's portrayal of women in discipleship roles suggests that his audience would have been able to identify with the experience of women who had faith in Jesus. John presents women such as the Samaritan woman, Martha and Mary of Bethany, and Mary Magdalene as examples of discipleship for women and men in his audience. Women, moreover, are linked to the confessions of faith of the Johannine tradition. The gospel is written to encourage the faith of women and men that Jesus is the Messiah, the Son of God, with the result that they may have life in his name (20.30-31).

John emphasizes the role of individual women and men who believe that Jesus is the Messiah.[12] Women and men left their families and community but also joined a new community founded on their relationship to Jesus. It is possible that John's emphasis on individual women may reflect a situation in which a number of women had joined the church but their husbands had not (cf. 1 Cor. 7.13-14; 1 Pet. 3.1-6). John does not depict any married couples who believe in Jesus, and the only married couple in the gospel is the parents of the blind man who are afraid of being excluded from the synagogue (9.22-23). In the account of the healing of the blind man (9.1-41) the man's parents are afraid to speak to the Pharisees, and they tell them to speak to their son because he is of age. In this narrative family relationships are broken. The fearful response of the man's mother and father to the religious authorities demonstrates the pressures experienced by the families of the members of John's community.[13] In first-century Graeco-Roman Palestine women and men found their identity through their family relationships and belonging to a household. John redefines the household of disciples by stating that those who believe in Jesus receive the power to become 'children of God' (1.12-13).

John's focus on the faith of individual women, however, does not suggest that he presents an individualistic form of discipleship. The individuals who joined the Johannine community found a new sense of belonging as members of the family of Jesus. John depicts the formation of the new discipleship community as an act of new creation. He associates the beginning of the discipleship community with the death of Jesus. Shortly before he dies, Jesus declares that his mother is now the mother of the Beloved Disciple, and he is now her son (19.25-27). In this passage the Beloved Disciple is an ideal figure who represents all the disciples. John's portrayal of Mary as 'mother' recalls the presentation of Eve as the 'mother of all who live' (Gen. 3.20) and the prophetic role of mother Zion (Isa. 49.20-22; 54.1; 66.7-8). John's portrayal of Mary as the 'mother' of the disciples suggests that she is venerated in the Johannine community.

---

[12] R. E. Brown (*The Churches the Apostles Left Behind* (London: Geoffrey Chapman, 1984), 84) proposes that the gospel's focus on the 'relation of the individual Christian to Jesus' characterizes the ecclesiology of the Johannine tradition.

[13] A. T. Lincoln, *Truth on Trial: The Lawsuit Motif in the Fourth Gospel* (Peabody, MA: Hendrickson, 2000), 278.

John, moreover, portrays the disciples as the 'sisters' and 'brothers' of Jesus. At the end of the gospel Jesus asks Mary Magdalene to tell his 'brothers and sisters' that he is ascending to God (τοὺς ἀδελφούς μου, 20.17). The disciples are brothers and sister of Jesus, and these relationships may replace the broken bonds with birth families (cf. Mk 3.31-35; 10.28-30). In other early Christian texts women and men become sisters and brothers of Jesus (cf. Rom. 16.1, 17, 23; 1 Cor. 1.10, 11, 26). Jesus has a unique role as Son but disciples are bound together through their relation to Jesus. In John's Gospel the disciples become sisters and brothers of Jesus, and they may replace his birth family. Similarly, the members of the Johannine community may have formed new family relationships to compensate for the loss of their former family relationships and community relations when they left the synagogue. The discipleship group became the primary locus relationship for the members of the Johannine community. The terms 'sister' and 'brother' express the close relationship between members of the group. These relationships may suggest a lack of hierarchy within the Johannine community since all members are brothers and sisters of Jesus.

John's concept of discipleship involves a community of women and men who are linked to one another through their individual relationships with Jesus. His portrayal of the discipleship community is influenced by his apocalyptic world view. Disciples are 'reborn' through the eschatological gift of the Spirit. In the resurrection narrative Jesus breathes the Spirit into his disciples and creates a new humanity (20.22). Jesus's gift of the Spirit unleashes the creative power of God into the world. In several narratives John links women with the gift of the Spirit. Jesus offers the Samaritan woman the 'living water' of the Spirit which indicates that women and men receive the Spirit (4.14). At the crucifixion Jesus hands over the Spirit to the mother of Jesus and the Beloved Disciple, and they are the representatives of the women and men in the new discipleship community (19.26-30). John writes for a charismatic community who place emphasis on the gift of the Spirit. In the gospel Jesus offers the Spirit to ordinary women and men. John's portrayal of the Spirit implies that this gift is given to all women and men who place their trust in Jesus, and it is not the preserve of male church leaders.

Our study has illustrated the ways in which John has presented women as examples of faith and discipleship. In the early church some women had the roles of prophets and teachers but in other early Christian communities some leaders attempted to restrict the speech of women (cf. 1 Cor. 14.33-35). The author of 1 Timothy states that he does not permit women to teach or to have authority over men, and he proposes that women should keep silent in church (2.12). The positive portrayal of women in John's Gospel suggests that it is unlikely that the Johannine community would have accepted the views expressed in 1 Timothy.[14] John does not restrict the speech of women, and he highlights their confessions of faith. Adela Yarbro Collins, moreover, observes that in John's Gospel the Paraclete remains with all the disciples and his role as the teacher of the disciples restricts the authority of any individual teacher (14.26).[15] In this way

---

[14] Brown, *Churches*, 94–5.
[15] A. Y. Collins, 'New Testament Perspectives: The Gospel of John', *JSOT* 22 (1982): 47–53.

the gift of the Spirit to individual women and men may challenge the power of male-appointed leadership to restrict the discipleship of women.

The Johannine focus on the Spirit may also have encouraged the community to be less concerned with the formal leadership positions that may be seen in later epistles such as 1 Tim. 3.1-13 and Tit. 1.5-9. John's association of the Paraclete with Jesus suggests that his community experience the gifts associated with the end-time in the present. His presentation of the Spirit indicates that each woman and man is given revelation directly from God, and each person has the ability to understand Jesus. Women and men receive the gift of knowledge, and they are able to share their wisdom with the members of the community. It is thus probable that women and men shared leadership in worship and teaching. John's focus on the role of the Spirit downplays the emphasis on hierarchical male structures of leadership that developed in the communities that produced the Pastoral Epistles.

In John's Gospel women are portrayed as examples of discipleship who represent the faith of those outwith the first group of male disciples. The faith of the women also foreshadows the faith of future disciples within the Johannine tradition. John's portrayal of women emphasizes that women respond to Jesus's figurative language and receive divine revelation. The conversations of women and Jesus have been designed by John to deepen the faith of his audience. John's audience would probably have identified with characters who meet Jesus. We see women and men receive life through their meetings with Jesus. John writes the gospel for people who are encouraged to believe in Jesus through the testimony of the disciples. These people have not seen Jesus themselves but they may experience an encounter with Jesus through listening to the narratives depicting the meetings of Jesus and women such as the Samaritan woman, Martha and Mary, and Mary Magdalene.

Conclusion

John's Gospel includes several narratives in which women recognize Jesus as the hidden Messiah and Son of God. The Samaritan woman wonders if Jesus could be the Messiah. Martha confesses her faith in Jesus as 'the Messiah, the Son of God, the one coming into the world', and Mary of Bethany anoints Jesus as the suffering Messiah. At the end of the gospel Mary Magdalene is the first person to recognize Jesus as the risen Lord. John's frequent use of the address 'woman' links the accounts that feature women, and it suggests that John is aware of the issue of gender. This address associates women characters with the figure of Eve who is identified as the 'woman' in Genesis. In the Old Testament Eve encouraged Adam to disobey God's commandment. In John's Gospel the requests of women lead Jesus to carry out signs which foreshadow the abundance of the new creation. The mother of Jesus prompts Jesus to perform his first sign, and he transforms water into the abundant wine of the new creation. The request of Martha and Mary leads Jesus to carry out his final sign, and he raises their brother from the clutches of death. The mother of Jesus, her sister, Mary of Clopas and Mary Magdalene, moreover, are present at the 'hour' of Jesus's death (19.26-27). John connects women characters with the decisive eschatological hour in which Jesus casts out the 'ruler of the world' and inaugurates the new creation (cf. 12.27; 13.1; 17.1-4).

The mother of Jesus is the woman who is most closely identified with Eve. At the crucifixion Jesus forms a new relationship between his mother and the Beloved Disciple. Jesus gives his Spirit to his mother and the Beloved Disciple, and these two figures form the basis of the new community of disciples. Eve is the 'mother of all who live' (Gen. 3.20), and Mary becomes the 'mother' of the group of disciples (19.26-27). John also associates Mary Magdalene with the figure of Eve in his resurrection account. At the end of the gospel Mary meets the risen Jesus in a garden, and he addresses her as 'woman' before he calls her by her name. John portrays Jesus as a second Adam who overcomes the power of death to bring humanity eternal life. John's allusions to Genesis indicate that Jesus not only brings salvation to humanity but also inaugurates the new creation. His association of women with the character of Eve indicates that women have a distinctive role in the new creation according to their gender. John depicts the new discipleship community that is formed at the cross as an act of new creation. The women and men who follow Jesus are reborn with the eschatological Spirit, and they are entrusted with the continuation of Jesus's mission.

Bibliography

Aitken, E. B. 'At the Well of Living Water: Jacob Traditions in John 4'. In *From Prophecy to Testament: The Function of the Old Testament in the New*, edited by C. A. Evans, 342–52. Peabody, MA: Hendrickson, 2004.
Alexander, L. 'Sisters in Adversity: Retelling Martha's Story'. In *Women in the Biblical Tradition*, edited by G. J. Brooke. Studies in Women and Religion 31, 167–86. Lewiston: Edwin Mellen Press, 1992.
Allison, D. C. *The New Moses. A Matthean Typology*. Edinburgh: T&T Clark, 1993.
Anderson, G. A. 'The Culpability of Eve: From Genesis to Timothy'. In *From Prophecy to Testament: The Function of the Old Testament in the New*, edited by C. A. Evans, 233–51. Peabody, MA: Hendrickson, 2004.
Archer, L. J. *Her Price Is Beyond Rubies: The Jewish Woman in Graeco-Roman Palestine*. Sheffield: JSOT Press, 1990.
Arndt, W. *A Greek-English Lexicon of the New Testament and Other Early Christian Literature*. Revised and edited by F. W. Danker, 3rd edn. London: University of Chicago Press, 2000.
Ashton, J. 'Riddles and Mysteries: The Way, the Truth, and the Life'. In *Jesus in Johannine Tradition*, edited by R. T. Fortna and T. Thatcher, 333–42. Louisville, KY: Westminster John Knox, 2001.
Ashton, J. *Understanding the Fourth Gospel*, 2nd edn. Oxford: Oxford University Press, 2007.
Balch, D. L. *Let Wives Be Submissive: The Domestic Code in 1 Peter*. Chico, CA: Scholars Press, 1981.
Barrett, C. K. *The Gospel according to St. John: An Introduction with Commentary and Notes on the Greek Text*, 2nd edn. London: SPCK, 1978.
Barrett, C. K. 'The Holy Spirit in the Fourth Gospel'. *JTS* 1 (1950): 1–15.
Bassler, J. M. 'Mixed Signals: Nicodemus in the Fourth Gospel'. *JBL* 108 (1989): 635–46.
Bauckham, R. (ed.). *The Gospels for All Christians: Rethinking the Gospel Audiences*. Edinburgh: T&T Clark, 1997.
Bauckham, R. *Jesus and the Eyewitnesses: The Gospels as Eyewitness Testimony*. Grand Rapids, MI: Eerdmans, 2006.
Bauckham, R. 'John for Readers of Mark'. In *The Gospels for All Christians: Rethinking the Gospel Audiences*, edited by R. Bauckham, 161–9. Edinburgh: T&T Clark, 1997.
Bauckham, R. 'Mary of Clopas (John 19:25)'. In *Women in the Biblical Tradition*, edited by G. J. Brooke. Studies in Women and Religion 31, 231–55. Lewiston: Edwin Mellen Press, 1992.
Bauckham, R. 'Response to Philip Esler'. *SJT* 51 (1998): 249–53.
Baumgarten, J. M. 'On the Testimony of Women in 1QSa'. *JBL* 76 (1957): 266–9.
Beasley-Murray, G. R. *John*, 2nd edn. WBC 36. Nashville, TN: Thomas Nelson, 1987.
Beirne, M. M. *Women and Men in the Fourth Gospel: A Genuine Discipleship of Equals*. JSNTSup 242. Sheffield: Sheffield Academic Press, 2003.

Brooten, B. J. *Women Leaders in the Ancient Synagogue: Inscriptional Evidence and Background Issues.* BJS 36. Chico, CA: Scholars Press, 1982.
Brown, J. K. 'Creation's Renewal in the Gospel of John'. *CBQ* 72 (2010): 275–90.
Brown, R. E. *The Churches the Apostles Left Behind.* London: Geoffrey Chapman, 1984.
Brown, R. E. *The Community of the Beloved Disciple. The Life, Loves, and Hates of an Individual Church in New Testament Times.* New York: Paulist Press, 1979.
Brown, R. E. *The Death of the Messiah. From Gethsemane to the Grave: A Commentary on the Passion Narratives in the Four Gospels*, 2 vols. ABRL. Garden City, NY: Doubleday, 1994.
Brown, R. E. *The Epistles of John.* AB30. Garden City, NY: Doubleday, 1982.
Brown, R. E. *The Gospel according to John*, 2 vols. AB29-29A. Garden City, NY: Doubleday, 1966–70.
Brown, R. E. 'Not Jewish Christianity and Gentile Christianity but Types of Jewish/Gentile Christianity'. *CBQ* 45 (1983): 74–9.
Brown, R. E. 'The Paraclete in the Fourth Gospel'. *NTS* 13 (1967): 113–32.
Brown, R. E., K. P. Donfried, J. A. Fitzmyer and J. Reumann (eds). *Mary in the New Testament: A Collaborative Assessment by Protestant and Roman Catholic Scholars.* London: Geoffrey Chapman, 1978.
Bull, R. J. 'An Archaeological Context for Understanding John 4.20'. *BA* 38 (1975): 54–9.
Bull, R. J. 'An Archaeological Footnote to "Our Fathers Worshipped on This Mountain" John IV.20'. *NTS* 23 (1977): 460–2.
Bultmann, R. *The Gospel of John.* Translated by G. R. Beasley-Murray. Oxford: Blackwell, 1971.
Byers, A. J. *Ecclesiology and Theosis in the Gospel of John.* Cambridge: Cambridge University Press, 2017.
Charlesworth, J. H. (ed.). *The Old Testament Pseudepigrapha*, 2 vols. Garden City, NY: Doubleday, 1983–5.
Coggins, R. J. 'The Samaritans and Acts'. *NTS* 28 (1982): 423–34.
Cohick, L. H. *Women in the World of the Earliest Christians: Illuminating Ancient Ways of Life.* Grand Rapids, MI: Baker Academic, 2009.
Collins, A. Y. 'New Testament Perspectives: The Gospel of John'. *JSOT* 22 (1982): 47–53.
Collins, J. J. *The Apocalyptic Imagination: An Introduction to the Jewish Matrix of Christianity.* New York: Crossroad, 1984.
Collins, J. J. *The Scepter and the Star: The Messiahs of the Dead Sea Scrolls and Other Ancient Literature.* Garden City, NY: Doubleday, 1995.
Coloe, M. L. *God Dwells with Us: Temple Symbolism in the Fourth Gospel.* Collegeville, PA: Liturgical Press, 2001.
Coloe, M. L. 'Theological Reflections on Creation in the Gospel of John'. *Pacifica* 24 (2011): 1–12.
Coloe, M. L. 'The Woman of Samaria: Her Characterization, Narrative, and Theological Significance'. In *Characters and Characterization in the Gospel of John*, edited by C. W. Skinner, 182–96. LNTS 461. London: T&T Clark, 2012.
Conway, C. M. *Behold the Man: Jesus and Greco-Roman Masculinity.* Oxford: Oxford University Press, 2008.
Conway, C. M. *Men and Women in the Fourth Gospel: Gender and Johannine Characterization.* SBLDS 167. Atlanta, GA: Society of Biblical Literature, 1999.
Corley, K. E. *Maranatha Women's Funerary Rituals and Christian Origins.* Minneapolis, MN: Fortress, 2010.

Cosgrove, C. H. 'A Woman's Unbound Hair in the Greco-Roman World, with Special Reference to the Story of the "Sinful Woman" in Luke 7:36-50'. *JBL* 124 (2005): 675-92.
Cullmann, O. *The Johannine Circle: Its Place in Judaism among the Disciples of Jesus and Early Christianity*. London: SCM, 1956.
Culpepper, R. A. *Anatomy of the Fourth Gospel: A Study in Literary Design*. Philadelphia, PA: Fortress, 1983.
Culpepper, R. A., and P. N. Anderson (eds). *John and Judaism: A Contested Relationship in Context*. Atlanta, GA: SBL Press, 2017.
Danby, H. *The Mishnah: Translated from the Hebrew with Introduction and Brief Explanatory Notes*. Oxford: Oxford University Press, 1933.
D'Angelo, M. R. 'A Critical Note: John 20:17 and Apocalypse of Moses 31'. *JTS* 41 (1990): 529-36.
D'Angelo, M. R. 'Reconstructing "Real" Women from Gospel Literature: The Case of Mary Magdalene'. In *Women and Christian Origins*, edited by R. S. Kraemer and M. R. D'Angelo, 105-28. Oxford: Oxford University Press, 1999.
D'Angelo, M. R. '(Re)Presentations of Women in the Gospels. John and Mark'. In *Women and Christian Origins*, edited by R. S. Kraemer and M. R. D'Angelo, 129-49. Oxford: Oxford University Press, 1999.
Daube, D. 'Jesus and the Samaritan Woman: The Meaning of συγχράομαι'. *JBL* 69 (1950): 137-47.
Daube, D. *The New Testament and Rabbinic Judaism*. London: Athlone Press, 1956.
Davies, W. D., and D. C. Allison. *The Gospel according to Saint Matthew*, vol. 2. Edinburgh: T&T Clark, 1991.
Deines, R. *Jüdische Steingefässe und pharisäische Frömmigkeit: ein archäologisch – historischer Beitrag zum Verständnis von Joh 2,6 und jüdischen Reinheitshalacha zur Zeit Jesu*. Tübingen: Mohr Siebeck, 1993.
De Boer, M. C. *Johannine Perspectives on the Death of Jesus*. Kampen: Kok Pharos, 1996.
De Boer, M. C. 'The Johannine Community under Attack in Recent Scholarship'. In *The Ways That Often Parted. Essays in Honor of Joel Marcus*, edited by L. Baron, J. Hicks-Keeton and M. Thiessen, 211-41. Early Christianity and Its Literature 24. Atlanta, GA: SBL Press, 2018.
De Boer, M. C. 'John 4:27 – Women (and Men) in the Gospel and Community of John'. In *Women in the Biblical Tradition*, edited by G. J. Brooke, 208-30. Studies in Women and Religion 31. Lewiston: Edwin Mellen Press, 1992.
De Jonge, M. 'Jewish Expectations about the "Messiah" according to the Fourth Gospel'. *NTS* 19 (1973): 246-70.
Dodd, C. H. *Historical Tradition in the Fourth Gospel*. Cambridge: Cambridge University Press, 1963.
Dschulnigg, P. *Jesus Begegnen. Personen und ihre Bedeutung im Johannesevangelium*. Münster: Lit Verlag, 2002.
Eisen, U. E. *Women Officeholders in Early Christianity: Epigraphical and Literary Studies*. Collegeville, PA: Liturgical Press, 2000.
Esler, P. F. 'Community and Gospel in Early Christianity: A Response to Richard Bauckham's *Gospels for All Christians*'. *SJT* 51 (1998): 235-48.
Esler, P. F., and R. Piper. *Lazarus, Mary and Martha. Social Scientific Approaches to the Gospel of John*. Minneapolis, MN: Fortress, 2006.
Fehribach, A. *The Women in the Life of the Bridegroom: A Feminist Historical-Literary Analysis of the Gospel of John*. Collegeville, PA: Liturgical Press, 1998.

Feuillet, A. *Johannine Studies*. New York: Alba House, 1965.
Fortna, R. *The Fourth Gospel and Its Predecessor*. Edinburgh: T&T Clark, 1989.
Freed, E. D. 'Did John Write His Gospel Partly to Win Samaritan Converts?' *NovT* 12 (1970): 241–56.
Frey, J. *Die Johanneische Eschatologie: Band II: Das Johanneische Zeitverständnis*. WUNT 110. Tübingen: Mohr Siebeck, 1998.
Friedmann, M. A. 'Babatha's *Ketubba*: Some Preliminary Observations'. *IEJ* 46 (1996): 55–76.
Gardner-Smith, P. *Saint John and the Synoptic Gospels*. Cambridge: Cambridge University Press, 1938.
Gaventa, B. R. *Mary: Glimpses of the Mother of Jesus*. Edinburgh: T&T Clark, 1999.
Giblin, C. H. 'Mary's Anointing for Jesus' Burial-Resurrection (John 12, 1-8)'. *Bib* 73 (1992): 560–4.
Giblin, C. H. 'Suggestion, Negative Response, and Positive Action in St John's Portrayal of Jesus (John 2.1-11; 4.46-54; 7.2-14; 11.1-44)'. *NTS* 26 (1980): 197–211.
Goodacre, M. S. 'Scripturalization in Mark's Crucifixion Narrative'. In *The Trial and Death of Jesus: Essays on the Passion Narrative in Mark*, edited by G. Van Oyen and T. Shepherd, 33–47. Leuven: Peeters, 2006.
Grey, M. *Redeeming the Dream. Feminism, Redemption and Christian Tradition*. London: SPCK, 1989.
Gundry, R. H. *Mark: A Commentary on His Apology for the Cross*. Grand Rapids, MI: Eerdmans, 1993.
Haenchen, E. *John*. 2 vols. Philadelphia, PA: Fortress, 1984.
Hakola, R. *Identity Matters. John, the Jews and Jewishness*. Supplements to Novum Testamentum 118. Leiden: Brill, 2005.
Hartenstein, J. *Charakterisierung im Dialog: Maria Magdalena, Petrus, Thomas und die Mutter Jesus im Johannesevangelium*. NTOA 64. Göttingen: Vandenhoeck & Ruprecht, 2007.
Heine, S. *Women and Early Christianity: Are the Feminist Scholars Right?* London: SCM Press, 1987.
Hjelm, I. *The Samaritans and Early Judaism*. JSNTSup 303. Sheffield: Sheffield Academic Press, 2000.
Hogan, P. N. *'No Longer Male and Female' Interpreting Galatians 3.28 in Early Christianity*. London: T&T Clark, 2008.
Hornsby, T. J. 'Anointing Traditions'. In *The Historical Jesus in Context*, edited by A.-J. Levine, D. C. Allison and J. D. Crossan, 339–42. Princeton, NJ: Princeton University Press, 2006.
Hoskyns, E. C. *The Fourth Gospel*, 2 vols. Edited by F. N. Davey. London: Faber, 1940.
Hoskyns, E. C. 'Genesis I-III and St John's Gospel'. *JTS* 21 (1920): 210–18.
Hylen, S. E. *Imperfect Believers: Ambiguous Characters in the Gospel of John*. Louisville, KY: Westminster John Knox, 2009.
Hylen, S. E. *Women in the New Testament World*. Oxford: Oxford University Press, 2019.
Ilan, T. *Jewish Women in Greco-Roman Palestine*. Peabody, MA: Hendrickson, 1996.
Ilan, T. 'Notes on the Distribution of Jewish Women's Names in Palestine in the Second Temple and Mishnaic Periods'. *JJS* 40 (1989): 186–200.
Karris, R. J. *Jesus and the Marginalized in John's Gospel*. Collegeville, PA: Liturgical Press, 1990.
Käsemann, E. *The Testament of Jesus: A Study of the Gospel of John in the Light of Chapter 17*. London: SCM Press, 1968.

Katz, S. T. 'Issues in the Separation of Judaism and Christianity after 70 C.E.: A Reconsideration'. *JBL* 103 (1984): 43–76.
Kimelman, R. 'Birkat Ha-Minim and the Lack of Evidence for an Anti-Christian Jewish Prayer in Late Antiquity'. In *Jewish and Christian Self-Definition. Vol. 2: Aspects of Judaism in the Graeco-Roman Period*, edited by E. P. Sanders with A. I. Baumgarten and A. Mendelson, 226–44. London: SCM Press, 1981.
King, K. L. 'The Gospel of Mary Magdalene'. In *Searching the Scriptures*, vol. 2, edited by E. Schüssler Fiorenza, 601–34. New York: Crossroad, 1994.
Kittel, G., and G. Friedrich (eds). *Theological Dictionary of the New Testament*, 10 vols. Translated by G. W. Bromiley. Grand Rapids, MI: Eerdmans, 1964–76.
Koester, C. R. *Symbolism in the Fourth Gospel. Meaning, Mystery, Community*. Minneapolis, MN: Fortress, 2003.
Kovacs, J. L. '"Now Shall the Ruler of This World Be Driven Out": Jesus' Death as Cosmic Battle in John 12:20-36'. *JBL* 114 (1995): 227–47.
Kraemer, R. S., and M. R. D'Angelo (eds). *Women and Christian Origins*. Oxford: Oxford University Press, 1999.
Lee, D. A. 'Abiding in the Fourth Gospel: A Case Study in Feminist Biblical Theology'. In *A Feminist Companion to John*, vol. 2, edited by A.-J. Levine with M. Blickenstaff, 64–78. London: Sheffield Academic Press, 2003.
Lee, D. A. 'Martha and Mary: Levels of Characterization in Luke and John'. In *Characters and Characterization in the Gospel of John*, edited by C. W. Skinner, 197–220. LNTS 461. London: T&T Clark, 2012.
Lee, D. A. *The Symbolic Narratives of the Fourth Gospel: The Interplay of Form and Meaning*. JSNTSup 95. Sheffield: JSOT Press, 1994.
Legault, A. 'An Application of the Form-Critique Method to the Anointings in Galilee (Lk 7, 36-50) and Bethany (Mt 26, 6-13; Mk 14, 3-9; Jn 12, 1-8)'. *CBQ* 16 (1954): 131–45.
Levine, A.-J. (ed.) with M. Blickenstaff. *A Feminist Companion to John*, 2 vols. London: Sheffield Academic Press, 2003.
Levine, A.-J. 'Second Temple Judaism, Jesus and Women: Yeast of Eden'. *BibInt* 2 (1994): 8–20.
Lieu, J. M. 'The Mother of the Son in the Fourth Gospel'. *JBL* 117 (1998): 61–77.
Lifshitz, B., and J. Schiby. 'Une Synagogue Samaritaine à Thessalonique'. *RB* 75 (1968): 268–78.
Lightfoot, R. H. *St. John's Gospel*. Oxford: Clarendon, 1956.
Lincoln, A. T. 'The Beloved Disciple as Eyewitness and the Fourth Gospel as Witness'. *JSNT* 85 (2002): 3–26.
Lincoln, A. T. *The Gospel according to Saint John*. Black's New Testament Commentaries. London: Continuum, 2005.
Lincoln, A. T. *Truth on Trial: The Lawsuit Motif in the Fourth Gospel*. Peabody, MA: Hendrickson, 2000.
Lindars, B. *The Gospel of John*. NCBC. London: Marshall, Morgan and Scott, 1972.
Lindars, B. 'Rebuking the Spirit. A New Analysis of the Lazarus Story of John 11'. *NTS* 38 (1992): 89–104.
Loader, W. 'Jesus and the Law in John'. In *Theology and Christology in the Fourth Gospel*, edited by G. Van belle, J. G. Van der Watt and P. Maritz, 149–54. Leuven: Leuven University Press, 2005.
Maccini, R. G. *'Her Testimony Is True': Women as Witnesses according to John*. JSNTSup 125. Sheffield: Sheffield Academic Press, 1996.

MacDonald, M. Y. *The Pauline Churches: A Socio-Historical Study of Institutionalization in the Pauline and Deutero-Pauline Writings*. Cambridge: Cambridge University Press, 1988.

Madigan, K., and C. Osiek (eds). *Ordained Women in the Early Church: A Documentary History*. Baltimore, MD: John Hopkins University Press, 2005.

Magen, Y. 'Mount Gerizim and the Samaritans'. In *Early Christianity in Context: Monuments and Documents*, edited by F. Manns and E. Alliata, 134–48. Jerusalem: Franciscan Printing Press, 1993.

Magen, Y. 'The Ritual Baths (Miqva'ot) at Qedumim and the Observance of Ritual Purity among the Samaritans'. In *Early Christianity in Context: Monuments and Documents*, edited by F. Manns and E. Alliata, 181–92. Jerusalem: Franciscan Printing Press, 1993.

Marcus, J. '*Birkat Ha-Minim* Revisited'. *NTS* 55 (2009): 523–51.

Marcus, J. *Mark 1–8. A New Translation with Introduction and Commentary*. AB27. Garden City, NY: Doubleday, 1999.

Marcus, J. *Mark 8–16: A New Translation with Introduction and Commentary*. AB27A. New Haven, CT: Yale University Press, 2009.

Marcus, J. 'Son of Man as Son of Adam'. *RB* 110 (2003): 38–61.

Martin, J. P. 'History and Eschatology in the Lazarus Narrative in John 11:1-44'. *SJT* 17 (1964): 332–43.

Martin, T. W. 'Assessing the Johannine Epiphet '"the Mother of Jesus"'. *CBQ* 60 (1998): 63–73.

Martinez, F. G., and E. J. C. Tigchekar (eds). *The Dead Sea Scrolls Study Edition*. Leiden: Brill, 1997–8.

Martyn, J. L. *History and Theology in the Fourth Gospel*, 2nd edn. New York: Crossroad, 1995.

McHugh, J. *The Mother of Jesus in the New Testament*. London: Darton, Longman and Todd, 1975.

McWhirter, J. *The Bridegroom Messiah and the People of God*. Cambridge: Cambridge University Press, 2006.

Meeks, W. A. 'The Man from Heaven in Johannine Sectarianism'. *JBL* 91 (1972): 44–72.

Meeks, W. A. *The Prophet-King: Moses Tradition and the Johannine Christology*. Leiden: Brill, 1967.

Meier, J. P. 'The Historical Jesus and the Historical Samaritans: What Can Be Said?' *Bib* 81 (2000): 202–32.

Methuen, C. 'Widows, Bishops and the Struggle for Authority in the *Didascalia Apostolorum*'. *JEH* 46 (1995): 197–213.

Metzger, B. M. *A Textual Commentary on the Greek New Testament: A Companion Volume to the United Bible Societies' Greek New Testament*, 3rd edn. London: United Bible Societies, 1975.

Miller, P. C. (ed.). *Women in Early Christianity: Translations from Greek Texts*. Washington, DC: Catholic University of America Press, 2005.

Miller, S. '"Among You Stands One Whom You Do Not Know" (John 1:26): The Use of the Tradition of the Hidden Messiah in John's Gospel'. In *The Ways That Often Parted. Essays in Honor of Joel Marcus*, edited by L. Baron, J. Hicks-Keeton and M. Thiessen, 243–63. Early Christianity and Its Literature 24. Atlanta, GA: SBL Press, 2018.

Miller, S. 'Anointing'. In *Dictionary of Jesus and the Gospels*, edited by J. B. Green, J. K. Brown and N. Perrin, 17–18. Leicester: Intervarsity, 2013.

Miller, S. 'Mary (of Bethany): The Anointer of the Suffering Messiah'. In *Character Studies in the Fourth Gospel*, edited by S. A. Hunt, D. F. Tolmie and R. Zimmermann, 473–86. WUNT 314. Tübingen: Mohr Siebeck, 2013.
Miller, S. 'The Woman at the Well: John's Portrayal of the Samaritan Mission'. In *John, Jesus, and History. Volume 2: Aspects of Historicity in the Fourth Gospel*, edited by P. N. Anderson, F. Just and T. Thatcher, 73–81. Atlanta, GA: Society of Biblical Literature, 2009.
Miller, S. *Women in Mark's Gospel*. JSNTSup 259. London: T&T Clark, 2004.
Minear, P. S. *Christians and the New Creation: Genesis Motifs in the New Testament*. Louisville, KY: Westminster John Knox, 1994.
Mitchell, M. M. 'Patristic Counter-Evidence to the Claim That "The Gospels Were Written for All Christians"'. *NTS* 51 (2005): 36–79.
Moloney, F. J. 'Can Everyone Be Wrong? A Reading of John 11.1-12.8'. *NTS* 49 (2003): 505–27.
Moloney, F. J. *The Gospel of John*. Sacra Pagina Vol. 4. Collegeville, PA: Liturgical Press, 1998.
Moloney, F. J. *Signs and Shadows. Reading John 5-12*. Minneapolis, MN: Fortress, 1996.
Mowinckel, S. *He That Cometh*. Oxford: Blackwell, 1956.
Munro, W. 'The Anointing in Mark 14:3-9 and John 12:1-8'. In *SBL Seminar Papers 1*, edited by P. J. Achtemeier, 127–30. Missoula, MT: Scholars Press, 1979.
Neirynck, F. 'John and the Synoptics: The Empty Tomb Stories'. *NTS* 30 (1984): 161–87.
Newsom, C. A., and S. H. Ringe (eds). *Women's Bible Commentary*, exp. edn. Louisville, KY: Westminster John Knox, 1998.
North, W. E. S. *A Journey Round John: Tradition, Interpretation and Context in the Fourth Gospel*. LNTS 534. London: T&T Clark, 2015.
North, W. E. S. *The Lazarus Story within the Johannine Tradition*. JSNTSup 212. Sheffield: Sheffield Academic Press, 2001.
O'Day, G. R. 'John'. In *Women's Bible Commentary*, exp. edn, edited by C. A. Newsom and S. H. Ringe, 381–93. Louisville, KY: Westminster John Knox, 1998.
O'Day, G. R. *Revelation in the Fourth Gospel: Narrative Mode and Theological Claim*. Philadelphia, PA: Fortress, 1986.
Okure, T. *The Johannine Approach to Mission: A Contextual Study of John 4:1-42*. WUNT 31. Tübingen: Mohr Siebeck, 1988.
Painter, J. *The Quest for the Messiah: The History, Literature and Theology of the Johannine Community*, 2nd edn. Edinburgh: T&T Clark, 1993.
Parsenios, G. L. *Departure and Consolation: The Johannine Farewell Discourses in Light of Greco-Roman Literature*. Supplements to Novum Testamentum 117. Leiden: Brill, 2005.
Pelikan, J. *Mary through the Centuries: Her Place in the History of Culture*. New Haven, CT: Yale University Press, 1996.
Perkins, P. '"I Have Seen the Lord" (John 20:18): Women Witnesses to the Resurrection'. *Int* 46 (1992): 31–41.
Plaskow, J. 'Anti-Judaism in Feminist Christian Interpretation'. In *Searching the Scriptures*, vol. 1, edited by E. Schüssler Fiorenza, 117–29. New York: Crossroad, 1993.
Pummer, R. *The Samaritans. A Profile*. Grand Rapids, MI: Eerdmans, 2016.
Purvis, J. D. 'The Fourth Gospel and the Samaritans'. *NovT* 17 (1975): 161–98.
Ramsey Michaels, J. *The Gospel of John*. NICNT. Grand Rapids, MI: Eerdmans, 2010.
Du Rand, J. A. 'The Creation Motif in the Fourth Gospel: Perspectives on Its Narratological Function within a Judaistic Background'. In *Theology and Christology*

in the Fourth Gospel: Essays by the Members of the SNTS Johannine Writings Seminar, edited by G. Van Belle, J. G. Van der Watt and P. Maritz, 21–46. BETL. 184. Leuven: Leuven University Press, 2005.

Reed, J. L. *Archaeology and the Galilean Jesus: A Re-examination of the Evidence*. Harrisburg: Trinity Press, 2000.

Reinhartz, A. *Befriending the Beloved Disciple: A Jewish Reading of the Gospel of John*. London: Continuum, 2001.

Reinhartz, A. '"Jews" and Jews in the Fourth Gospel'. In *Anti-Judaism and the Fourth Gospel*, edited by R. Bieringer, D. Pollefeyt and F. Vandecasteele-Vanneuville, 213–27. Louisville, KY: Westminster John Knox, 2001.

Reinhartz, A. 'Women in the Johannine Community: An Exercise in Historical Imagination'. In *A Feminist Companion to John*, vol. 2, edited by A.-J. Levine with M. Blickenstaff, 14–33. London: Sheffield Academic Press, 2003.

Reinhartz, A. *The Word in the World: The Cosmological Tale in the Fourth Gospel*. SBLMS 45. Atlanta, GA: Scholars Press, 1992.

Rena, J. 'Women in the Gospel of John'. *Église et Théologie* 17 (1986): 131–47.

Resseguie, J. L. 'The Beloved Disciple: The Ideal Point of View'. In *Character Studies in the Fourth Gospel*, edited by S. A. Hunt, D. F. Tolmie and R. Zimmermann, 537–49. WUNT 314. Tübingen: Mohr Siebeck, 2013.

Reynolds, B. E. *The Apocalyptic Son of Man in the Gospel of John*. WUNT 249. Tübingen: Mohr Siebeck, 2008.

Reynolds, B. E., and G. Boccaccini (eds). *Reading the Gospel of John's Christology as Jewish Messianism. Royal, Prophetic, and Divine Messiahs*. Ancient Judaism and Early Christianity 106. Leiden: Brill, 2018.

Ricci, C. *Mary Magdalene and Many Others: Women Who followed Jesus*. Kent: Burns and Oates, 1994.

Rowland, C. *The Open Heaven: A Study of Apocalyptic in Judaism and Early Christianity*. New York: Crossroad, 1982.

Ruether, R. R. *Women and Redemption: A Theological History*. London: SCM Press, 1998.

Russell, D. S. *The Method and Message of Jewish Apocalyptic 200 B.C.-A.D. 100*. London: SCM Press, 1964.

Schnackenburg, R. *The Gospel according to St. John*, 3 vols. London: Burns and Oates, 1968–82.

Schneiders, S. M. 'Death in the Community of Eternal Life: History, Theology, and Spirituality in John 11'. *Int* 41 (1987): 44–56.

Schneiders, S. M. 'The Foot Washing (John 13:1-20): An Experiment in Hermeneutics'. *CBQ* 43 (1981): 76–92.

Schneiders, S. M. 'John 20:11-18: The Encounter of the Easter Jesus with Mary Magdalene – A Transformative Feminist Reading'. In *What Is John? Vol. 1*, edited by F. F. Segovia, 155–68. Atlanta, GA: SBL Symposium Series, 1996.

Schneiders, S. M. *The Revelatory Text: Interpreting the New Testament as Sacred Scripture*. New York: HarperCollins, 1991.

Schneiders, S. M. 'Women in the Fourth Gospel and the Role of Women in the Contemporary Church'. *BTB* 12 (1982): 35–45.

Schnelle, U. *Antidocetic Christology in the Gospel of John: An Investigation of the Place of the Fourth Gospel in the Johannine School*. Translated by L. M. Maloney. Minneapolis, MN: Fortress, 1992.

Schottroff, L. *Let the Oppressed Go Free: Feminist Perspectives on the New Testament.* Louisville, KY: Westminster John Knox, 1993.
Schottroff, L. *Lydia's Impatient Sisters: A Feminist Social History of Early Christianity.* Louisville, KY: Westminster John Knox, 1995.
Schüssler Fiorenza, E. 'The Ethics of Biblical Interpretation: Decentering Biblical Scholarship'. *JBL* 107 (1988): 3–17.
Schüssler Fiorenza, E. *In Memory of Her: A Feminist Theological Reconstruction of Christian Origins*, 2nd edn. New York: Crossroad, 1995.
Schüssler Fiorenza, E. (ed.). *Searching the Scriptures: A Feminist Commentary*, vol. 2. New York: Crossroad, 1994.
Scott, M. *Sophia and the Johannine Jesus*. JSNTSup 71. Sheffield: Sheffield Academic Press, 1992.
Seim, T. K. 'Roles of Women in the Gospel of John'. In *Aspects on the Johannine Literature*, edited by L. Hartman and B. Olsson, 56–73. ConB. 18. Uppsala: Almqvist and Wiksell International, 1987.
Senior, D. *The Passion of Jesus in the Gospel of John*. Leominster: Gracewing/Fowler Wright Books, 1991.
Siliezar, C. R. S. *Creation Imagery in the Gospel of John*. LNTS 546. London: Bloomsbury, 2015.
Sim, D. C. 'The Gospels for All Christians? A Response to Richard Bauckham'. *JSNT* 84 (2001): 3–27.
Sim, D. C. *The Gospel of Matthew and Christian Judaism: The History and Social Setting of the Matthean Community*. Edinburgh: T&T Clark, 1998.
Smith, D. M. 'Johannine Christianity: Some Reflections on Its Character and Delineation'. *NTS* 21 (1975): 222–48.
Smith, D. M. *John*. Nashville, TN: Abingdon, 1999.
Smith, D. M. *John among the Gospels*, 2nd edn. Columbia: University of South Carolina Press, 2001.
Smith, D. M. *The Theology of the Gospel of John*. Cambridge: Cambridge University Press, 1995.
Soards, M. L. 'Appendix IX: The Question of a PreMarcan Passion Narrative'. In *The Death of the Messiah. From Gethsemane to the Grave: A Commentary on the Passion Narratives in the Four Gospels*, vol. 2. edited by R. E. Brown. ABRL, 1492–1524. Garden City, NY: Doubleday, 1998.
Stanton, G. *The Gospels and Jesus*, 2nd edn. Oxford: Oxford University Press, 2002.
Stibbe, M. W. G. 'A Tomb with a View: John 11.1-44 in Narrative-Critical Perspective'. *NTS* 40 (1994): 38–54.
Swidler, L. *Biblical Affirmations of Women*. Philadelphia, PA: Westminster, 1979.
Taylor, J. *Jewish Women Philosophers of First-Century Alexandria – Philo's 'Therapeutae' Reconsidered*. Oxford: Oxford University Press, 2003.
Temple, W. *Readings in St. John's Gospel*. London: Macmillan, 1941.
Theissen, G. *The First Followers of Jesus: A Sociological Analysis of the Earliest Christianity*. London: SCM Press, 1978.
Thomas, J. C. *Footwashing in John 13 and the Johannine Community*. JSNTSup 61. Sheffield: JSOT Press, 1991.
Thompson, M. M. *John. A Commentary*. Louisville, KY: Westminster John Knox, 2015.
Thompson, M. M. 'Lazarus: "Behold a Man Raised Up by Christ"'. In *Character Studies in the Fourth Gospel*, edited by S. A. Hunt, D. F. Tolmie and R. Zimmermann, 460–72. WUNT 314. Tübingen: Mohr Siebeck, 2013.

Thyen, H. *Das Johannesevangelium*. Tübingen: Mohr Siebeck, 2005.
von Wahlde, U. C. *The Gospel and Letters of John*, vol. 2. Grand Rapids, MI: Eerdmans, 2010.
von Wahlde, U. C. '"The Johannine Jews": A Critical Survey'. *NTS* 28 (1982): 33–60.
Wardle, T. 'Samaritans, Jews, and Christians: Multiple Partings and Multiple Ways'. In *The Ways That Often Parted: Essays in Honor of Joel Marcus*, edited by L. Baron, J. Hicks-Keeton and M. Thiessen, 15–39. Early Christianity and Its Literature 24. Atlanta, GA: SBL Press, 2018.
Warner, M. *Alone of All Her Sex: The Myth and the Cult of the Virgin Mary*. London: Weidenfeld and Nicolson, 1976.
Wegner, J. R. *Chattel or Person? The Status of Women in the Mishnah*. Oxford: Oxford University Press, 1988.
White Crawford, S. 'Mothers, Sisters, and Elders: Titles for Women in Second Temple Jewish and Early Christian Communities'. In *The Dead Sea Scrolls as Background to Post Biblical Judaism and Early Christianity*, edited by J. R. Davila, 177–91. Leiden: Brill, 2003.
Wilckens, U. *Das Evangelium nach Johannes*. Göttingen: Vandenhoeck and Ruprecht, 1998.
Williams, C. H. *I Am He: The Interpretation of 'Anî Hû' in Jewish and Early Christian Literature*. WUNT 113. Tübingen: Mohr Siebeck, 2000.
Williams, C. H., and C. Rowland (eds). *John's Gospel and Intimations of Apocalyptic*. London: T&T Clark, 2013.
Wire, A. C. *The Corinthian Women Prophets: A Reconstruction through Paul's Rhetoric*. Minneapolis, MN: Fortress, 1990.
Witherington, B. *Women in the Ministry of Jesus: A Study of Jesus' Attitudes to Women and Their Roles as Reflected in His Earthly Life*. Cambridge: Cambridge University Press, 1984.
Wyatt, N. '"Supposing Him to Be the Gardener" (John 20,15): A Study of the Paradise Motif in John'. *ZNW* 81 (1990): 21–38.
Yadin, Y., J. C. Greenfield and A. Yardeni. 'Babatha's *Ketubba*'. *IEJ* 44 (1994): 75–101.
Zimmermann, R. 'The Narrative Hermeneutics in John 11. Learning with Lazarus How to Understand Death, Life, and Resurrection'. In *The Resurrection of Jesus in the Gospel of John*, edited by C. R. Koester and R. Bieringer, 75–101. WUNT 222. Tübingen: Mohr Siebeck, 2008.

Index of References

BIBLE

Old Testament
Genesis
1.1–2.3	30, 132
1.1 LXX	5, 30
1.2	53, 114
1.4	5
1.5	5
1.9	5
2.2 LXX	113, 146
2.7 LXX	5, 77
2.8	133
2.15-17	112, 133, 145
2.15	133, 146
2.16-17	31
2.22-23	53
3.1-22 LXX	53
3.1-7	146
3.2	133
3.4	31
3.8	112, 133, 145
3.15	112, 133, 145
3.16-18	30
3.20	31, 113, 146, 148, 151
3.22-24	76, 134
8.21	90
24.10-61	39
24.22-27	39
29.1-20	39
29.10-12	39
38	40
50.2-3 LXX	95

Exodus
2.15-21	39
3.14 LXX	47
10.1-2	29
16.7-10	32
20.17	32, 45
28.41	88
29.18	90

Leviticus
2.2	90
14.5-6	44
14.50-52	44
15.13	44

Numbers
14.22	29
18.20	92
19.17	44

Deuteronomy
7.19	29
12.12	92
14.27	92
15.11	89
18	46
18.15-18	45
18.15	45, 67
18.18	67
19.15	124
32.39	47

Judges
11.12	23
14.6 LXX	44
14.19 LXX	44
15.14 LXX	44

Ruth
1.16	129

1 Samuel
9.15–10.1	88
10.1	88
10.10 LXX	44

16.1	88	Isaiah	
16.12-13	88	1.23	21
17.13 LXX	44	2.2	64
18.21	110	10.3	21
25	92	26.17	114
		27.12-13	56
2 Samuel		32.15	44
14.1-20	48	41.4	47
16.10	23	43.3	50
19.23	23	43.10	47
		43.11	50
1 Kings		44.3	44
1.45	88	45.15	50
17.17-24	76	45.19 LXX	47
17.18	23	45.21	50
19.16	88	46.4	47
		49.14-22	113
2 Kings		49.20-22	148
3.13	23	49.26	50
4.32-37	76	52.6 LXX	47
17	38, 41	54.1-3	113
17.30-32	38	54.1	148
		54.4-8	32
2 Chronicles		54.4-5	41
6.14	89, 90	60.16	50
35.21	23	62.4-5	32
		62.5	41
Esther		65.17	5
4.17 LXX	89	66.7-13	113
		66.7-8	148
Psalms		66.22	5
2.7	110		
23.5	88	Jeremiah	
33.6	5	2.2-3	41
37.11 LXX	106	14.8	50
42.5	69	22.3	21
87.8 LXX	106	31.12	20, 26, 96
118.26	67	31.31-34	129
Proverbs		Ezekiel	
9.3	2	11.19	44
13.14	43	36.25-27	44
16.22	43	36.26-27	114
18.4	43	37.15-23	42, 56
Ecclesiastes		Daniel	
2.15 LXX	133	12.2	76
9.7	88	10.40 LXX	24
		10.45 LXX	24

Index of References

Hosea		8.14-15	8, 62
2.21-22	96	8.29	23
11.11	56	9.17	20
13.4	50	9.18-26	1, 8
14.7	20, 26	9.30	68
		9.37-38	51
Joel		10.1-4	62
2.28-29	44, 114	10.5-6	15, 38, 42, 58
		10.5	55
Amos		10.6	55
9.13-14	20, 26, 96	11.2-6	65
		11.3	67
Micah		12.46-50	8
4.1	64	12.46	22
		13.55-56	22
Zechariah		14.13-21	20
7.10	21	15.21-28	140
8.12	96	15.24	55
9.9	90	15.28	23
9.13	41, 56	16.13-20	61, 71
10.6-7	42, 56	16.14	46
		16.16	71
Apocrypha		16.18	71
1 Maccabees		16.19	72
13.51	90	16.21-23	71
		18	108
2 Maccabees		20.2	88
1.27	56	21.9	67
10.7	90	21.21-28	1
14.4	90	22.1-14	32, 41
		22.23-33	40, 76
Sirach		24.8	114
15.3	43	24.51	92
24.21	43	25.1-13	41
24.23-29	43	26.6-13	83, 84
24.23-34 LXX	133	26.6	62
49.16	32	26.8	86
50.25-26	38	26.10-13	87
		26.12	95
Tobit		26.13	87
7.12	110	26.14-16	87
14.5	54	26.36-46	90
		26.56	101, 107
Wisdom of Solomon		26.63	66
9.1	5	27.54	107
		27.55-56	8, 63, 101
New Testament		27.55	105
Matthew		27.56	104, 139
8.11	32	27.62-66	126

28.1-10	8, 131	14.1-11	61
28.1	123	14.3-9	60, 83, 84
28.9-10	121, 122, 127	14.3	62, 85
28.9	128	14.4	86
28.10	128	14.5	68
28.16-20	131	14.6-9	87
28.16-18	126	14.7	85
28.19	56	14.9	84, 87, 95
		14.10-11	87
Mark		14.32-42	90
1.4-8	13	14.35	24
1.14-15	13	14.38	24
1.24	23, 72	14.41	24
1.29-31	8, 62	14.50	101, 107
1.43	68	14.61	66
2.22	20, 32	15.21	104
3.13-19	62	15.29-32	106
3.20-35	61	15.29	107
3.31-35	8, 149	15.39	107
3.35	17, 129	15.40-41	8, 63, 86, 98, 101
5.7	23	15.40	62, 101, 102, 104, 105, 106
5.21-43	1, 8, 61		
6.3	22, 102	15.41	105
6.35-44	20	16.1-8	8, 121, 122, 131
6.37	13	16.1	123
6.38	13	16.5	126
6.43	13		
6.44	13	Luke	
6.50	13	4.34	23, 72
7.24-30	1, 140	4.38-39	8, 62
8.27-30	61, 71	5.37-39	20
8.28	46	6.12-16	62
8.29	71	7.11-17	1
8.31-33	71	7.18-23	65
9.3	126	7.19	67
9.30	13	7.36-50	84
9.35	98	7.37	89
10.1	13	7.40-50	84
10.28	149	8.1-3	8, 63, 101
10.30	117, 118	8.2-3	104
10.32	13	8.3	62, 105, 139
10.43	98	8.19-21	8
10.45	98	8.19-20	22
10.46	13	8.28	23
11.9	67	8.40-56	1, 8
11.12-25	61	9.12-17	20
12.18-27	40, 76	9.18-20	61, 71
12.41-44	21	9.19	46
13.8	114	9.20	71

Index of References

9.21-22	71	1.21	46
9.51-56	55	1.26	27
10.12	51	1.29	16, 30, 90
10.29-37	38	1.31-34	27
10.38-42	1, 12, 59, 140	1.33	27
10.39	59	1.35-51	136
10.40	59	1.35-42	29
10.42	60	1.35	30
12.37	92	1.36	16, 90
12.46	92	1.38	130
13.12	23	1.39	70
14.7-11	41	1.41	29, 66, 72, 88
15.8-10	8	1.43-51	29, 62
16.19-31	60	1.43	30
17.8	92	1.45	21
17.11-19	38, 55	1.46	27, 70, 124
17.18	55	1.47-51	41
18.1-8	8, 21, 48	1.49	29, 41, 66, 80, 88
19.38	67	1.50-51	29
20.27-40	40, 76	1.51	4, 29, 66, 128
21.1-4	21	2.1-12	108, 116, 146
22.5	87	2.1-11	1, 6, 12, 19, 41, 42,
22.16-18	32		51, 53, 61, 96, 101,
22.67-70	66		102, 111, 112, 139
23.47	107	2.1	21, 23, 30, 31, 32, 108
23.49	8, 101, 104, 106	2.3	21, 22, 23, 31, 63, 141
24.1-10	8, 121	2.4	19, 20, 23, 24, 25, 31,
24.1	124		53, 69, 110, 108, 110,
24.10	123		112, 122, 126, 133,
24.11	124, 135		140, 141, 145
24.12	122	2.5	21, 23, 24, 31, 34
24.13.35	126	2.6	34
24.13-32	103	2.9–2.10	96
24.24	122	2.9	27, 47, 53
24.31	126	2.10	27, 32, 95
		2.11	19, 20, 26, 29, 30, 32,
John			70, 78, 88, 94, 111,
1.3	30		116, 145
1.4	77	2.12	21, 23, 30, 31, 115
1.5	6, 77	2.19-21	32, 54
1.9	6, 67, 77	2.19	54
1.10-11	6 n.21	2.23-25	29, 131
1.12-13	129, 148	2.23	20
1.12	6	3.1-21	123
1.13	113	3.2	29, 123
1.14	14, 32	3.3	113
1.17-18	34 n.46	3.5	115, 129
1.18	47	3.13	128
1.19-36	13	3.16-17	67

3.16	134	4.40	32
3.17	50	4.42	1, 12, 37, 55, 67, 81, 132
3.18	66		
3.25	134	4.45	20
3.31	67	4.46-54	24, 63
4.1-42	1, 6, 12, 16, 61, 62, 139, 147	5.1-9	63, 89
		5.10-13	90
4.1-26	121, 123, 125	5.17-18	129
4.2-9	58	5.18	6, 90
4.3	13	5.20	146
4.4	32	5.24	76
4.5-6	42	5.25-47	129
4.6	54	5.25-29	4
4.7-26	64–79	5.25	25, 76
4.7-9	43	5.29	76
4.7	43, 50, 54, 144	5.36	113, 146
4.9	17, 40, 43, 123	6.1-71	72
4.10	37, 43, 52, 65, 74	6.1-15	96
4.11-12	133	6.1-14	79
4.11	44, 47, 53	6.1	11
4.12	42, 123	6.7	13
4.13-14	44	6.9	13
4.14	44, 52, 144, 149	6.10	13
4.15	143	6.13	13
4.16-19	131	6.14-15	46, 56
4.17-18	141	6.14	66
4.17	40	6.15	90
4.19	44, 124	6.20	13, 47
4.20	123	6.26	96
4.21-24	58	6.35	5, 12, 47, 52, 65, 74, 79, 130
4.21	23, 53, 122, 126, 140, 145	6.37	129
4.22	44, 114	6.39	4, 76
4.23-24	145	6.40	4, 76, 129
4.23	25, 39, 51, 53	6.41-51	128
4.24	44	6.41	17 n.69
4.25	46, 67	6.42	21
4.26	47, 48, 57, 144	6.44	4, 76
4.27	11, 50, 51, 58, 94, 136	6.52	17 n.69
4.28	47	6.53-54	115
4.29	1, 37, 41, 46, 47, 99, 126, 131, 140, 142	6.54	4, 76
		6.60-65	128
4.32	51	6.60	136
4.33	51	6.66-71	144
4.34	20, 113	6.69	61, 66, 72, 80, 82
4.35	51	6.71	60
4.38	51	7.1-9	141
4.39-42	69	7.2-14	24
4.39	88, 125	7.2	16

7.3	136	9.35	65
7.5	115	9.38	46, 81, 131
7.10-14	13	9.39	67
7.18	78	9.41	147
7.20	143	10.1-6	127, 130
7.24	109	10.1	11
7.25-31	18, 90	10.7	47
7.27	27, 28	10.9	12, 47, 65
7.30	24	10.10	52, 65, 67, 90, 95, 130, 134
7.31	70		
7.32	64, 90	10.11	12, 65, 90, 92
7.33-34	89	10.15-18	89
7.37-39	44, 54, 115	10.15	92
7.37	16	10.17-18	92
7.38-39	143, 145	10.17	92
7.38	44	10.18	92
7.39	111, 129	10.19-21	18
7.40-44	18	10.19	70
7.43	70	10.22-42	75
7.45-52	97	10.22	16
7.48-49	90	10.30	65, 129
7.48	90	10.33	6, 90
7.50	60	10.39	64
7.52	46	10.42	70
8.12	5, 12, 47, 65, 74, 77, 130	11.1–12.8	1, 21
		11.1-44	6, 24, 139
8.14	27	11.1-27	121, 125
8.18-20	129	11.2	60, 61, 87
8.20	24, 143	11.3	63
8.24	47	11.4	64, 74, 77, 78
8.28	47	11.5	73
8.40	70	11.6	74
8.48	55	11.11	73
8.54	78	11.14-15	74
8.58	47	11.15	64
9.1-41	62, 148	11.16	75, 93
9.1-12	63	11.17-27	64
9.1-7	79, 89	11.20	59, 79
9.3-4	146	11.21	64, 68, 74
9.5	74, 79	11.22	64
9.13-17	25	11.23	64, 143
9.16	29, 70	11.24	4, 64, 76
9.17	46	11.25-27	79
9.22-23	148	11.25-26	65
9.22	17, 64, 66 n.17, 72, 75, 80	11.25	1, 12, 47, 65, 70, 75, 77, 81, 144, 145
9.27	136	11.26	65
9.29	27	11.27	12, 59, 61, 65, 72, 78, 79, 81, 83, 88, 94, 99,
9.35-41	79		

	125, 126, 131, 132, 140, 142	13.1	24, 90, 91, 108, 112, 143, 151
11.28-37	68	13.3	90
11.28	136, 143	13.5	91
11.31	69, 124	13.8	92
11.32	59, 68, 74	13.12-17	93
11.33	68	13.12	92
11.34	70	13.12-20	93
11.35	70	13.19	47
11.37	74	13.21	69
11.39	70	13.23	60, 108, 109
11.40-42	70	13.25	109
11.40	70, 77, 145	13.31-32	26, 27, 32, 143, 145
11.44	77	13.33	89, 92
11.45-54	80	13.34-35	93, 109
11.45-53	75	13.36-38	94
11.45-46	18, 25, 29	13.36	94
11.45	70	14.1	69
11.49	60	14.6	5, 12, 52, 65, 130
11.55	16	14.9	89
11.57	83	14.10	146
12.1-8	6, 12, 59, 60, 84, 139	14.16	14
12.1	91	14.26	14, 149
12.2	59, 98	14.27	69
12.3	84, 85, 90, 91, 97–7	14.30	6, 31, 67, 69, 145
12.5	88	14.31	11
12.6	89	15.1	12, 65, 74
12.7-8	148	15.12-14	73, 93
12.7	89, 94, 96, 97	15.15	73
12.8	84, 85, 89, 92	15.17	109
12.9-11	80, 90	15.18–16.4	5
12.12-19	75, 99	15.18-25	118
12.13	67, 83, 90	15.26	14
12.23-24	24, 90	16.1-4	118
12.23	108, 112, 143, 145	16.1-2	72
12.24	70, 96	16.2	17, 66 n.17, 80
12.26	98	16.4-5	89
12.27-33	89	16.7	74, 111, 129
12.27-28	24, 143	16.11	31, 67, 69, 113, 145
12.27	67, 69, 151	16.21	114
12.31-32	5	16.27	66
12.31	6, 31, 32, 67, 69, 78, 113, 134, 145	16.28	74
		16.32	143
12.37-43	25	16.33	118
12.42	17, 66 n.17, 72, 80	17.1-5	19, 26, 78, 90, 108, 112, 143
12.47	67		
12.48	4	17.1-4	151
13.1-20	84, 99, 100	17.1	24, 32, 143
		17.4	113, 146

17.5	5	19.38	97, 103
17.11	72	19.39	97
17.24	5	19.40	95
18.1	133	19.41	133
18.4	90	20.1-18	1, 6, 8, 21, 97, 101, 103, 139
18.5	21, 47		
18.6	47	20.1	32, 132
18.7	21	20.2	109, 123
18.8	21, 47, 107	20.6-7	77
18.11	111	20.8	109, 121, 122, 124
18.14	60	20.11-18	12
18.15-18	107	20.11-13	126
18.15	109	20.12	126
18.17	107	20.13	23, 126, 145
18.19	107	20.14-17	126
18.25-27	107	20.15	23, 122, 126, 127, 130, 133, 140, 141, 145
18.33-40	83		
18.33-38	91		
18.33	90	20.16	126, 127, 136, 141, 143
18.36-37	90		
18.37	67	20.17	127, 128, 129, 149
19.1-2	54	20.18	1, 12, 121, 126, 131, 132, 137, 140, 142
19.7	90		
19.9	27	20.19-25	128
19.14-16	90	20.19-23	131, 135
19.14-15	90	20.19	107, 126, 132
19.14	54	20.22	5, 112, 129, 149
19.19	21, 83, 90, 108	20.24-29	128
19.23	107	20.24	144
19.24-25	107	20.25	137
19.25-27	1, 6, 8, 19, 23, 25, 108, 139, 146, 148	20.26	126
		20.27	128
19.25-26	133	20.28	71
19.25	21, 93, 101, 108, 139	20.29	66, 125
19.26-30	149	20.30-31	11, 29, 130, 136, 148
19.26-29	135	20.31	66, 66 n.17, 67, 72, 79, 134
19.26-27	101, 108, 130, 150, 151		
		21.1-14	135
19.26	30, 109, 110, 112, 122, 124, 140, 145	21.2	136
		21.4	126
19.27	19, 108, 110, 111, 145	21.7	136, 137
19.28-30	111	21.14	135
19.28	54, 90	21.20-23	109, 136
19.30	54, 111, 113, 116, 146	21.24-25	16
19.34-37	114	21.24	14, 106
19.34	25, 60, 60		
19.35	14	Acts	
19.36	90	1.14	22, 102
19.38-42	90, 96, 124	2.14-42	71

2.33-35	128	5.17	5
3.17	46	6.4	34, 98
5.31	128	11.2-3	33, 98
7.55-56	128	11.23	34
8	51		
8.4-25	38	Galatians	
8.14-25	71	1.11-16	134
8.21	92	1.19	22
11.1-18	71	2.11-14	71, 116
12.1-19	71	3.27-28	9
12.2	117	4.21–5.1	114
12.17	116	6.15	5
15.13-21	116		
21.8	116	Ephesians	
21.9	99	5.21–6.9	10
21.10-11	99	5.22-24	142
23.8	76		
		Philippians	
Romans		1.1	34, 98
10.9	131, 142	1.2	2.11 131, 142
12.6-8	99		
16.1	10, 35, 117, 129, 149	Colossians	
		3.11	9
16.3	10, 52, 117	3.18–4.1	10
16.7	10, 52	4.7	34, 98
16.17	129, 149	4.10	22
16.23	129, 149		
		1 Thessalonians	
1 Corinthians		4.13-18	74
1.10	129, 149		
1.11	129, 149	1 Timothy	
1.26	129, 149	2.8-15	33
3.5	34, 98	2.11-15	10
7.13-14	148	2.12	149
7.15	117	3.1-13	10, 150
9.1-12	134	5.9-14	142
9.5	22, 52, 62		
11.2-16	89, 99, 100	Titus	
12.3	131, 142	1.5-16	10, 150
12.13	9	2.3-5	142
12.29-30	99		
14.26-32	99	James	
14.31	99	2.15	117
14.33-35	10, 149		
15.8-11	134	1 Peter	
		2.18–3.7	10
2 Corinthians		3.1-6	142, 148
2.14	95	3.22	128
3.6	34, 98		

1 John		1 Enoch	
2.1	14	10.19	20, 26
2.10-11	129	48.1	43
2.28	14	48.6	28, 143
3.10	129	49.1	43
3.13-17	129	62.4	114
4.17	14	62.7	113
4.20-21	129	90.28-29	54
5.16	129	91.16	5

2 John		4 Ezra	
1	117	4.42	114
13	117	7.26-28	28, 143
		7.30-36	5
3 John		14.13	95
3	130		
5	130	Joseph and Aseneth	
10	130	10.4	89
15	73	13.15	92
		20.15	92

Revelation		Jubilees	
2.20	99, 117	1.17	54
2.23	117		
3.10	24	Life of Adam and Eve	
5.6	16	3.1	33
5.8	16	5.2	33
5.12	16	11.3	32
6.1	16	26.2	33
6.16	16	35.3	33
7.9	126		
7.13-14	126	Sibylline Oracles	
12.1	30	3.378	95
12.7	30	8.208	95
19.9	32		
20.6	92	Testaments of the Twelve Patriarchs	
21.8	92		
22.19	92	Testament of Benjamin	
		9.2	54

OTHER ANCIENT SOURCES
Old Testament Pseudepigrapha

Apocalypse of Moses		Testament of Judah	
20.1-2	32	25.4	95
20.2	32		
21.6	32	Dead Sea Scrolls	
		1QS	
2 Baruch		3.6-9	44
3.7	5	4.20-26	44
29.3	26	4.20-23	32
29.5	20, 26	4.20-22	44

9.11	46	2.559-61	9
1QSa		Rabbinic Writings	
1.11	124	Mishnah	
		'Abot	
1QH		1.5	50, 140
1.15	32		
		Berakot	
11QT		7.1	43
29.8-10	54		
		Niddah	
CD		4.1	43
3.16	43		
3.18-20	32	*Qiddušin*	
6.4-11	43	4.3	55
19.34	43		
		Šabbat	
4QD^e7 I		23.5	89
13-15	116		
		Yebamot	
Philo		16.5-7	22
Against Flaccus		16.5	125
72	106		
		Tosefta	
On the Contemplative Life		*Pe'ah*	
68-69	62	4.19	89
Josephus		Babylonian Talmud	
Antiquities		*Bekorot*	
4.219	125	46b	125
9.201	37		
9.277-91	56	*Berakot*	
9.288	41	43b	50, 140
9.291	38, 55		
11.340-41	37	*'Erubin*	
11.340	38	53b	48, 50, 140
17.74	23		
17.76	23	*Ketubot*	
17.93	125	74b	125
17.196-99	90		
17.199	89	*Nedarim*	
18.14	76	20a	140
18.85-89	46		
		Pesaḥim	
Jewish War		5a	95
1.538	125		
2.162-63	76	*Qiddušin*	
2.253	106	75a-6a	56

Šabbat
151b 95

Sukkah
49b 89

Yebamot
115a 22

Further Rabbinic References
Exodus Rabbah
1.26 46

Ruth Rabbah
5.6 46

Ecclesiastes Rabbah
1.28 46
7.1 95

Samaritan Writings
Memar Marqah
2.12 55
4.1 46
4.6 55
6.2 55

Early Christian Writings
Barnabas
15.8-9 133

1 Clement
42.4 35

Didache
14.1-3 35

Gospel of Thomas
114 103, 135

Ignatius,
To the Romans
7 16

To the Trallians
2 35

Protevangelium of James
9.2 22

17.1–18.1 22

Classical and Ancient Christian Writings
Apostolic Constitutions
3.9.1-4 35
3.16.1-2 35

Didascalia Apostolorum
3.9 35
3.12 35

Dio Chrysostom
Servants (Or. 10)
27.3 21
29.5 21

Trojan Discourse (Or. 11)
10.107 21
55.3 21

Epiphanius
Refutation of all Heresies
78.17-19 33
78.23 20, 34
79 20, 34
79.2.3-4.1 35

Eusebius
Demonstration of the Gospel
989 85

Ecclesiastical History
3.11.1 103
3.32.1-6 103
4.22.4 103

Herodotus
Histories
6.19 92

Irenaeus
Against Heresies
3.1.1 15
3.22.4 30
5.22.4 34

Justin
First Apology
1.65.5 35

Dialogue with Trypho
8.4	28
100.4-6	32
100.5	30
110.1	28

Ovid
Metamorphoses
583-99	89

Petronius
Satyricon
69	88
111	89

Plutarch
Moralia
142CD	140
267	89
318F	21

Pompeius
73.6-7	92

Solon
27.7.5	21

Suetonius
Tiberius
61	106

Tacitus
Annals
6.10	106
6.19	106

Virgil
Aeneid
365	89

Index of Authors

Aitken, E. B. 42
Alexander, L. 60 n.2
Allison, D. C. 46, 55–6
Anderson, G. A. 33 n.41
Anderson, P. N. 16 n.67, 56 n.58
Archer, L. J. 6 n.23
Arndt, W. 85
Ashton, J. 4, 11, 25, 28, 66 n.17, 143 n.5

Balch, D. L. 10
Bammel, E. 95
Barrett, C. K. 11 n.49, 12, 20, 43, 59, 66, 72, 83, 85, 86, 105 n.11, 110, 112, 112 n.30, 113, 115, 135
Bassler, J. M. 97
Bauckham, R. 15, 15 n.61, 60, 102, 103, 104
Baumgarten, J. M. 124 n.4
Beasley-Murray, G. R. 23, 25, 110
Beirne, M. M. 3, 108
Beyer, H. 98
Boccacini, G. 4 n.13
Brown, J. K. 5, 53, 113, 132, 133
Brown, R. E. 2, 11, 14, 15, 16, 17, 22 n.11, 23–4, 28, 29, 31, 32, 37, 41, 43 n.25, 45, 47, 55, 60, 65, 68, 69, 76, 77, 83, 86, 90, 92, 93, 95, 98, 102, 105, 108, 110, 111, 112 n.30, 113, 114, 127, 129, 134, 147, 148, 149
Bull, R. J. 38 n.6
Bultmann, R. 6 n.21, 20, 33, 78, 95, 101–2, 108, 109
Byers, A. J. 129

Coggins, R. J. 55
Cohick, L. H. 8
Collins, A. Y. 149
Collins, J. J. 4 n.15, 65, 143
Coloe, M. L. 42, 54 n.50, 132–3
Conway, C. M. 3, 7, 23, 24, 67, 70, 110, 124, 131

Corley, K. E. 124 n.1
Cosgrove, C. H. 89 n.21
Cullmann, O. 51
Culpepper, R. A. 3 n.7, 16 n.67

D'Angelo, M. R. 3, 7 n.25, 117, 128, 135
Daube, D. 43, 89
Davies, D. C. 55–6
Deines, R. 34 n. 45
De Boer, M. C. 17 n. 73, 50, 66
De Jonge, M. 27 n.25, 143
Dodd, C. H. 86
Donfried, K. P. 22 n.11, 110
Dschulnigg, P. 79–80

Eisen, U. E. 35 n.47, 100
Esler, P. F. 15, 73

Fehribach, A. 2, 19, 41
Feuillet, A. 31
Fitzmyer, J. A. 22 n.11, 110
Fortna, R. 20
Freed, E. D. 45
Frey, J. 4 n.16
Friedmann, M. A. 9 n.37

Gardner-Smith, P. 13, 85
Gaventa, B. R. 20 n.7
Giblin, C. H. 24, 96
Goodacre, M. S. 106
Greenfield, J. C. 9 n.37
Grey, M. 7 n.27
Gundry, R. H. 102

Haenchen, E. 23, 41, 60, 93, 115, 134–5
Hakola, R. 17 n.73
Hartenstein, J. 135
Heine, S. 7 n.25
Hjelm, I. 37–8
Hogan, P. N. 9 n.39
Hornsby, T. J. 88

Hoskyns, E. C. 107, 114, 133
Hylen, S. E. 8, 74, 140 n.1

Ilan, T. 6 n.23, 9, 21, 40 n.10, 50, 62 n.7, 103, 104, 125, 140

Johnson, M. D. 128

Karris, R. J. 89 n.19
Kasemann, E. 144
Katz, S. T. 80 n. 50
Kimelman, R. 80 n.50
King, K. L. 10, 135
Koester, C. R. 44
Kovacs, J. L. 4–5, 31 n.38, 67 n.20, 145 n.7
Kraemer, R. S. 7 n.25

Lee, D. A. 7, 43, 66 n.15, 70
Legault, A. 86, 88
Levine, A.-J. 7 n.25, 9
Lieu, J. M. 25
Lifshitz, B. 57
Lightfoot, R. H. 29, 54
Lincoln, A. T. 12 n.50, 41, 47, 95, 109, 111, 124, 136, 148
Lindars, B. 11 n.49, 28, 30, 40, 60, 68, 91, 111
Loader, W. 34 n.46

Maccini, R. G. 2, 23
MacDonald, M. Y. 10
Madigan, K. 35 n.47
Magen, Y. 38 n.6, 44 n. 26
Marcus, J. 32, 80 n.50, 85, 105
Martin, J. P. 74, 76
Martin, T. W. 21
Martyn, J. L. 17, 80, 147
McHugh, J. 31
McWhirter, J. 39
Meeks, W. A. 56, 128 n.12
Meier, J. P. 37, 55
Methuen, C. 35
Metzger, B. M. 43 n.21
Miller, P. C. 33, 35
Miller, S. 28 n.26, 56, 84 n.4, 89 n.20, 98 n.44
Minear, P. S. 5 n.19
Mitchell, M. M. 15
Moloney, F. J. 44, 65, 66, 68

Mowinckel, S. 27 n.25
Munro, W. 86

Neirynck, F. 127–8
Newsom, C. A. 7 n.25
North, W. E. S. 12 n.50, 73, 75

O'Day, G. R. 19, 40, 50, 51, 73, 96, 116, 130
Okure, T. 41
Osiek, C. 35 n.47

Painter, J. 127
Parsenios, G. L. 11 n.47
Pelikan, J. 20 n.7
Perkins, P. 131
Piper, R. 73
Plaskow, J. 9
Pummer, R. 37 n.4
Purvis, J. D. 57

Ramsey Michaels, J. 24, 87
Du Rand, J. A. 5 n.19
Reed, J. L. 34 n.45
Reinhartz, A. 3, 6, 17–18, 80, 117, 132, 136, 147
Rena, J. 2
Resseguie, J. L. 109
Reynolds, B. E. 4 n.13
Ricci, C. 7 n.25
Ringe, S. H. 7 n.25
Rowland, C. 4 n.13, 4 n.15
Ruether, R. R. 10
Russell, D. S. 5

Schiby, J. 57
Schnackenburg, R. 27, 44, 46, 68, 90 n.23, 102
Schneiders, S. M. 2, 3, 7 n.27, 50, 74, 78, 93, 127, 129, 133, 134, 147
Schnelle, U. 70
Schottroff, L. 7 n.24, 106
Schüssler Fiorenza, E. 7 n.24, 7 n.25, 7 n.26, 8, 10, 37, 72, 84, 87
Scott, M. 2
Seim, T. K. 10–11, 50
Senior, D. 114
Siliezar, C. R. S. 5, 133
Sim, D. C. 15, 72

Smith, D. M. 14, 16, 51, 67, 93, 109, 128
Soards, M. L. 13 n.55
Stanton, G. 14
Stibbe, M. W. G. 65
Swidler, L. 8 n.32

Taylor, J. 9 n.36
Temple, W. 69
Theissen, G. 63
Thomas, J. C. 92
Thompson, M. M. 13, 16 n.6, 77
Thyen, H. 43 n.20

von Wahlde, U. C. 16–17, 22

Wardle, T. 37 n.14
Warner, M. 20 n.7, 33 n.42
Wegner, J. R. 9
White Crawford, S. 116, 117
Wilckens, U. 40
Williams, C. H. 4 n.13, 47 n.36
Wire, A. C. 99
Witherington, B. 8 n.32
Wyatt, 133 n.27

Yadin, Y. 9. n.37
Yardeni, A. 9 n.37

Zimmermann, R. 70

www.ingramcontent.com/pod-product-compliance
Lightning Source LLC
Chambersburg PA
CBHW061835300426
44115CB00013B/2397